Warfare in History

THE CIRCLE OF WAR IN THE MIDDLE AGES

Essays on Medieval Military and Naval History

Warfare in History

General Editor: Matthew Bennett
ISSN 1358–779X

Already published

The Battle of Hastings: Sources and Interpretations
edited and introduced by Stephen Morillo

Infantry Warfare in the Early Fourteenth Century:
Discipline, Tactics, and Technology
Kelly DeVries

The Art of Warfare in Western Europe during
the Middle Ages, from the Eighth Century to 1340 (second edition)
J.F. Verbruggen

Knights and Peasants:
The Hundred Years War in the French Countryside
Nicholas Wright

Society at War:
The Experience of England and France during the Hundred Years War
edited by Christopher Allmand

THE CIRCLE OF WAR IN THE MIDDLE AGES

Essays on Medieval Military and Naval History

Edited by
Donald J. Kagay and L. J. Andrew Villalon

THE BOYDELL PRESS

First published 1999
The Boydell Press, Woodbridge

ISBN 0 85115 645 2

The Boydell Press is an imprint of Boydell & Brewer Ltd
PO Box 9, Woodbridge, Suffolk IP12 3DF, UK
and of Boydell & Brewer Inc.
PO Box 41026, Rochester, NY 14604–4126, USA
website: http://www.boydell.co.uk

A catalogue record for this book is available
from the British Library

Library of Congress Cataloging-in-Publication Data
The circle of war in the Middle Ages : essays on medieval military and
naval history / edited by Donald J. Kagay and L.J. Andrew Villalon.
    p.   cm. – (Warfare in history, ISSN 1358–779X)
Includes bibliographical references
ISBN 0–85115–645–2 (hardback : alk. paper)
    1. Military history, Medieval.   2. Military art and science –
History — Medieval, 500–1500.   3. Naval history.   I. Kagay,
Donald J.   II. Villalon, L. J. Andrew.   III. Series.
D128.C57   1999
355'.009182'20902 – dc21   98–56265

This publication is printed on acid-free paper

Printed in Great Britain by
St Edmundsbury Press Ltd, Bury St Edmunds, Suffolk

CONTENTS

I. Aspects of Medieval Warfare Reconsidered

II. Medieval Warfare as a Divine Tool

III. The Orders of Society at War

IV. War at Sea

ILLUSTRATIONS

CONTRIBUTORS

Bernard S. Bachrach, University of Minnesota

Paul E. Chevedden, University of California, Los Angeles

Kelly DeVries, Loyola College of Maryland

Douglas Haldane, Institute of Nautical Archaeology, Alexandria

Kent G. Hare, Louisiana State University

Steven Isaac, Louisiana State University

Steven G. Lane, University of Chicago

Stephen Morillo, Wabash College

Lawrence V. Mott, University of Minnesota

Edward G. Schoenfeld, University of Minnesota

Jean A. Truax, University of Houston

Theresa M. Vann, Hill Monastic Manuscript Library, St. John's University

ACKNOWLEDGEMENTS

The editors would like to thank the contributors of this volume for their long-suffering patience and thorough professionalism. They would also like to express their warm appreciation to Ms. Susan-Dykstra-Poel and Ms. Caroline Palmer for their calm and friendly assistance in the solution of a number of routine and emergency problems which this book has occasioned. They would also like to extend their fervent thanks to President Portia Holmes Shields, Dean James Hill, of the School of Arts and Sciences, Dean Lee Formwalt, of the Graduate School, and Professor Nyota Tucker of Albany State University, for their invaluable aid in attaining subvention funds for this volume.

PREFACE

The Vietnam War – from its initial hollow jingoism in the Gulf of Tonkin Resolution to the demeaning statement of weary American surrender in the Peace of Paris[1] – has formed a sad backdrop before which the political and social trends of the late twentieth century have been played out. Far from the madding crowd of such political consumerism, however, the conflict in southeast Asia also provided a starting point for the surging intellectual, and sometimes anti-intellectual, trends which have forced American academia to confront its old prejudices and values on a long and anguished journey that has not yet come to an end.

The immediate victors in this process were such understudied minority groups as women, homosexuals, Afro-Americans and native Americans and any other body which could make a case that it was an amorphous "other" class which American mainstream society had for so long either attacked or ignored. A great loser in this war for academic attention and patronage was military history which in the view of many intellectuals was stained by a shameful connection to the "military-industrial complex."[2] In an irony that only Clio could fashion, this trend toward "otherness" in American university curricula eventually led to a growing international focus, and in the train of an army of "world studies" courses, military history has ridden back into favor – or at least into grudging acceptance.[3]

This volume is the direct result of the upsurge of academic interest in matters military. This collection of papers – many of which were first presented at one of the annual conferences of the Medieval Institute or at the meetings of other smaller regional conferences including the Texas Medieval Association – is divided into four sections.

In the first, section (Aspects of Medieval Warfare Reconsidered), "closed" historiographical questions focusing on army demography, strategy, siegecraft, cavalry and infantry are reopened with the admixture of new interpretations and

---

1   Douglas Welsh, *The History of the Vietnam War* (London, 1981); Ralph B. Smith, *An International History of the Vietnam War* (New York, 1983); Stanley Karnow, *Vietnam, A History* (New York, 1985); Thomas D. Boettcher, *Vietnam: the Valor and the Sorrow* (New York, 1985).
2   Paul A. Koistinen, *The Military-Industrial Complex: A Historical Perspective* (New York, 1980); Gregg D. Walker, David A. Bella, Stephen J. Sprecher, eds, *The Military Industrial Complex: Eisenhower's Warning Three Decades Later* (New York, 1992).
3   Walter Millis, *Military History* (Washington, 1969); David A. Charters, Marc Miliner and J. Brent Wilson, eds, *Military History and the Military Profession* (Westport CT, 1992); Paul Kennedy, "The Fall and Rise of Military History," *The Yale Journal of World Affairs* 1, no. 2 (1989): 12–19.

evidence. In the first paper of this section, Bernard Bachrach attacks a standard idea of nineteenth-century historiography (especially as posited by Hans Delbrück), that large field armies did not exist in the Middle Ages. Destroying the basis of demographic arguments which depend on Delbrück, Bachrach calls for a review of evidence based, not on nationalistic assumptions but on an unbiased assessment of the sources.

In the second paper of this section, Theresa Vann indirectly touches on the question of army size in medieval times, though her principal focus is the issue of the existence of strategy in the armies of the Middle Ages. By investigating the twelfth- and thirteenth-century Castilian reconquest around the pivotal city of Toledo, she tests the hypothesis that strategic planning did, indeed, exist on the medieval battlefield. By assessing the "defense in depth" policy of Castilian kings, she asserts that these monarchs were acting in line with a clear strategy of avoiding pitched battles except when unavoidable and extending the defensive "screen" of fortresses to the south and east of Toledo into Muslim *al-Andalus*.

In this section's third offering, Paul Chevedden attacks the view of R.C. Smail that no significant military technology emerged during the era of the crusades. Using the citadel of Damascus as a focal point to discredit Smail's arguments, Chevedden proceeds to review how the city's fortifications were altered by Saladin's brother Al-'Adil in reponse to the spread of the counterweight trebuchet through Byzantium into the Muslim world. Al-'Adil's defensive plan for Damascus was marked by the use of towers especially adapted to the use of trebuchets. Unlike Smail's view that the twelfth and thirteenth centuries consistuted a technologically-arid era in the Middle East, Chevedden convincingly argues that the crusades served as a catalyst for the spread of military technology between combatants of different faith, thus changing the "face of battle" in the process.

In this section's fourth paper, Stephen Morillo challenges the widespread nineteenth-century view that the Middle Ages were "an age of cavalry" – an idea which still has a great effect on popular and textbook images of the medieval era. Morillo reexamines the theory of the influence of the stirrup as posited by Heinrich Brunner and Lynn White, rejecting their view that cavalry held pride of place on the medieval battlefield until the fifteenth century. In Morillo's view, infantry forces had a far greater influence during the Middle Ages than most historions have been willingly to concede. He finds very similar patterns of infantry dominance over cavalry in the contemporary societies of China and Japan.

In the last paper of the section, Edward Schoenfeld reexamines the status and political nature of the "farmer warriors" (*agrarii milites*) of tenth-century Saxony. Reviewing the vast array of German scholarship of the last century which largely identified these militiamen with the *ministeriales*, the servile troops of the Ottonian period, Schoenfeld continues this argument by assessing certain burghal documents of Henry I (919–36) and Otto I (936–73) for Saxony.

In the second section (Medieval Warfare as a Divine Tool), two papers explore the early medieval perceptions of God's influence on the outcome of battles in which war itself becomes a metaphor for a soul caught between two opposing hosts – one celestial and the other demonic.

In the first of these, Kent Hare explores the influence of saintly apparitions on the battlefield, classifying their activities into advisory, defensive and offensive. He argues that these intrusions of saintly influence into war became more strident and proactive during the First Crusade when saintly armies led by St. Michael and other holy warriors intervened to destroy the infidel.

In the second article, Kelly DeVries focuses on the problem of defeat in medieval battle and its ultimate cosmic implications, that is, is God still on our side? While the action of divine aid toward the granting of victory could be as unlimited as the Almighty himself, defeat could also be a complicated matter, usually explained by the injustice of the vanquished's cause or his crying need for reform. In this regard, even the enemies of God could be used to chastise his children who had temporarily lost the path of righteousness.

In the third section (The Orders of Society at War), the authors clearly demonstrate that, despite its own idealized paradigm of the three orders,[4] medieval society was far from perfect and seemed even less so under the strain of war. What these papers show instead is that nobles were not always simple feudatories but could be professional soldiers who fought for the highest bidder and, on the other hand, such "helpless" (*inermis*) populations as women and villagers could constitute small but essential cogs in a military machine.

In the first paper of this section, Steven Isaac investigates the identification of mercenary troops in the twelfth-century Anglo-Norman world. By carefully analyzing the patterns of their alliances to lords during the turbulent era of Stephen (1135–57) and Matilda (1135–1154), Isaac concludes that the Flemish troops of William of Ypres, far from being the mercenary "wolves" and "kites" of contemporary chronicles, were more influenced by feudal considerations of allegiance and loyalty than they were by greed.

In the second article, Jean Truax deals with another significant, but often overlooked, element of Anglo-Norman warfare: noble women. Eschewing the expansive claims of much modern feminist historiography, Truax is careful to tread no further than the evidence (largely comprised of twelfth-century cronicles) will lead her arguments. Even with this careful methodology, Truax is able to find a great number of Anglo-Norman women who rallied troops in defeat, commanded castle garrisons or led fullfledged armed assaults with large numbers of male soldiers under their command. Though these "Amazons" were not the rule in Anglo-Norman warfare, there were enough of them to make male adversaries take them seriously.

In the last paper of this section, Stephen Lane deals with another under-reported party to medieval war, the rural militia. Exploring the Lombard countryside of the twelfth-century, an era when the great cities of the region

---

4 Georges Duby, *The Three Orders: Feudal Society Imagined*, trans. Arthur Goldhammer (Chicago, 1980).

broke away from the dominance of the Holy Roman Emperor, Frederick I Barbarossa (1152–90), Lane concludes that the village communities of this exposed
land had little option but to throw in their lot with the cities which assessed
fiscal and military obligations on them in exchange for urban protection.
Though the village militiamen rendered most of their war service either in
digging ditches or supplying front-line troops, they occasionally demonstrated
effectiveness in their own right, challengeing either imperial or urban oppressors
as the need arose.

In the fourth section (War at Sea), the battle for the Mediterranean is chroni-
cled in articles which trace the spread of naval technology and expertise from
older powers to newer ones, and between societies often at war with one another.

In the first paper of this section, Douglas Haldane traces the journey of the
great military secret, "Greek Fire," across enemy lines from Byzantium to
Islam. He asserts that the first use of this predominantly naval incendiary among
Muslim troops took place in the ninth century on the western fringes of Islam's
power base, the Abbasid empire. By the twelfth century, this deadly technology
was well known in the Muslim world and provided a cruel surprise to the European crusaders who often found their land advantages outflanked by a Muslim
naval superiority, bolstered by the sudden impact of "Greek Fire." The importance of this incendiary, however, cannot be measured by ultimate victory or
defeat, but instead as an example of the inexorable passage of technology
among peoples – even those who happen to be at war with each other.

In the last of this section's papers, Lawrence Mott deals with the emergence
of the Crown of Aragon as a Mediterranean power during the War of the Sicilian
Vespers (1282–1302). Mott's principal focus is the pivotal sea battle of Malta (8
June 1283), in which the Aragonese fleet under the brillant Sicilian admiral,
Roger de Lauria, soundly defeated the forces of Charles of Anjou, the ousted
ruler of Sicily. Mott claims that this great victory was due to an inherent superi-
ority of Aragonese ships and crews over most naval contenders in the western
Mediterranean, including the Angevins.

Barring the unthinkable – that Fukuyama is right and history will indeed
"end"[5] – it is hoped that this collection will spur even further interest in military
affairs during the "medieval centuries," and tie this development to the ever-
increasing body of scholarship on modern *militaria*.

---

[5] Francis Fukuyama, *The End of History and the Last Man* (New York, 1992).

ABBREVIATIONS

AHR   *American Historical Review.*

ASB   *Vita Sancti Neoti, Acta Sanctorum Bollandiana.* 1731.

ASC   *Anglo-Saxon Chronicle,* trans. G.N. Garmonsway. London, 1990.

CAI   *Chronica Adefonsi Imperatoris,* eds Emma Falque, Juan Gil, and Antonio Maya, in *Chronica hispana saeculi XII.* Turnhout, 1990.

EH   Bede, *Ecclesiastical History of the English People,* ed. and trans. Bertram Colgrave and R.A.B. Mynors. Oxford, 1969.

EHD   *English Historical Documents.* London, 1953– .

EHR   *English Historical Review.*

GFH   *Gesta Francorum et aliorum Hierosolimitanorum,* ed. and trans. Rosalind Hill. London, 1962.

GR   William of Malmesbury, *De Gestis Regum Anglorum,* ed. William Stubbs, 2 vols. London, 1887–1889.

GS   *Gesta Stephani,* trans. K.R. Potter, ed. R.H.C. Davis. Oxford, 1976.

HF   Gregory of Tours, *The History of the Franks,* trans. Lewis Thorpe. London, 1974.

HFI   Raymond d'Aguilers, *Historia Francorum Qui Ceperunt Iherusalem,* trans. John Hugh Hill and Laurita L. Hill. Philadelphia, 1968.

HN   William of Malmesbury, *Historia Novella,* ed. and trans. K.R. Potter. London, 1955.

HR   Simeon of Durham, *Historia Regum,* ed. Thomas Arnold, *Symeonis Monachi Opera Omnia,* 2 vols. London, 1882–1885.

JEH   *Journal of Ecclesiastical History.*

MGH   *Monumenta Germaniae Historica inde ab a.c. 500 usque ad a. 1500,* ed. G.H. Pertz et al. Berlin–Hanover, Hahn, 1825– .

AA   *Auctores Antiquissimi.*

DHI   *Diplomatum Henrici I.*

DOI   *Diplomatum Ottonis I.*

Epp   *Epistolae.*

Lib   *Libelli de lite.*

SRG   *Scriptores rerum germanicarum in usum scholarum.*

SS   *Scriptores.*

OV   Ordericus Vitalis, *Historia ecclesiastica,* ed. and trans. Marjorie Chibnall, 6 vols. Oxford, 1978.

PL   *Patrologia Latina,* ed. J.P. Migne, 217 + 4 index vols. Paris, 1841–64.

RCEA   *Répertoire chronologique d'épigraphie arabe,* ed. Gaston Weit, Jean Sauvaget and Etienne Combe, 17 vols. in progress. Cairo, 1931– .

RHF   *Revue d'Histoire de l'Eglise de France.* Paris, 1910.

RIS   *Rerum Italicarum Scriptores.*

RS   *Rerum Britannicarum Medii Aevi Scriptores,* 99 vols. London, 1858–1911. Rolls Series.

MAJOR BATTLES MENTIONED IN THIS VOLUME

Battle	Date	Combatants*
Cannae	216 B.C.	Carthaginians (Hannibal) vs Romans
Vercellae	105 B.C.	Romans (Marius) vs Cimbri and Teutones
Chalons	451	Romans (Aetius) vs Huns (Attila)
Milvian Bridge	312	Constantine I vs Maxentius
Adrianople	378	Visigoths vs Romans (Valens)
Dyle	891	Germans (Arnulf) vs Norse
Riade	933	Germans (Henry I) vs Magyars
Lechfeld	955	Germans (Otto I) vs Magyars
Manzikert	1071	Seljuk Turks vs Byzantines (Romanus Diagones)
Zallaqa	1086	Almoravids vs Castile (Alfonso VI)
Bremule	1119	French (Louis VI) vs English (Henry I)
Lincoln	1141	English (Matilda) vs English (Stephen)
Mansura	1249	Mamlukes vs French (Louis IX)
Benevento	1266	French (Charles of Anjou) vs Germans/Sicilians (Manfred)
Las Rosas	1281	Catalans vs French (naval battle)
Malta	1283	Catalans (Roger de Llauria) vs French (naval battle)
Courtrai (Battle of the Spurs)	1302	French (Philip IV) vs Flemish/English

* Victorious forces listed first

Part I

ASPECTS OF MEDIEVAL WARFARE RECONSIDERED

EARLY MEDIEVAL MILITARY DEMOGRAPHY: SOME OBSERVATIONS ON THE METHODS OF HANS DELBRÜCK

Bernard S. Bachrach

DURING the past century, due in large part to the work of Hans Delbrück, whose books have dominated the field of medieval military demography, scholars have come to reject as basically unreliable the figures found in narrative sources and even to regard with great suspicion the numbers found in a great variety of documentary sources. This *Tendenz* has resulted in the armies of medieval Europe and especially those mustered and put into the field prior to the First Crusade, the period addressed in this study, being viewed as tiny forces, indeed, little more than undisciplined warbands.[1]

It will be argued here that Delbrück's methods were fundamentally unsound. Thus, if the critique presented in this essay is successful, reference to Delbrück's arguments for the purpose of providing support to sustain generalizations concerning the size of medieval armies must abandoned and conclusions concerning medieval military demography that have been based upon his researches in already published studies must be substantially reworked if not completely jettisoned.[2]

Delbrück's "obsession with numbers," to use M.I. Finley's ungenerous phrase,[3] was, in large part, a reaction to the uncritical scissors and paste use of

---

[1] Hans Delbrück, *Geschichte der Kriegskunst im Rahmen der politischen Geschichte*, 6 volumes (Berlin, 1900–1936) of which volumes 1, 2, 3 are relevant to the present study. These are now available in English translation by Walter J. Renfroe as *History of the Art of War: Within the Framework of Political History*, vols. 1, 2, 3 (Westport, Conn., 1975–1982). For the incremental influence of Delbrück's views see, for example, Ferdinand Lot, *L'Art militaire et les armeés au Moyen Age et dans la Proche-Orient*, 2 vols. (Paris, 1946); Charles Oman, *History of the Art of War in the Middle Ages*, 2 vols. (2nd edn. 1924 rpt. New York, 1964); J.F. Verbruggen, *De Krijgskunst in West-Europa in de Middeleeuwen, IXe tot begin XIVe eeuw* (Brussels, 1954), trans. as *The Art of War in Western Europe during the Middle Ages, from the Eighth Century to 1340*, trans. Sumner Willard and S.C.M. Southern, 2nd edn. revised and enlarged (Woodbridge, 1997) – the translation adds a treatment of the eighth century whereas the original began in the ninth century – and Philippe Contamine, *War in the Middle Ages*, trans. Michael Jones (Oxford, 1984).

[2] See Bernard S. Bachrach, "Medieval Siege Warfare: A Reconnaissance," *The Journal of Military History* 58 (1994): 119, n. 1, where I provide a very brief preview of the thesis to be presented here.

[3] M.I. Finley, *Ancient History: Evidence and Models* (New York, 1986), p. 71.

sources by military historians who wrote during much of the nineteenth and early twentieth centuries.[4] These early scholars generally viewed the later Roman empire and the early Middle Ages as a Dark Age in which the vigorous denizens of the German forests replaced effete Romans as the rulers of the West.[5] Delbrück essentially agreed with this "noble savage" approach but refused to believe that such a primitive "feudal" society which emerged in the Germanic West and which based its economy on barter could possibly have had large armies.[6]

This picture of the later Roman empire and the early Middle Ages, i.e. a primitive Dark Age dominated by small feudal armies[7] and supported by a barter economy,[8] is fundamentally inconsistent with the vast body of research

---

[4]   See, for example, *Art of War*, II, 133–34, where Delbrück levels his guns on General von Peucker's "widely used book" *Das deutsche Kriegswesen der Urzeiten* (Berlin, 1860).

[5]   See the brief but valuable survey by Bryce D. Lyon, *The Origins of the Middle Ages: Pirenne's Challenge to Gibbon* (New York, 1972), where a broad spectrum of works are examined concerning the decline and fall of the Roman empire and the emergence of the so-called "Dark Ages."

It must be noted here that a curious phenomenon developed following World War II which has seen some medievalists adopt an "anthropological" attitude toward the early Middle Ages. This has resulted in some very unfortunate comparisons of the early medieval world with non-literate, sub-Saharan African societies. Such an anthropological approach is particularly inappropriate when studying the early medieval military. For a preliminary critique of this terribly misleading anthropological distraction see Bernard S. Bachrach, "Anthropology and Early Medieval History: Some Problems," *Cithara* 34 (1994): 3–10.

[6]   *Art of War*, II, 214–17.

[7]   There has to date been no systematic attack on the methods used by Delbrück for establishing the size of early medieval armies although many revisionist studies have been published recently which focus on one or another particular topic. See, for example, the series of articles dealing with the later Roman empire and the early Middle Ages by Bernard S. Bachrach: "The Hun Army at the Battle of Chalons (451): An Essay in Military Demography," in *Ethnogenese und Übrerlieferung: Angewandte Methoden der Frühmittelalterforschung*, edd. Karl Brunner and Brigitte Merta (Vienne–Munich, 1994), pp. 59–67; "Grand Strategy in the Germanic Kingdoms: Recruitment of the Rank and File," in *L'Armée romaine et les barbares du IIIe au VIIe siècle*, edd. Françoise Vallet and Michel Kazanski (Paris, 1993), pp. 55–63 in 4o; "Angevin Campaign Forces in the Reign of Fulk Nerra, Count of the Angevins (987–1040)," *Francia* 16.1 (1989): 67–84; "Some Observations on the Military Administration of the Norman Conquest," pp. 1–25 in *Anglo-Norman Studies VIII*, ed. R. Allen Brown (Woodbridge, 1986); "On the Origins of William the Conqueror's Horse Transports," *Technology and Culture* 26 (1985): 505–31; and (with Rutherford Aris), "Military Technology and Garrison Organization: Some Observations on Anglo-Saxon Military Thinking in Light of the Burghal Hidage," *Technology and Culture* 31 (1990): 1–17.

[8]   For a survey of medieval economic history relevant to the matter of discrediting the notion that the medieval economy was a barter economy, see Georges Duby, *Rural Economy and Country Life in the Medieval West*, trans. Cynthia Postan (London, 1968). More recently the magisterial study by Jean Durliat, *Les finances publiques de Dioclétien aux Carolingiens (284–889) [with a preface by K.F. Werner]* (Sigmaringen, 1990) breaks much new ground regarding late antique and early medieval financial administration. See the very favorable review by Bernard S. Bachrach in *Francia* 19.1 (1992): 276–77. However, the death knell of autarky was sounded in the pioneering work of Alfons Dopsch, *Die Wirtschaftsentwicklung der Karolingerzeit vornehmlich in Deutschland* (orig. published 1911–1913, 2nd. edn.

produced since World War II. Thus, it remains to be seen if Delbrück's methods of source criticism and models for military organization can be sustained in light of the very different economic conditions which are now known to have prevailed during the half-millennium prior to the first Crusade.

Delbrück begins his critique of military demography, as studied in the nineteenth century and earlier, with the observation that previous scholarship has failed to grasp the several essential idiosyncracies which operate throughout the history of Western civilization and determine how historians have used numbers in the context of warfare. He observes, for example, that although strategists such as Clausewitz advocate the doctrine of overwhelming force this is not the way in which "people conceive and hand down their military exploits." Rather, according to Delbrück, "nothing gives more pleasure to the soul of the people, and nothing is related by the narrator more willingly, than that a small host has conquered a greater."[9]

Indeed, Delbrück contends that this principle is "deeply rooted in the human mind" and that it "pervades, governs and renders difficult the transmission of the history of war." He goes on to assert:

> The greatest of all warlike virtues is bravery, and bravery in a struggle of the minority against a majority, or, indeed, in a conquest of the majority by the minority, appears most marked and unquestionable. For this reason the most unreliable and incredible of all the many inaccuracies handed down to us in the chronicles is the number of the armies.[10]

Delbrück's insight, although not universally valid, as he admits, nevertheless is intriguing. The general rule he posits is that a chronicler who is depicting his side as the victor must make the defeated enemy larger, perhaps even very much larger, than the army of his own people in order to assure the desired glory about which his readers want to be informed. Conversely, an account written from the perspective of the losing side requires the victorious army to be described as very much larger than the defeated force for there is little shame in losing to overwhelming odds. Indeed, at Thermopylae the Spartans under Leonidas gained immortality in their defeat as did the Texans at the Alamo.

This rule, however, does not result inexorably only in the upward exaggeration of military numbers by chroniclers. Rather, as Delbrück observes, military commanders are wont to complain that they do not have enough troops and this cliche also influences the way numbers are recorded in the narrative sources. By complaining before a battle, the general attempts to absolve himself of blame if

---

Weimar, 1922, and rpt. Weimar, 1962), 2 vols. Dopsch's general views are more easily accessible in *Wirtschaftliche und Soziale Grundlage der Europäischen Kulturentwicklung aus der Zeit von Caesar bis auf Karl den Grossen* (Vienna, 1924) and translated from the abridged German of Erna Patzalt by M.G. Beard and N. Marshall as *The Economic and Social foundations of European Civilization* (London, 1937).

9 Hans Delbrück, *Numbers in History* (London, 1913), pp. 11–12.

10 Delbrück, *Numbers in History*, p. 14.

he should lose and if he should win his glory in victory is that much greater because he fought with inadequate numbers against superior forces.[11] This tendency obviously has the effect of lowering rather than raising the numbers found in the narrative sources. It is of course possible the general may well simply complain of the insufficient size of his army in relation to the exaggerated numbers which he has attributed to his adversary.

Indeed, stated more broadly, Delbrück's principles for criticizing narrative sources give rise to several corollaries. For example, those chroniclers who are describing their own people losing a battle or a war have the option either to provide a grossly exaggerated figure for the enemy army while recording a more or less accurate number for the size of their own forces or they may provide a more or less accurate figure for the size of the enemy force and an exaggerated undercount for their own army. These corollaries provide a sort of internal control mechanism on the patterns of "abuse" practiced by the authors of narrative sources by providing information regarding military demography which, however, Delbrück does not explicitly recognize but which implicitly he employs.

The likelihood that authors will at once exaggerate the number of the enemy grossly while at the same time providing a substantial undercount of his own forces is small. It is Delbrück's view that the people at home are likely to have a firmer idea concerning the size of their own forces and thus misinformation, if purveyed, will probably concern the size of the enemy army. Conversely, a chronicler who describes his people as the winner is more likely to provide an ostensibly accurate figure regarding this force, and for the same reasons adumbrated above, than a chronicler on the losing side, concerning the enemy army. In short, the audience is likely to get better or more accurate information concerning matters about which it is already better informed.[12] This principle is a variation on a theme, discussed by the Roman historian Sallust (*Cat.* 3) and popularized during the early Middle Ages by Gregory of Tours, which suggests that audiences are inclined to believe those things that are consistent with their personal knowledge while learning about matters concerning which they are ignorant raises skepticism.[13]

---

11 Delbrück, *Art of War*, II, 227.

12 As will be seen below, Delbrück understands this pattern but for some reason or reasons, which are not adumbrated, he did not see fit to expose the underpinnings of his thinking on this matter. If the likelihood that the "hometown" chronicler normally can be expected to have provided numbers of the correct order of magnitude for his own people is accepted as a working principle, this, of course, would mean that when such a source indicates big numbers these too would have to be given considerable respect. Thus, if large numbers cannot be dismissed out of hand, as is Delbrück's wont, and each figure must be evaluated in its wide variety of contexts, his frequent though carefully selected *a priori* assertions that an army must be markedly smaller than the number provided by the source would carry considerably less weight.

13 The fact that both Sallust and Gregory (*Hist.*, bk VII, ch. 1) focus their remarks on personal virtue and individual self-knowledge does not obviate the general epistemology identified above.

Although Delbrück was driven to emphasize the unreliability of narrative sources, especially in contexts where the numbers obviously are too large, he was well aware that "without approximately accurate figures an exact knowledge and true understanding of martial proceedings are absolutely impossible." He laments, moreover, that even modern commanders, i.e. those of the eighteenth and nineteenth centuries, while reporting troop strengths in their memoirs, succumb to the tendency to "increase their fame by the help of inaccurate numerical returns."[14] Indeed, he asks with obvious rhetorical exaggeration: "How . . . is one to obtain accurate numbers, when only incorrect ones have been handed down to us?"[15]

Delbrück certainly was not wrong to emphasize that at least some and perhaps even many authors of narrative sources exaggerate, surely in certain contexts and not always in an upward manner, whether or not we accept his causal model. However, the canons for the acceptance of information, which are employed by Delbrück, highlight his very careful selection of particular narrative sources to prove his point. On occasion, these canons or controlling assumptions appear to be of a rather curious cast. For example, Delbrück asserts: "Sometimes we have, though indeed seldom enough, numbers which are subjectively beyond every doubt, like the statements of Thucydides concerning the number of the armed citizens of Athens. . . ."[16] This approach appears almost mystical, especially when dealing with a writer who made up speeches and admitted doing so. However, Delbrück goes on to observe that "the official numbers of the Roman Census, which Livy and other writers have preserved for us" also "are subjectively beyond every doubt."[17] It would seem, therefore, that in a rather convoluted manner Delbrück implicitly is recognizing the observations regarding his method made above, i.e. one can not easily exaggerate in an outrageous manner in works that are represented as history with a claim to numerical accuracy for the home folks about matters concerning which they are well informed. However, the notion that a particular author in a particular context was seeking to be regarded by his audience as providing "accurate" numbers is not a matter which Delbrück examines.[18]

Indeed, from specific examples which Delbrück provides, additional "principles" may be inferred regarding how he believes narrative sources are to be

---

14 *Numbers in History*, pp. 14–15.
15 *Numbers in History*, p. 14.
16 *Numbers in History*, p. 16.
17 *Numbers in History*, pp. 16–17, where Delbrück makes clear that the scholarly world is not of one mind in determining what these numbers really mean. For a more modern appraisal of the problems raised by Roman census figures see P.A. Brunt, *Italian Manpower, 225 B.C.–A.D. 14* (Oxford, 1971).
18 In this vein see the efforts of Walter Goffart, *Barbarians and Romans, A.D. 418–584: The Techniques of Accommodation* (Princeton, 1980), pp. 231–34, to discredit what on their face value would seem to be reliable numbers provided by an author who had no apparent reason to exaggerate or misinform an audience which in any event was likely to be aware of the order of magnitude of the population under discussion.

criticized from the perspective of military demography. For example, although Delbrück almost obsessively rejects very large numbers provided by narrative sources, he ostensibly accepts immense figures regarding the Roman and Carthaginian forces which engaged at the battle of Cannae in 216 B.C. Delbrück takes this unusual position despite the efforts of some of his predecessors and contemporaries to reduce dramatically the numbers given in the sources for both forces.[19] Thus, in defense of his position, Delbrück argues that the 50,000 figure for Hannibal's army is provided by the Carthaginian writer Silenos concerning whom he asks rhetorically: "What reason would Silenos have had for exaggerating the Carthaginian forces?" Regarding the Roman army, Delbrück observes, "the 86,000 figure for the Romans stems, as Appian proves, drawing on Roman sources, from their own side, and . . . no objective reason exists to cause us to doubt the strength of that army."[20]

Delbrück's treatment of the discussion by Roman writers of the size of Celtic and German armies, including Caesar's own writings, follows this pattern of seeking "objective" reasons either to accept or reject a particular figure. For example, he observes: "all Roman sources agree in the assertion that first Marius defeated hundreds of thousands of Teutons and Cimbri at Aquae Sextiae and Vercellae, and fifty years later Caesar defeated just as many Gauls and Germans."[21] These figures, Delbrück argues, are to be rejected as fantastic. However, by contrast, Caesar's information provided in the *Commentaries* that the Celtic chief, Ambiorix, commanded forces which were of the same order of magnitude as those in the Roman army and caused the loss of one and a half legions, i.e. some 8,000–10,000 effectives, can be accepted. It is Delbrück's argument here that Caesar would have no point in exaggerating his own losses to a force of equal size.[22] Also, it is important to note here that Delbrück finds it not only plausible but acceptable, despite the rather primitive technology commanded by the forces under consideration, to see a battle which involved some 60,000 effectives suffering 30% casualties.

In trying to get beyond the exaggerations found in some sources and the ambiguities presented by numbers which are very likely correct, Delbrück articulated or implied several additional methodological principles. For example, he argued: "All numbers control each other mutually; not only the numbers from the same time and the same event, but also those from the most remote periods of time." Thus he asks rhetorically: "How could Attila the Hun

---

[19] Delbrück, *The Art of War*, I, 325, provides a thorough going critique of Cantalupi's effort to reduce vastly the number of troops that are indicated to have participated in the battle Cannae by the authors of the narrative sources.

[20] *The Art of War*, I, 326–27. The purpose here is neither to defend nor to attack either Delbrück's view of the sources or the size of the opposing forces but merely to illustrate his methods and models. Parenthetically, as will be seen below, among the "objective" criteria to be considered are logistics as Delbrück, himself, recognizes in principle but puts into practice only when it suits his argument.

[21] *Numbers in History*, pp. 46–47.

[22] *Numbers in History*, p. 46.

have led 700,000 men from Germany over the Rhine into France to the Plain of Châlon," if in 1870, "Moltke was able to move some 500,000 with such difficultly over the same road" despite the fact that he enjoyed the benefits of modern technology and staff planning which obviously the Hunnic ruler in the mid-fifth century lacked?[23]

This all too brief comparison of the vastly different situations faced by von Moltke and Attila nevertheless, at least from a rhetorical perspective, suffices for the reader to reject the obviously exaggerated claims found in the medieval sources concerning the size of the Hunnic army. The likelihood that these figures may have been based upon a contemporary source to which these later historians had access does not impinge upon Delbrück's judgment here.[24] In addition, we are required to consider the possible upper limits of an army's size in relation to its logistic infrastructure as conditioned by such variables as technology, time, and distance. Thus, Delbrück's discussion of Xerxes' army, which is reported by Herodotus to have been comprised of 5,100,000 men, when considered within the broadly understood logistic realities which obtained at the time, easily convinces us that a certain amount of common sense is necessary for modern scholars to write history even if "seldom in these 2500 years had this number been doubted, and even up to date [1913] it has found defenders. . . ."[25] Delbrück, however, provides detailed studies of neither late Roman nor early medieval logistics. He merely follows the prescription illustrated by the von Moltke-incident, discussed above.[26]

There is little doubt that debunking absurdly large numbers such as armies in the millions or even many hundreds of thousands, provided by near contemporary, contemporary, and even eyewitness sources, is made much easier today because of Delbrück's efforts. However, since Delbrück provides a rather systematic rationale, both explicitly and implicitly, for examining the validity of numbers provided by narrative sources, it is also more difficult to reject out of hand armies said to have numbered in the several tens of thousands. For the Greeks, Romans, Celts and Germans, prior to the so-called crash of the third century, Delbrück obviously is prepared to accept large figures, i.e. battles involving 50,000 to 100,000 combatants, found in the narrative sources. The logistic "realities" required to sustain such numbers on the march and in the field apparently gave Delbrück no "objective" reason to raise doubts among his readers.[27]

---

23 *Numbers in History*, pp. 19–21.
24 Now see Bachrach: "The Hun Army at the Battle of Chalons," pp. 59–67.
25 *Numbers in History*, pp. 22–23.
26 See for a very different view, Bernard S. Bachrach, "Logistics in Pre-Crusade Europe," in *Feeding Mars: Logistics in Western Warfare from the Middle Ages to the Present*, ed. John A. Lynn (Boulder, 1993), pp. 57–78.
27 Although, from time to time, Delbrück makes a desultory effort to provide a quantitative approach to logistics in dealing with armies in the ancient world, his work is far inferior to more modern studies. See, for example, the classic work by Donald W. Engels, *Alexander the Great and the Logistics of the Macedonian Army* (Berkeley, 1978); and regarding the early

Delbrück developed a matrix of criteria for the evaluation of narrative sources. As a result of the new "method" he then proceeded to press his arguments regarding the order of magnitude of armies during the period prior to what he regards as the "Decline and Dissolution of the Roman Military System," i.e. the early third century A.D. However, in his treatment of the later Roman empire and much of the Middle Ages, Delbrück ostensibly abandoned the system of "controls" he had so laboriously created when dealing with the Ancient World. His major reason for believing that the rules, which he assumed worked so well for the Ancient World and which had permitted him to accept the historicity of some of the very large armies identified in the narrative sources, did not apply to the later period, was his conviction that during the third century A.D. the West went from a money economy to a barter economy, i.e. the all too familiar autarky so much favored by late nineteenth and early twentieth-century economic historians. Delbrück asserted the new "rule" that "it is impossible to feed large armies on a barter economy basis" and thus the economy of the later Roman empire and the Middle Ages could not support military forces of the order of magnitude that had been under arms in Ancient World.[28]

Delbrück argued for and showed that in the Ancient World there was an important correlation between the size of polity's population and the order of magnitude of its armies. Despite the fact that he recognized that the population of the West during the *floruit* of the Republic likely was smaller than it had been in the mid-third century A.D., he insisted that the armies of the latter period were smaller than those of the former. Delbrück even admitted that the effect of a barter economy, to which he was so firmly wedded, "was probably not very fast or strong in either one direction or the other."[29] Thus, it is striking when Delbrück asserts, contrary to Mommsen, that the number of men under arms in the later empire was much smaller than those of the Republic and early empire.[30]

Delbrück rejects Mommsen's researches which put the size of the imperial army at the beginning of the third century, under Septimius Severus, at 300,000 and the early fifth-century army of the Roman empire somewhere between 500,000 to 600,000.[31] The latter figure is provided not by narrative sources but by documentary evidence, e.g. the *Notitia Dignitatum*: indeed, documents

---

Middle Ages, see two works by Bernard S. Bachrach, "Animals and Warfare in Early Medieval Europe," *Settimane di Studio del Centro Italiano di Studi sull'alto Medioevo* 31 (Spoleto, 1985), 1: 707–64. Reprinted in *Armies and Politics in the Early Medieval West* (London, 1993); and "Logistics in Pre-Crusade Europe," pp. 57–78.

[28] *Art of War*, II, 214–17, and 227 for the quotation.

[29] *Art of War*, II, 220–24.

[30] *Art of War*, II, 226–29. See Theodor Mommsen, "Das römischen Militärwesen seit Diocletian," *Hermes* 24 (1889), 195–279. Indeed, most recent scholars, as their work is summarized by Dietrich Hoffmann, *Das spätrömische Bewegungsheer und die* Notitia Dignitatum (*Epigraphische Studien*, 7, 1 and 2, Düsseldorf, 169/70), see the armies of the later Roman empire as very large.

[31] Mommsen, "Das römischen Militärwesen," pp. 195–279.

which both then and now are regarded as providing sound and reliable data.[32] The sole "reason" Delbrück adduces for his position that the armies of the later Roman empire were "not larger but considerably smaller than in the period of Augustus and Tiberius" rests on the often asserted rule: "it is impossible to feed large armies on a barter economy basis."[33]

It is clear, moreover, that Delbrück's notions regarding the nature of the economy of later Roman empire and the early Middle Ages, which were controversial even when he wrote early in the twentieth century, have even less currency today.[34] Nevertheless, it is important to see how Delbrück dealt with various types of information provided by the sources, in light of his assumptions, when he did not simply reject the source *a priori* as was the case with the *Notitia Dignitatum*, mentioned above. This examination of Delbrück's methods is required, although his premises are seriously flawed, e.g. particularly those regarding the economy, because many of his conclusions are nevertheless still in vogue.

An exceptionally informative example of Delbrück's method is provided by his discussion of Ammianus Marcellinus' account of Roman operations against the Alamanni in 357 which ended with Julian's victory at Strasbourg. As Ammianus tells the story, the Roman plan was to catch the Alamannic army, which was drawn from a confederation of seven major groups, in a pincer between Julian's contingent of some 20,000 effectives, which would move eastward from Sens and the surrounding region, where they had wintered, toward Strasbourg, and Barbatio's force of some 25,000 effectives which was supposed to move north from their Rhaetian winter encampment. Thus, according to Ammianus, the Romans planned to put a force of some 40,000–45,000 troops into the field against the Alamanni during the campaigning season of 357.[35]

First, in discussing the Roman force, Delbrück believes that Ammianus, who tells his readers that Julian led 13,000 effectives in his victory over the Alamanni at the battle of Strasbourg, obtained this information from the general, himself. Secondly, Delbrück asserts, according to his traditional method, that Julian probably provided an undercount to Ammianus so as to give himself and to the Romans greater glory in their victory.[36] Delbrück then goes on to argue:

> But even if we assume that Julian actually did state too small a number, we
> may still conclude from this figure that it was no longer armies of 60,000 and

---

32 See now Hoffmann, *Das spätrömische Bewegungsheer, passim.*

33 *Art of War*, II, 227.

34 See, for example, Durliat, *Les finances publiques de Dioclétien aux Carolingiens (284–889), passim.*

35 Bk XVI, 11.1–15; 12.1–70, tells the basic story. Note that although Julian only arrived at Strasbourg with some 13,000 troops, Ammianus makes clear that many units had been detached from this main body at the beginning of the campaigning season and the force with which he went into battle was far smaller than the one with which he began the campaign.

36 *Art of War*, pp. 267–68, indicates a rather simplistic view of the sources available to Ammianus. See on this point John Matthews, *The Roman Empire of Ammianus* (Baltimore, 1989), p. 300.

80,000 men that fought the great decisive battle of that day. Even underestimates and exaggerations must still take into account prevailing contemporary
notions, and Julian could not give a number so distorted that his contemporaries would immediately have realized that. If he wanted to boast, he could of
course, have increased the strength of the Alamanni even more. Without considering his figure of 13,000 as absolutely credible, I still believe that from
this figure we may conclude with certainty that smaller forces were engaged
in this battle, and therefore also in this whole epoch, than in the wars of Caesar
and Germanicus.[37]

Delbrück goes on to conclude: "Ammianus tells us that Julian's army was
13,000 strong, and we have already explained . . . that this number may perhaps
be somewhat too small but was at any rate not very far from the true figure. If
we say between 13,000 and 15,000, we shall be on safe ground."[38]

Thus, after providing a lengthy rationale for Ammianus or Julian having provided an undercount of the Roman army, it seems that the figure cited by the
former is not really open to serious question as being so grossly low as to be
considered a massive exaggeration. Delbrück gives no reason for his calculations here other than his earlier assertion that he is certain that the armies of the
later Roman empire, putatively sustained by a barter economy, could not
possibly be as large as those of Augustus. Indeed, the number for Julian's force
provided by Ammianus is, according to Delbrück, approximately a 15% undercount at most and may well even be an absolutely accurate figure despite the
"rule" that narrative sources in such a context are not to be trusted.

More important, however, is Delbrück's articulation of the principle that
"even underestimates and exaggerations must still take into account prevailing
contemporary notions, and Julian could not give a number so distorted that his
contemporaries would immediately have realized that." Clearly, Delbrück
believed that Julius Caesar did not think in this way when that Roman general is
"accused" of grossly exaggerating the size of the Celtic armies against which he
fought. Delbrück obviously did not press this principle when dealing with the
large numbers provided in the *Gallic Wars*. Rather, in that context, he preferred
to focus on the principle that Caesar puffed up enemy numbers to enhance his
own glory. In short, some not so very subtle changes are to be noted in Delbrück's methods as he downsizes the armies of the later Roman empire in
accord with the demands of a barter economy. Indeed, the principle of "prevailing contemporary notions" is an important one but obviously Delbrück
believed that it could only be applied selectively.

Delbrück is likely correct in concluding that Julian fought at Strasbourg with
a force which was no larger than two of Julius Caesar's somewhat augmented
legions, i.e. somewhere between 13,000 to 15,000 effectives. However, Delbrück
ignores the fact that, according to Ammianus, Julian left his winter camp to

---

[37] *Art of War*, II, 226.
[38] *Art of War*, II, 226.

begin the campaign against the Alamanni with a force of some 20,000 effectives, i.e. a force larger than three of Caesar's legions.[39]

More importantly, however, Delbrück fails to give full attention to the fact that the Roman plan called for an imperial army of some 45,000 men to attack the Alamanni. Such a scenario very likely presumed an enemy Alamannic force at least half the size of the projected Roman army and very likely considerably larger (see below). Thus, in a worst case situation from a numerical perspective, the imperial planners envisioned a battle between the united forces of Julian and Barbatio, on the one hand, and the seven kings of the Alamanni, on the other hand, as resulting in the engagement of some 65,000 to 70,000 effectives. Obviously, the imperial staff, which in the winter of 356–357 planned the forthcoming campaign against the Alamanni, envisioned a clash, which from the point of view of combat effectives met the numerical criteria, adumbrated above by Delbrück, for the battles in which Caesar and Germanicus had fought.[40]

Ammianus puts the army of the Alamannic confederation led by seven kings and including both mercenaries and allied forces at 35,000 effectives available for the battle of Strasbourg (XVI, 12.26). Delbrück asserts: "The 35,000 Alamanni we can eliminate at once; this is the usual exaggeration." He then attempts to strengthen this argument with the observation: "There was never a time when 13,000 Romans were able to defeat 35,000 Germans in open battle and most certainly not in the fourth century."[41] Following this line of reasoning, if such nationalistic drivel can be considered reasoning, Delbrück confidently asserts that "the strength of the Alamanni was between 6,000 and 10,000 men."[42] If this order of magnitude is to be accepted for the Alamannic army then each of the seven kings, mentioned above, commanded on average about 1,200 or so effectives. By contrast, if Ammianus' figure is found plausible then each Alammanic ruler commanded about six to seven thousand effectives, i.e. a force of the same order of magnitude as a Roman legion of the Republican era.

Whatever we may conclude, even tentatively, regarding Ammianus' account of the size of the Alamannic force, the major question at this point in the discussion requires that we ask: Why has Delbrück jettisoned the important principle, articulated only a few pages earlier in his account: "even underestimates and *exaggerations* (my italics) must still take into account prevailing contemporary notions, and thus Julian could not give a number so distorted that his contemporaries would immediately have realized that"? If Delbrück were correct in

---

[39] See the discussion by Matthews, *The Roman Empire*, p. 317.

[40] Delbrück, *Art of War*, I, 471, 481–82, 491, 499–505, 544–49, regarding Caesar and concerning Germanicus, *Art of War*, II, 99, 100, 119, 227.

[41] *Art of War*, II, 227.

[42] *The Art of War*, II, 262. Delbrück's assertion that Ammianus says that Julian's forces outnumbered the Germans is a misreading of the text. Actually, Ammianus makes clear that Julian attacked while the Alamanni had not yet all moved into position. Some Alamanni were still on the other side of the river. Ammianus is well known for his superb military knowledge and for treating military matters in a highly nuanced manner. See on this Bernard S. Bachrach, "Some Observations on the 'Goths' at War," *Francia* 19.1 (1992): 205–14.

arguing that Ammianus' audience would not tolerate a distortion of more than 15% in undercounting the Roman army we can hardly assume that this same audience would not balk at accepting a 300% to 600% overcount in the number of the Alamanni – heroics against overwhelming odds not withstanding!

Delbrück's lack of consistency in his treatment of Ammianus' numbers is not compensated for by his "nationalistic" assertions regarding the military superiority of the Germans. Indeed, during the two centuries following Julian's victory at Strasbourg, imperial forces were successful in the overwhelming majority of their encounters with so-called "barbarian" armies, in general, and against the Germans in particular.[43]

Ammianus' observation (XVI, 12.47) that the Roman army was superior to the Alamanni in discipline at the battle of Strasbourg takes note of a tactical advantage which cannot be ignored in any evaluation of the question of the number of effectives involved in the conflict. The annals of military history are so overcrowded with examples of large undisciplined armies being defeated by much smaller but well disciplined forces that making lists would be superfluous.

There are several other problems with Delbrück's treatment of the Strasbourg campaign of 357. For example, it should be made clear that Ammianus' figure of 13,000 for Julian's army is an indication of the size of the imperial force known to the Alamanni prior to the battle, but does not include several units that had been detached from Barbatio's force. These troops joined Julian before the battle but only after the intelligence was provided to the Alammanic kings that put the imperial forces at 13,000 effectives. Thus, the Alammanic kings are depicted as deploying their forces under the false assumption that Julian was going into battle with only 13,000 men.[44] In addition, while the total army of the Alamanni is put at 35,000, it is clear from Ammianus' account that Julian attacked well before the full enemy force had crossed the Rhine and deployed for combat.[45]

Finally, it must be reiterated that the Romans initially devised a strategy which required a force of 45,000 effectives under imperial commanders to be sent against the Alamanni during the campaigning season in 357. In short, if Delbrück's assertion that the Alamannic forces numbered between 6,000 and

---

[43] The list below is not intended to be exhaustive. The emperor Valentinian brought the Visigoths to their knees in several major campaigns during the 360s, early in the fifth century Alaric I was defeated at Pollentia and Verona. Radegasius' huge army was slaughtered in 406, Constantius routed the Alamanni near Arles in 413 and brought the Visigoths to terms in 416. Aetius' forces consistently defeated the Visigoths and Franks during the two decades prior to his great victory on the Cataluanian plains in 451. Aegidius dominated the Franks in north-eastern Gaul until his death in 481 and during Justinian's reconquest in Africa and Italy, Vandal and Ostrogothic armies consistently were defeated by imperial forces. Imperial losses to German armies, such as the defeat suffered at Adrianople in 378, were very few and very far between.

[44] Matthews, *The Roman Empire*, p. 300.

[45] Delbrück, *Art of War*, II, 263–64, simply does not seem to know how to deal with this information provided by Libanius (*Or.* 18.56).

10,000 effectives is to be accepted then some good reason must be given as to why the Romans were preparing to use two armies totaling some 45,000 troops against such a small enemy force. In this context, one may believe, with Delbrück, that it took 45,000 Romans to defeat 6,000 to 10,000 Alamanni. However, it may be suggested that Julian, Barbatio and their advisors had received inaccurate intelligence regarding the Alamannic army and thus erroneously concluded that an Alamannic force of perhaps 30,000 to 35,000 would have to be engaged. If such were the explanation then an Alamannic army of an order of magnitude which could result in a battle of 70,000 combatants or even more surely was plausible to late Roman commanders even if they were mistaken regarding the particular campaign under consideration here. The most obvious conclusion, however, is that the Alamannic army was of an order of magnitude of 30,000 to 35,000 effectives.

According to Delbrück, the barter economy, which so weakened the Roman world and made large imperial armies impossible, continued well into the Middle Ages. He asserts that the "barter economy governed the civilized world not for just a few generations [as Max Weber had argued] but for much longer than a thousand years."[46] Indeed, Delbrück assumes that the earlier Middle Ages were even more economically backward than the last centuries of imperial antiquity. The barter economy and its putatively deleterious effect on the size of military forces thus forms the "evidential" undergirding or more accurately the controlling assumption for further discussions of the size of military forces in Western Europe until the first Crusade, the terminus of this study, and even beyond.[47]

The various Germanic and other peoples who invaded the later Roman empire all, are argued by Delbrück, to have had small armies. Indeed, their economies obviously were even more primitive than that of the Romans in the West during the last centuries of the empire. Delbrück sums up this view: "From start to finish, the Germans were principally warriors and not farmers."[48] Thus, having "established" by assertion that it was economically impossible for the Germans, who invaded the Roman empire in the fourth and fifth centuries, to field large armies, Delbrück turns to the written evidence. Here he employs his customary technique in dealing with the large numbers, which he finds in the narrative sources but are unacceptably high, and cites some obviously fantastic figures, e.g. 500,000 or 700,000 for the Huns at the battle of Châlons.[49] He then reiterates the types of derisive observations regarding the unreliability of the narrative sources, which are sprinkled through earlier chapters, and implies that anyone who would accept such figures as accurate must be considered a fool.[50] This tactic would seem to have been intended to inhibit the reader from accept-

---

46 *Art of War*, II, 237.
47 *Art of War*, II, 214, 227, 237, 326; and III, 55, n. 3, 169, 314.
48 *Art of War*, II, 292.
49 *Art of War*, II, 286.
50 *Art of War*, II, 285–99.

ing any number, even perhaps "reasonable ones," which are provided by what Delbrück believes to be chronically unreliable narrative sources.[51]

By reasonable numbers, in this context, I mean those of an order of magnitude which Delbrück already has accepted for forces which operated in the West during the Roman Republic and early empire, i.e. before the putative advent of the feudal barter economy. In these cases, and there are many, Delbrück falls back on the type of argument, described above, with regard to the imperial and Alammanic forces which are reported by Ammianus Marcellinus to have been mustered for the campaign which ended at Strasbourg in 357, e.g. a barter economy cannot sustain large armies. Thus, the narrative sources, invariably of imperial origin, are biased to exaggerate the size of the enemy force. Indeed, in his treatment of the battle of Adrianople in 378, where the field army of the emperor Valens was defeated by a unified force of Goths and their Alan allies, Delbrück argues, contrary to the information found in the sources and the conclusions of most other scholars, then and now, that the numbers of each force must be reduced to about 15,000 effectives.[52]

As part of his argument for this "reduction" of forces at Adrianople, Delbrück relies upon his earlier arguments for a "reduction" at Strasbourg. Without a hint of qualification, he asserts: "At Strasbourg a considerable numerical advantage on the side of the Romans is well attested. . . ."[53] Thus, after examining the only two battles of this period concerning which he considers that there is sufficient information available for estimating the size of the armies, Delbrück concludes: "It is impossible to arrive at any kind of average or normal figure for the various tribes we encounter. Only this much is certain, that we may never exceed 15,000 warriors for any of the migrating tribal armies."[54]

For Delbrück it followed naturally that the new kingdoms, which the Germanic invaders established with their small warrior bands and barter economies throughout the erstwhile western half of the Roman empire, fielded small armies. Indeed, he believed that these military forces became even smaller as the warrior spirit, which had sustained the Germans during the migrations and brought them victory over the Roman empire, was gradually attenuated during some two and a half centuries of settlement in civilian life.[55] The tribal warrior army gradually disappeared and was replaced by "a class of large estate owners" who were surrounded by their personal armed retainers. As Delbrück put it: "this warrior class was able to survive only in the status of vassals under the class of large estate owners." Thus, the real military force in this new Europe gradually fell to an aristocratic warrior elite of German descent who were joined

---

[51] A very good example of Delbrück's technique of intimidation (*Art of War*, III, 643–46) is found in his appendix dealing with the work of General Köhler.
[52] *Art of War*, II, 269–83. For the contemporary state of the question with the relevant literature see Hoffmann, *Das spätrömische Bewegungsheer und die Notitia Dignitatum*, I, 444.
[53] *Art of War*, II, 279.
[54] *Art of War*, II, 293.
[55] *Art of War*, II, 387–405.

by a very small smattering of others who adopted a new "feudal" ethos based upon mounted combat.[56]

This feudal military organization, Delbrück contends, was fully developed in the reign of Charlemagne if not earlier.[57] Indeed, Delbrück argues that the notices in contemporary texts of farmers and townsmen at war generally describe incompetent, untrained, and undisciplined local militiamen who were of no importance on the battlefield in the circumstances of a gradually emerging feudal world. Therefore they are not worthy of study in a proper history of the art of war.[58]

Delbrück believed that "The true feudal system was based on a pure barter economy" and thus this objective factor made it impossible for feudal armies to be large.[59] Therefore, he argues that the regulations found, for example, in various Carolingian documents for calling up a militarily viable general levy, i.e. a non-feudal force by his definition, was not a military matter but a fiscal matter. These summons were, in Delbrück's view, merely an excuse, a subterfuge, to collect a "disguised tax," i.e. the fine owed by those men who did not appear at the muster. This approach to the problem of the levy, which obviously had the potential to produce large numbers of non-feudal troops, was vulnerable on two counts. Delbrück treated the plethora of information on the levies, which is to be found in both documentary and narrative sources, in a highly selective manner. Secondly, the fine of 60 *solidi*, which Delbrück does discuss, was a huge sum to pay as a fine and the punishment of enslavement, with which he does not deal, strongly suggests that the Carolingians were interested in deterring non-compliance and not in establishing a hidden tax.[60]

Perhaps because he understood the weaknesses of his position regarding the "disguised tax levy," Delbrück developed a second line of attack in order to sustain his views that Charlemagne never led more than 10,000 effectives on campaign.[61] Thus, he asserts that Carolingian administration was so primitive that it could not possibly hope to maintain the lists of those eligible for service. He writes: "Let us imagine an administration whose leaders are all ignorant of the written language, who are dependent on their scribes as translators for every bit of information, every list, every report, every account. It was absolutely impossible for the central government to obtain a reliable idea of how many men were available in each district with how much property."[62] Even if we were to indulge Delbrück's imagination, and it not only is pure imagination but

---

56 *Art of War*, II, 427–59, pp. 428 and 439, respectively, for the quotations.
57 *Art of War*, III, 13, 49, 644.
58 *Art of War*, II, 387–426, and III, 97–98.
59 *Art of War*, III, 169.
60 Delbrück, *Art of War*, III, 17–18, 30–42. Regarding payments and enslavement see F.L. Ganshof, *Frankish Institutions under Charlemagne*, edd. and trans. Bryce and Mary Lyon (Providence, R.I., 1968), pp. 67–68.
61 *Art of War*, III, 22–23.
62 *Art of War*, III, 18.

imagination contrary to fact,[63] how would such a central government hope to collect the "disguised tax" it putatively worked so hard and deviously to establish through the issue of numerous regulations for the mustering of a large non-feudal levy?

Delbrück found his views that early medieval armies were small most severely tested in his account of the Carolingian conquest of Saxony. He writes: "Now that we have become convinced of how small Charlemagne's armies were, there arises with renewed persistence this question: How could he succeed in subjugating those Germanic peoples against whom the Romans, with their so much larger, economically so much stronger empire, and their perhaps tenfold stronger, disciplined armies had previously failed?"[64] Thus, Delbrück takes the only line of argument open to him, the Saxons were not "the same kind of men the Cherusci, Bructeri, Marsi, and Angrivarii had once been," i.e. "The strength of the early Germanic tribes was based on absolute barbarism, in which the man is only a warrior and only the warrior is a man. This condition had already disappeared by the eighth century."[65] Needless to say, this formulation is pure hyperbole for which Delbrück cites no evidence and for which no evidence exists.

For the Carolingians as throughout much of the Middle Ages, Delbrück asserts, the reader "shall be shown again and again what a difference in military strength is caused by an interval of a few stages of civilization."[66] Thus, the argument for small armies in the Middle Ages is complete. "Feudal warriorhood was the product of the barter economy" which made large armies impossible and concurrent "progress" from barbarism to feudalism reduced the numbers of

---

[63] For this old view, which was sustained into the early 1950s, see, for example, F.L. Ganshof, "Charlemagne et l'usage de l'écrit en matière administrative," *Le Moyen Age* LVII (1951): 1–25; and translated as "The Use of the Written Word in Charlemagne's Administration," in F.L. Ganshof, *The Carolingians and the Frankish Monarchy*, trans. Janet Sondheimer (London, 1971). However, for the new and very different state of the question see now Rosamund McKitterick, *The Carolingians and the Written Word* (Cambridge, 1989); and the favorable review by Bernard S. Bachrach, *Journal of Interdisciplinary History* 21 (1990): 321–23. Cf. the recent demurrer by Michael Richter, " '. . . *quisquis scit scirbere, nullum potat abere labore*'. Zur Laienschriftlichkeit im 8. Jahrhundert," in *Karl Martell in Seiner Zeit*, edd. Jörg Jarnut, Ulrich Nonn and Michael Richter (Sigmaringen, 1994), pp. 393–404. Richter's conclusion, based upon a study of Saint Gall charters inscribed before 789, that lay scribes were not an important factor in the writing of documents prior to the period of major Carolingian educational legislation does not affect the argument made here. The lay or religious status of the scribes and other agents available to the Carolingians is not of significance. Indeed, even Richter cannot deny that the educational legislation introduced by Charlemagne had an important impact on lay literacy. There is no argument regarding the literacy of the army of clerical bureaucrats in the Carolingian government. With regard to high levels of scientific knowledge see Bruce Stansfield Eastwood, "The Astronomy of Macrobius in Carolingian Europe: Dungal's letter of 811 to Charles the Great," *Early Medieval Europe* 3 (1994): 117–34.

[64] *Art of War*, III, 65.

[65] *Art of War*, III, 66.

[66] *Art of War*, III, 67.

warriors as "the inherent natural laws of warriorhood had changed them into feudal lords. . . ."[67] In light of this neat conceptual framework all information provided in the narrative sources and the documentary sources which provide reason to believe that armies were not small is, according to Delbrück, to be rejected and modern scholars have by and large obliged.[68]

Between 1911 and 1913, Alfons Dopsch published a massive and magisterial study of the Carolingian economy which destroyed previous arguments for a barter economy.[69] A second edition of Dopsch's *Wirtschaftsentwicklung der Karolingerzeit* appeared in 1922, and by 1923, when Delbrück published the second edition of *Geschichte der Kriegskunst*, the notion that a so-called "barter economy" prevailed in early medieval Europe was dead. Delbrück's response illustrates his fundamental misunderstanding of historical methodology as he asserted in an obviously circular argument against Dopsch: "I find on the contrary, the conclusions of my studies on the changes in military organization to be a new confirmation of the *accepted concept* [my italics]. The transition from the Roman legionary to the medieval knight is not conceivable without the shift of the ancient money economy into a barter economy." He then goes on to conclude that since armies were small a barter economy must have existed.[70]

How has it come about that a view of medieval military demography so lacking in methodological cogency has so dominated the field for so long? First, it is clear that many medieval narrative sources are unreliable when it comes to providing numbers. In so far as Delbrück provided a needed critique of the work of previous scholars, who often accepted or at the least did not reject numbers that were of an obviously impossible order of magnitude, he contributed valuable service and there was no need to look too closely at his methods. With a nod to Delbrück, subsequent specialists in medieval military history simply discounted the numbers found in the narrative sources and often even rejected figures found in documentary sources.[71]

The time for a revaluation of Delbrück's methods in dealing with late antique and early medieval military demography is long overdue. Scholars no longer

---

67 *Art of War*, II, 387, III, 166, for the quotations, respectively.
68 Karl Ferdinand Werner, "Heeresorganization und Kriegsführung im deutschen Königreich des 10. und 11. Jahrhunderts," *Settimane di Studio de Centro Italiano sull'alto Medioevo* 15 (Spoleto, 1968): 813–14, vigorously chides modern scholars for uncritically accepting the arguments for small numbers put forth by Delbrück and observes: "in contrast to the extraordinary mistrust of critical efforts which accompany every effort to establish a greater troop strength, it must be emphasized that the effective scholar does not gain distinction simply because he estimates the smallest possible number for an army but because his methods bring him closer to the truth and, in addition, he can prove his point."
69 *Die Wirtschaftsentwicklung der Karolingerzeit vornehmlich in Deutschland.* Dopsch's general views are more easily accessible in *Wirtschaftliche und Soziale Grundlage.*
70 *Art of War*, III, 54–55.
71 See, for example, Horst Zettel, *Das Bild der Normannen und der Normanneneinfälle in westfränkischen, östfränkischen und angelsächsischen Quellen des 8. bis II. Jahrhunderts* (Munich, 1977), and the critical review of his treatment of Viking numbers by Bernard S. Bachrach, *Speculum* 55 (1980): 613–15.

may look safely to Delbrück's work for an understanding of medieval military demography and reference to his arguments for the purpose of providing support for generalizations concerning the size of medieval armies must be abandoned. It is now time to rework fundamentally our assessment of the order of magnitude of medieval armies and it is time for Delbrück's work on this subject to be consigned to a chapter in the history of history writing.

TWELFTH-CENTURY CASTILE
AND ITS FRONTIER STRATEGIES

Theresa M. Vann

MEDIEVAL strategy is considered an oxymoron by military historians who write general surveys. These surveys consist of an exhaustive description of ancient and classical strategy, followed by a short, apologetic chapter on the Middle Ages focusing on the superior attributes of the Normans, who are depicted as an exception to the generally poor quality of medieval strategists. The author of the general history then turns with relief to the seventeenth century, when proper strategy begins again.[1] The justification for this schema is that medieval warfare, with its emphasis on taking and holding fortified places, could not and did not employ the grand strategy practiced by large armies.[2] Feudal warfare consisted of knights, who engaged in single combat according to

---

[1] B.H. Liddel Hart, *Strategy* (1954; reprint, New York, 1967), 75–82 admits to passing over medieval wars, ostensibly through lack of information but in reality because he believed that "the spirit of feudal chivalry was inimical to military art." Hans Delbrück, *Medieval Warfare* (Lincoln NE, 1982), also has a chapter devoted to strategy, in which he wonders if people in the Middle Ages were aware that open battle is the truly decisive action, and that the first law of strategy is to assemble and unite all of one's forces on the battlefield (325–26). Delbrück finds such battles rare and sieges far more common in medieval warfare, which he also characterizes as "knightly warfare." Philippe Contamine, *War in the Middle Ages*, trans. Michael Jones (Oxford, 1984), 219–28, characterizes medieval strategy as fearing pitched battle in open country and preferring the siege. He notes that medieval generals "were capable of conceiving and executing 'grand strategy' " which involved mastery of terrain (227). These same authors never specifically mention the Iberian reconquest, because they unquestionably accept that Europe stops at the Pyrenees. Closer to Spain, James F. Powers, *A Society Organized for War: The Iberian Municipal Militias in the Central Middle Ages, 1000–1284* (Berkeley, 1988), relies heavily upon these and other interpretations and does not analyze strategy as utilized by the municipal militias in Spain. Ambrosio Huici Miranda, *Las grandes batallas de la reconquista durante las invasiones africanas* (Madrid, 1956), has studied the great battles of the reconquest and attempted to recreate them using Christian and Muslim sources.

[2] W.C. Oman, *The Art of War in the Middle Ages*, ed. John Beeler (1885; reprint, Ithaca, 1953), 60, cites medieval examples where commanders who followed simple tactical precepts such as retaining a reserve or selecting a good position were considered to be exemplars of military leadership. He does not say, however, if this was an attitude expressed by contemporaries or one commented on by military historians. Strategy, says Oman, was non-existent in the Middle Ages. John Keegan, *A History of Warfare* (New York, 1993), attributes this depreciation of medieval military aptitude to Clausewitz, who assumed that war would be fought between states that had the resources to fight a total war.

the code of chivalry. Feudal levies of footsoldiers served for a limited period of time, which prohibited the formation of great armies. Campaigns themselves served a limited purpose in the acquisition of territory. No "master plan" existed whereby individual campaigns served a purpose that utilized all the resources of a nation.

These authors are following Clausewitz's definition of war and strategy, which focused on the total war practiced by eighteenth- and nineteenth-century European nation-states. A new generation of historians, however, recognize that medieval warfare was waged under different circumstances. Feudal kingdoms lacked the organization and the resources available in the later era. Medieval society could not support a large army for an extended period of time, and no medieval kingdom could practice total warfare without destroying itself. Not even the Iberian kingdoms, which have been characterized as a "society organized for war," could engage in total war year in, year out, year round. Most of the fighting consisted of skirmishes, and most of the military action consisted of sieges. A kingdom could rarely muster the resources to mount a large, set-piece battle. Scholarly assumptions about the formation of Iberian armies, however, continue to incorporate all the strategic drawbacks of medieval warfare by patriotically exalting the contributions of municipal militias and ignoring the role of professional forces. The resulting model does not reconcile the problems of raising armies with the idea of continual military expansion. The municipal militias were governed by lawcodes that influenced the size of armies and, presumably, the conduct of major campaigns, by setting three-month limits on military service. Yet, at the same time, the Christian kings pursued a policy of military expansion despite innumerable delays caused by these time constraints.[3]

The conduct of the Castilian reconquest during the twelfth century appears to follow a different path: a strategy of defense in depth, similar to that used by the Romans and by the Byzantines on their frontiers.[4] The military objective was to maintain a perimeter, or a screen defense, which would deflect the enemy's assaults against the main target. This strategy avoided large-scale pitched battles while it reacted to the enemy's seasonal predations. After the initial investment in fortifications, the perimeter could be maintained by militias raised by the frontier settlers. Only on rare occasions – approximately once a generation – did the Christian kingdoms raise a large army to protect or extend the perimeter defenses. This necessitated the mustering of the entire lay and ecclesiastical resources of the kingdom, and, by the thirteenth century, employed the use of the "bull of crusade" (*bula de cruzada*) to exploit the money and the manpower

---

[3] Powers, 116.

[4] For "defense-in-depth" strategy, see Edward N. Luttwak, *The Grand Strategy of the Roman Empire from the First Century A.D. to the Third* (Baltimore, 1978), 127–90; Arther Ferrill, *The Fall of the Roman Empire: The Military Explanation* (London, 1988), 45–46; Mark C. Bartusis, *The Late Byzantine Army: Arms and Society, 1204–1453* (Philadelphia, 1992), 296–97.

of western Christendom. Thus, the mustering of a grand army was a rare event, undertaken in response to a grave emergency, and not a common undertaking.

The resources available to the Christian kingdoms dictated this strategy, not ignorance of classical warfare. The thirteenth-century Castilians knew of Vegetius and Roman military strategy and tactics. Alfonso X borrowed from Vegetius when he discussed the management of armies in the *Siete Partidas*. He urged his generals to select the battlefield carefully, taking into account the direction of the wind, the sun, and the terrain.[5] He mentioned battle formations that Vegetius had described, such as the wedge and the wall, and introduces the *citara* as a Spanish innovation.[6] Alfonso X, however, assumed the successful general was already familiar with Vegetius, so he omitted such elements as the importance of keeping a reserve.[7] Alfonso wrote the *Siete Partidas* as a comprehensive codification of law, not as a military manual, so he was more concerned with defining words and events than with explaining maneuvers. For example, Alfonso observed that military terminology had changed since the days of Vegetius; that while the Latin used the word *combatir* to apply to all engagements, whether in the field, attacking a town or castle, or when engaging in single combat, the Spanish only used *combatir* to mean capturing a fortress. In comparison, Alfonso indicates that the Spanish used the word "fight" (*lidiar*) to mean single combat or combat between any number of men without commanders. A battle took place when both sides had kings who displayed banners to mark their divisions and who had an advanced guard, a main body, and a rearguard.[8] Such specialized vocabulary implies that the Castilians had a well-developed idea of the methods and principles of warfare. Alfonso had commanded armies, and his experience shows in the section on the logistics of an army on the march. It was apparent to Alfonso that an army on the move was an exposed army, and he was far more comfortable when the army was within the walls of a fortress. His concern must have been shared by generations of Iberian monarchs who knew the possibilities for ambush in Spain's mountainous terrain.[9]

---

5   Alfonso X, *Siete Partidas*, II, 23, vii; Vegetius, *Epitome de re militari*, III, 12, 13.
6   Ibid., xvi. Delbrück, 638–39, comments on Alfonso X's use of Vegetius and concludes that it could not have much relation to the warfare of the time. He especially cites Alfonso's interpretation of the wall, in which the feet of the infantrymen forming the wall were tied together, and takes Alfonso to task for assuming that the resultant inability to retreat indicated the Roman's scorn for the enemy.
7   Vegetius, *Epitome*, III, 16.
8   Alfonso X, *Partidas*, II, 23, xxvii.
9   The Spanish terrain left an army on the march at the mercy of irregular forces that could strike suddenly and withdraw. Emma Falque, Juan Gil, and Antonio Maya, eds., *Chronica Adefonsi Imperatoris* [*CAI*] (Turnholt, 1990), bk II, chaps. 21–23, describes such an encounter of the early 1130s in the Lucena countryside between the municipal militias of Avila and Segovia, numbering some 2000 men, and an Almoravid expedition against Toledo led by Tāshufīn. Tāshufīn had encamped when the militias stumbled across him. After taking "divine" council, they pitched their tents, left one half of the footsoldiers to guard them, and used their remaining forces to attack the Almoravid encampment at night. Powers, 1–3, cites

Twelfth-century fortifications in Castile © Theresa Vann

Ambushes could be successful, as we shall see, but no monarch was able to build a strategy around their continued success. As the work of Randall Rogers has emphasized, most medieval warfare consisted of sieges of castles or fortified towns, and the Castilian reconquest was no exception.[10] The Castilian chronicles contain numerous accounts of sieges; in contrast, there are very few accounts of large-scale battles taking place in open terrain. Motivated by the desire to expand or recapture screen defenses, twelfth-century Castilians took, settled, held (and periodically lost) strategic areas along the Tagus River, as if

this encounter as a typical example of the sort of service that municipal militias provided and as proof that these militias had mastered tactics and the division of spoils, as well as possessing all the capacities of a smooth, well-running army.
[10] Randall Rogers, *Latin Siege Warfare in the Twelfth Century* (Oxford, 1992), 1–9.

engaged in a giant game of chess. The Spanish preferred siege warfare because the sequence of events was predictable and a siege could be conducted without a large loss of life on either side.[11] A fortified position was either tenable or not, and one fortified position could be held with a comparatively small garrison. In contrast to the incremental positions won or lost by sieges, a full-scale field battle was a gamble that could win or lose kingdoms. So in general, the king's army served either to mount or relieve sieges, and not to engage in largescale military campaigns.

Twelfth-century Castilian strategy focused on retention of the city of Toledo, which Alfonso VI (1072–1109) had recaptured in 1085. During the same period, the Almoravids and the Almohads targeted the city for recapture.[12] The geography of the area played an important role in the positional fighting that took place along the Tagus River. The city of Toledo was defensively sited on a high escarpment surrounded on three sides by the Tagus. It had an extensive system of walls and towers, and its bridge across the river was defended on the opposite side by the castle of San Servando. Beyond San Servando other, secondary fortresses such as Aceca, Calatrava, Escalona, and Oreja guarded the routes to Toledo and acted as focal points for settlement.

Each fortress in this line of defense was part of a screen that absorbed Muslim raids. Individual fortresses might fall; San Servando and other outlying perimeter fortresses fell with distressing regularity to Muslim raiding parties.[13] But as long as the screen held, these individual fortresses could be retaken and Toledo was safe. By contrast, one major defeat that exhausted the resources of the defenders could signal the collapse of the screen, which would endanger Toledo. It could take a generation to replace the human loss from such a defeat.

This is demonstrated by the aftermath of the major battles in the area. Alfonso VI's defeat at the battle of Zalaca in 1086 left the road to Toledo open

[11] For example, see accounts of the militia of Ávila in Amparo Hernández Segura, ed., *Crónica de la población de Avila* (Valencia, 1966). The anonymous author seems genuinely surprised when any member of the militia is killed in action. This suggests that the militia primarily engaged in low-level raiding activity. Based upon municipal complaints, it seems that most militias preyed upon their Christian neighbors by stealing their cattle and disrupting their markets.

[12] Alfonso VI had taken Toledo in 1085 from al-Qadir by systematically attacking its hinterlands and by manipulating internal discontent against the Muslim king. The capture of Toledo precipitated the invasion of the Almoravids, who conquered the remaining Muslim kingdoms, and then launched an attack against Alfonso. For the Toledo campaign, see Charles Julian Bishko, "The Spanish and Portuguese Reconquest, 1095–1492," in *A History of the Crusades*, ed. Kenneth M. Setton et al., 6 vols. (Madison, 1976), 3:399–98; Bernard F. Reilly, *The Medieval Spains* (Cambridge, 1993), 96–97.

[13] After the capture of Toledo in 1085, Alfonso VI gave the castle of San Servando to the papal legate to serve as a monastery. But the papacy gave it back after Almoravid assaults against Toledo captured the monastery. The *Anales Toledanos* indicate that each Muslim attack against the city included the capture of San Servando. Other fortresses that were continually threatened or lost were Talavera and Calatrava.

to the Almoravids, but they chose not to follow up on their victory.[14] After his defeat at Uclés in 1108, Alfonso lost Toledo's eastern and southern perimeter devices and he did not have the resources to regain them.[15] His successors were too preoccupied with Aragonese intrusion in the area, leaving the Castilian settlers to their own defenses. For the first half of the twelfth century, Toledo was continually besieged by Muslim and Aragonese forces. Alfonso VI had lost most of the outlying fortresses at the battles of Uclés and Zalaca. After his death in 1106, his daughter and successor, Urraca (1109–26), focused most of her energies on fighting her husband, Alfonso I of Aragon (1104–34) and subduing rebellions at home. Alfonso VI's grandson, Alfonso VII (1126–57), first had to arrange a treaty with his stepfather before he could resume fighting to regain the fortresses in Toledo's hinterlands.

For their part, the Almoravid and later the Almohad states were based in North Africa and could not always devote their full resources to taking Toledo. During most of the twelfth century, they placed pressure on Toledo by raiding and similar strategic maneuverings, thus disrupting its life and isolating it from the rest of Castile. The Muslims recognized the strategic importance of securing Toledo's outlying screen fortresses before laying siege to Toledo itself, and their campaigns in the area indicate that they targeted specific Castilian fortresses.

The twelfth-century *Cronica Adefonis Imperatoris* is the best narrative source for studying the positional maneuvering that took place on the Toledo frontier, since it identifies fortresses that served as Almoravid bases for attacks on Toledo and which therefore had to be retaken by Christian forces.[16] For example, during the 1130s while Alfonso VII (1126–1157) was preoccupied with other matters, the Almoravid general, Tāshufīn ibn 'Alī b. Yāsuf, enjoyed considerable success against the local forces holding Toledo and its environs. The castle of Aceca, destroyed by Tāshufīn in 1133, was not rebuilt until 1138.[17] He also destroyed the castle of Talavera. In 1138 he attacked Escalona, Alfamin, and captured the castle of Mora through what the chronicle described as negligence on the part of the governor of the fortress who had not finished and provisioned it in a timely fashion.[18]

Toledo was so hazardous a posting that Alfonso VII appointed a rebel noble

---

[14] For Zalaca, see Bernard F. Reilly, *The Kingdom of León-Castilla under King Alfonso VI, 1065–1109* (Princeton, 1988), 187–90; Joseph F. O'Callaghan, *A History of Medieval Spain* (Ithaca, NY, 1975), 208–9. The loss of Zalaca also caused Toledo's eastern screen to fall, including Cuenca.

[15] For Uclés, see Reilly, 348–51. The loss of Uclés gave the Muslims the southern bank of the Tagus River.

[16] Rogers, 175–76, relies upon the *Chronica Adefonsi Imperatoris* to describe Alfonso VII's siege operations.

[17] *CAI*, p. 166, bk II, chaps. 33–35; pp. 201, 211, bk II, chaps. 14, 24–25.

[18] Ibid., p. 216, bk II, chap. 46. The governor, Munio Alfonso, eventually redeemed himself, and was made second-in-command at Oreja in 1139.

as its military governor because his predecessors had been killed.[19] Alfonso was not able to secure the southern perimeter of his kingdom until the late 1130s when he began to re-take and resettle the fortifications south of Toledo. He built a castle, Penna Nigra, to serve as a counter against Mora in 1138.[20] He undertook the siege of Oreja, a prominent Almoravid base against Toledo, and captured it in 1139.[21] The settlement *fuero* of Oreja (1139) makes it clear in its preamble that Alfonso's primary goal was the establishment of an effective force for the defense of Toledo.[21a] In the 1140s, he extended Toledo's southern screen into the valley of the Guadiana River. Here, his most important achievement was the capture of the castle and village of Calatrava in 1147.[22] Calatrava, situated on the Guadiana River near Ciudad Real, was strategically located on the road between Andalusia and Toledo. Just south of of the mountains, the castle, like Oreja, had been the origin for Muslim raids against the city of Toledo. It was vital for the Christians to retain Calatrava in order to defend Toledo's eastern flank, and the Muslims recognized that Calatrava had to be recaptured in order to mount future sieges against the city.[23]

Despite these successes, Alfonso VII lacked the resources to maintain an army in his newly-reconquered lands. Therefore, with the help of the archbishop of Toledo he resettled the territories, using the fortresses as strategic centers. This policy of resettlement also formed part of the Castilian strategy of defense-in-depth. The king required the settlers to raise militias that served with him for a specified period of time. The towns could engage in their own raids, capture booty, and extend their own territories. But the militia was only recognized as such when it performed service with the king or his representative.

The most successful militias, those of Ávila, Segovia, and Toledo, participated in royal campaigns and used these opportunities to present petitions to the king and to ask royal favor. It is doubtful if these three cities could have carried the burden of the reconquest unaided. The crown and the church subsidized their fortification, and the church frequently underwrote campaigns for defense and

---

19 Ibid., bk II, chap. 23.

20 Ibid., p. 217, II, 48.

21 The *CAI* describes the activities of the Almoravid governor of Oreja, Farax, against the Christians of Toledo. It also describes an unlikely story in which the Muslims, hoping to distract Alfonso VII from Oreja, attempted a siege of Toledo itself, but were dissuaded by Alfonso's consort, Berenguela, on the grounds that taking a city from a woman was an unchivalrous and unworthy thing to do.

21a C. Gutíerrez del Arroyo, "Fueros de Oreja y Ocaña," *Anuario de Historia del Derecho Español* 17 (1946), 654.

22 Rodrigo Jiménez de Rada, *Historia de rebus Hispaniae sive historia gothica*, ed. Juan Fernández Valverde (Turnhout, 1987), bk 7, chap. 4, says that Alfonso VII besieged Calatrava with war machines, because it posed a very great danger to the kingdom of Toledo.

23 Ambrosio Huici Miranda, ed. and trans., *"Al-Hulal al Mawsiyya": Cronica arabe de las dinastias Almoravide, Almohade y Benimerin* (Tetuan, 1951), 91: "Su cabeza es Toledo y su pico Calatrava y sus garras Granada y sus alas, la derecha el poniente y la izquierda el levante."

expansion.[24] The city militias could also draw upon the forces from the villages in their hinterlands, so as to ensure their self-defense.[25]

Without the support of the royal army, Toledo's small outlying fortresses could still be wiped out periodically. The narrative sources and the sequence of settlement charters indicate that, indeed, these fortresses had to be settled and resettled several times by different groups of people.[26] The legal endorsement of settlement by family groups and the emphasis on colonization suggests that settlers were too valuable a resource to waste in a full-scale battle.

Alfonso VII's grandson, Alfonso VIII (1158–1214), continued the policy of securing Toledo by garrisoning strategically-placed fortresses in 1177. He extended Toledo's screen by besieging and capturing Cuenca, the next fortified city to the east. This also opened up a new area to Castilian resettlement and defense. Alfonso's task was made easier by the birth in 1157/1158 of the first native Iberian religious military order, the Order of Calatrava. This organization was formed when Abbot Ramón of Fitero along with the city of Toledo and its archbishop pooled their resources to hold the castle of Calatrava against an expected Muslim siege that never materialized.[27] During the 1170s and 1180s Alfonso VIII gave to the military religious orders of Calatrava and Santiago many of the fortresses that Alfonso VII had originally captured and settled, such as Uclés, Ocaña, Aceca, and Zorita. As a result of this policy, these military religious orders held a swath of lands along the Tagus frontier that barred Muslim advance. The knights of the orders provided professionally trained and well-supplied forces for a wide range of offensive or defensive undertakings without limitations.

For almost thirty years, Alfonso VIII successfully conducted sieges and positioned his forces along the frontier. His first pitched battle against the full force of the Almohad army was an unmitigated disaster. In 1195, the Almohad caliph Ya'qūb al-Mānsur (1184–1199) invaded the peninsula and marched on Toledo.

---

[24] For example, the *CAI* and the *Anales Toledanos* report that Alfonso VI and Alfonso VII extended the walls of the town; Alfonso VIII allocated part of the royal revenues in the city to the maintenance of its walls. Thus the major cities of the kingdom did not have to bear unaided the cost of their own defense. The archbishop of Toledo was interested not only in the reconquest but also in protecting his financial investments in the area. The Toledan church underwrote the defense of Calatrava in 1157/58; Rodrigo Jiménez de Rada undertook major campaigns in Moya in 1210.

[25] It should be noted that the royal and ecclesiastical underwriting of city defenses ensured that the municipalities would never become a force to challenge royal power. It is doubtful that the towns would have done so anyway, since the trend in the twelfth and the thirteenth centuries was for the militias to resist military service.

[26] The city and the archbishop of Toledo provided settlers, but by the 1150s most of the settlers were Mozarabs, Arabic-speaking Christian refugees from the Almoravid empire.

[27] For the origins of the Order, see Joseph F. O'Callaghan, "The Affiliation of the Order of Calatrava with the Order of Cîteaux," in *The Spanish Military Order of Calatrava and its Affiliates* (London, 1975). Alfonso VII had entrusted the fortress to the Templars, but they apparently did not trust his successor, Sancho III, to relieve them in the face of the expected siege.

Alfonso VIII met his adversary at the unfinished fortress of Alarcos, hoping to forestall the threatened siege against the city of Toledo.[28] In July, Alfonso VIII gave premature battle, committing every mistake medieval strategists have been accused of. He did not wait for promised Leonese reinforcements and during the battle he did not keep a reserve. After losing the battle and with it his army, he and the small remnants of his forces fled to Toledo.[29] The city's defensive fortresses and lands were once again under attack.

With the loss of the Castilian army, the Almohads captured all of Toledo's southern fortresses in the Guadiana valley and conducted raids into Toledo's hinterlands until Alfonso VIII made a peace treaty in 1197.[30] If Alfonso made strategic errors, the Almohads also erred by not pursuing him to Toledo and immediately besieging the city. The main contingent of the Almohad army, however, returned to North Africa, leaving Alfonso to ruminate over an important learning experience. Alfonso's contemporaries did not blame a lack of battle strategy for the defeat, but a lack of siegecraft know-how: Alfonso's mistake was his insistence upon holding an unfinished fortress. By contrast, the king was determined that in future he would avoid the mistakes of Alarcos by meeting a major Almohad army with equivalent force.

Alfonso was fortunate to have a second chance against a full Almohad army at Las Navas de Tolosa in 1212.[31] This major Christian victory has been well-studied. It marked the end of Almohad power in the peninsula; it secured the Toledo frontier; it permitted resettlement in the valley of the Guadiana; and it ended a century of stalemate. Las Navas demonstrates that Alfonso could assemble an extraordinary force, drawing upon extra-peninsular resources, in order to fight a full scale battle. Initially, Alfonso was reluctant to encounter the Almohads for a second time on the battlefield, but Pope Innocent III (1199–1216) insisted that the Christian kings of Spain put aside their differences and start to fight the Muslims. Innocent, who pledged the resources of the Church, demanded that the campaign be resumed after the five-year treaty had run out. Papal aid eventually materialized as a bull of crusade, which raised money and troops for the endeavor throughout Europe.[32] Alfonso also secured

---

28 See the account in the *Crónica latina de los reyes de Castilla* (Valencia, 1964), 29–30, in which Alfonso VIII based his defense on the castle of Alarcos.

29 Huici Miranda, *Las grandes batallas de la reconquista*, 155.

30 See Jiménez de Rada, *Historia de rebus hispanie*, bk 7, chap. 30. The year following Alarcos the Almohads besieged Toledo, Madrid, Alcalá, Cuenca and Uclés; the third year after Alarcos, they besieged Toledo, Maqueda and Talavera, successfully attacking Santa Olalla (where many Toledans owned property) and taking Plasencia, Santa Cruz, Monténchez and Trujillo. It was at this point that Alfonso sought a treaty, so that he could deal with his neighboring Christian kings.

31 Reilly, 135–36; O'Callaghan, 245–49.

32 See José Goñi Gaztambide, *Historia de la bula de la cruzada en España* (Vitoria, 1958), 110–32. The papal sponsorship of the Las Navas campaign has been well established, including the pope's role in assembling a large army that contained units from outside the peninsula. Alfonso VIII and the archbishop of Toledo, Rodrigo Jiménez de Rada, obtained a bull of

the help of the neighboring kingdoms of Navarre and León, through treaties and alliances that he entered into in 1207, 1209, and 1211.

Concurrent with these international preparations, Alfonso also reorganized his local defenses and enhanced strategic positions around Toledo. In 1207, he decreed that all villages within the Toledo's territory owed service with the militia of the city. He further asserted that the forces organized by the archbishop of Toledo would be separate and that the Toledo militia would exercise no authority over the archbishop's men.[33] He gave additional properties south of Ocaña to the Order of Calatrava, for the stated purpose of defending against Muslim incursions.[34] In March, 1207, he extended his protection to the monastery of San Clemente in order to offset Muslim forays.[35] He obtained money in 1208 by selling at least two villages to the municipalities of Segovia and Cuenca for a combined sum of 4,500 *maravedís*.[36] By 1209, Alfonso was ready to begin provoking the Almohads by raiding the provinces of Jaen and Murcía. Shortly thereafter, he settled Moya. Concurrently, Pedro II of Aragon (1196–1213) captured parts of Valencia. The new caliph, Muḥammad al-Nāṣir (1199–1213) responded by landing in the peninsula and capturing the castle of Salvatierra (in the Guadiana) in 1211. He then returned to Córdoba, giving Alfonso VIII time to prepare for a major battle.

The army that gathered in Toledo in the winter of 1211–1212 consisted of contingents from Aragon, Navarre, León, and France as well as Castilian troops and the troops of the military religious orders. Descriptions of the battle indicate that the Christians used the classical strategy of managing large armies. The army was divided into three sections, each led by one of the three participating monarchs: Pedro II of Aragon, Sancho VII of Navarre, and Alfonso, who led the rearguard. Alfonso scattered the militia men among more-experienced troops.[37] This army recaptured the fortresses of the Guadiana and caught the Muslims encamped in the open at Las Navas. The battle that followed fully justified Alfonso X's concerns for an army out in the open, and it could be described as a sophisticated ambush. The Christians captured the caliph's tent; once that position was taken the battle was over and the Almohads withdrew.

Clausewitz would have recognized Las Navas de Tolosa as a proper battle, one that employed grand armies and necessitated planning and strategy. But it is the exception which proves the rule: that such battles were beyond the normal resources of a medieval kingdom. The Castilians alone could not muster for a

---

crusade and publicized the projected campaign through Europe. This bull of crusade attracted recruits and enabled Alfonso to finance his campaign.

[33] Julio González, *El reino de Castilla en la época de Alfonso VIII*, 3 vols. (Madrid, 1960), 3:391–93, no. 793.

[34] Ibid., 3: 393–95, no. 794. (1210) He gave them Huerta de Valdecarávanos and the Galiana palace in Toledo.

[35] Ibid., 3: 397–400, no. 797.

[36] Ibid., 3: 451, 458–59, nos. 827, 831.

[37] Ibid., 3: 566–72, 572–74, nos. 897, 898, for accounts of the battle written by Alfonso VIII and his daughter, Berenguela.

grand battle, and it took years for them to gain additional support from the pope and several other realms.

The departure of the French, or non-Iberian troops, before the end of the campaign appears to have been a cause of considerable concern. Las Navas was viewed as a holy war, an international effort, and not just a Castilian attempt to increase territory. Therefore, accounts of the battle contained in letters from Alfonso VIII and his daughter, Berenguela, to both the pope and to the French court, emphasized French abandonment of the Iberian troops. The same letters also stress that Iberian troops brought the crusade to its successful completion, and provide the best evidence for the employment of classical strategy at Las Navas.

Engagements like Las Navas were rare in the reconquest, since most warfare consisted of raids and movements against weaker forces and fortresses. The Christians and the Muslims both knew the rules of siege warfare well, and they knew the likelihood for success and survival. Large-scale engagements were chancy, and not undertaken unless absolutely necessary. We should remember that the reconquest was not a continual triumphant progression, and that during distinct periods the Christians were happy to hold what they had, rather than embarking on futile attempts to expand their territory. They had not the resources of an early modern state that could sacrifice subjects in the name of glory; their goal was to preserve their human resources in order to have settlers on the frontier.

FORTIFICATIONS AND THE DEVELOPMENT
OF DEFENSIVE PLANNING DURING
THE CRUSADER PERIOD

Paul E. Chevedden

THE study of medieval military architecture – Islamic, Byzantine, Western, and crusader – has received much attention, but the major emphasis has been placed on architectural description and archeological investigation. Little attention has been devoted to the development of fortifications during the Middle Ages. R.C. Smail's *Crusading Warfare, 1097–1193* was not primarily devoted to the subject of fortifications and the development of defensive planning in the crusader states, but his comments on this topic have been extremely influential and have served to stifle further discussion on this important subject.[1]

The Middle Ages saw notable changes in the design of fortifications, yet Smail denied that any changes in defensive planning occurred during this period. According to Smail, the scientific principles of fortifications remained unchanged during the crusader period, only the details of fortification and construction were modified. Smail states:

> At first sight, a Château Gaillard, a Crac [Hisn al-Akrād], or a Caerphilly bear little resemblance to the motte and bailey castles of the early twelfth century or to the earthworks of primitive peoples, but the principles of defense which their respective architects sought to express were unchanged.[2]

Smail's static view of medieval fortifications has been echoed in Geoffrey Parker's *The Military Revolution*, and P.M. Holt, also relying on Smail's seminal study, has stated that in the crusader period there were "no significant developments in military technology or tactics."[3] The sequel to Smail's work, Christopher Marshall's *Warfare in the Latin East, 1192–1291*, inherits Smail's approach to fortifications. While observing that the crusaders built, or rebuilt, a number of castles on concentric principles during the thirteenth century,

[1] Research on this article has been supported by a grant from the National Endowment for the Humanities, an independent federal agency. I would like to thank Les Eigenbrod, Vernard Foley, Werner Soedel and Donald Kagay for their discussion on the topics discussed in this paper.
[2] R.C. Smail, *Crusading Warfare, 1097–1193* (Cambridge, 1956), 217.
[3] Geoffrey Parker, *The Military Revolution: Military Innovation and the Rise of the West, 1500–1800* (Cambridge, 1988), 7; P.M. Holt, *The Age of the Crusades: The Near East from the Eleventh Century to 1517* (London, 1986), 76.

Marshall, nevertheless, states that for the period considered in his study, "there appears to have been little change in the methods of attack and defence which were employed."[4]

Although primitive earthworks, motte and bailey castles, and castles with a concentric plan all have in common a defensive enclosure to ward off hostile intruders, the defensive principles upon which they were constructed vary considerably. The vast changes in weaponry and siege methods made over the centuries were countered by corresponding changes in the design of fortifications, and this is particularly true of the era of the crusades.

The development of fortifications in any period is closely connected with corresponding developments in siegecraft, and an understanding of the one is essential to an understanding of the other.[5] Although it may seem obvious that new or improved offensive devices greatly affect the character of defensive systems, many of the available studies on medieval fortifications in the Middle East – by Deschamps, Creswell, Johns and Sauvaget – focus primarily on architectural concerns and ignore the continuous interaction of offensive and defensive planning which spurred developments and counter-developments in both fields.[6]

At the beginning of the thirteenth century military architecture underwent a radical change. To counter the destructive effects of a new and more powerful piece of artillery, military architects developed a new system of defensive planning. The new fortifications had two basic aims: (1) to resist the effects of the new artillery, and (2) to employ the new artillery against attackers. The earliest unequivocal manifestation of this new defensive scheme is the citadel of Damascus, rebuilt between 1203 and 1216 by Saladin's brother and successor al-Malik al-ʿĀdil Sayf al-Dīn Ahmad ibn Ayyūb (1196–1218).[7]

---

4 Christopher Marshall, *Warfare in the Latin East, 1192–1291* (Cambridge, 1992), 100, 212.
5 My methodology is not novel, but is patterned after the approach taken to the study of Greek fortifications by F.E. Winter, *Greek Fortifications* (Toronto, 1972) and A.W. Lawrence, *Greek Aims in Fortification* (Oxford, 1979).
6 Paul Deschamps, *Les châteaux des croisés en Terre Sainte*, 3 vols. (Paris, 1934–73); K.A.C. Creswell, *Early Muslim Architecture*, 2nd edn, vol. 1 in 2 parts (Oxford, 1969), and *The Muslim Architecture of Egypt*, 2 vols. (Oxford, 1952–59); C.N. Johns, "Medieval ʿAjlūn," *Quarterly of the Department of Antiquities in Palestine* 1 (1932): 21–33; idem, "Excavations at Pilgrims' Castle, ʿAtlit (1932): The Ancient Tell and the Outer Defences of the Castle," *Quarterly of the Department of Antiquities in Palestine* 3, no. 4 (1933): 145–64; Jean Sauvaget, "La citadelle de Damas," *Syria* 11 (1930): 59–90; 216–41.
7 Sauvaget, "Citadelle"; D.J. Cathcart King, "The Defenses of the Citadel of Damascus; a Great Mohammedan Fortress of the Time of the Crusades," *Archaeologia* 94 (1951): 57–96; ʿAbd al-Qādir al-Rīhāwī, *Qalʿat Dimashq: taʾrīkh al-qalʿah wa-āthāruhā wa-funūnuhā al-miʿmārīyah* (Damascus, 1979); Paul E. Chevedden, "The Citadel of Damascus" (Ph.D. diss., University of California, Los Angeles, 1986); Hanspeter Hanisch, "Der Nordwestturm der Zitadelle von Damaskus," *Damaszener Mitteilungen* 5 (1991): 183–233; idem, "Die seldschukischen Anlagen der Zitadelle von Damaskus," *Damaszener Mitteilungen* 6 (1992): 479–99; idem, "Der Nordostabschnitt der Zitadelle von Damaskus," *Damaszener Mitteilungen* 7 (1993): 233–96; idem, *Die ayyubidischen Toranlagen der Zitadelle von Damaskus: ein Beitrag zur Kenntnis des mittelalterlichen Festungsbauwesens in Syrien* (Wiesbaden, 1996).

To appreciate the novelty of al-ʿĀdil's defensive system and the radical transition in fortification design which it represents, one must first become acquainted with the system of defensive planning current in the twelfth century. During the twelfth century many defensive circuits were fortified with towers similar in dimensions to those found in Roman Syria, averaging 5.0 to 6.0 meters in width and projecting 3.50 to 4.0 meters from the wall. In accordance with the Roman scheme of defensive planning, these towers were positioned at roughly 30-meter intervals. The city walls of Damascus and Homs, rebuilt by Nūr al-Dīn (1147–74) during the middle of the twelfth century, conform to this arrangement. The city wall of Cairo and its citadel, built by Saladin (1169–93), follow a similar plan but with towers spaced at even greater distances.

Al-ʿĀdil, drastically altered the construction of defensive circuits and the building of towers, which became larger, higher, thicker, and more closely spaced. His towers, found on the citadels of Damascus, Cairo, and Bosra, are immense, as large as 30 meters square. As yet the only explanation offered for these abrupt and radical changes has been the advances made in ballistic technique.[8] What brought about al-ʿĀdil's new system of defensive planning was the

Clive Foss, in his study on the citadel at Kütahya in western Anatolia, has suggested that the addition of numerous close-set solid towers during the great rebuilding of period II was the result of the introduction of the counterweight trebuchet. This machine, argues Foss, "demanded a solid platform to support [its] great weight, and an open space to give the arm room to swing" (*Survey of Medieval Castles of Anatolia*, I: *Kütahya* [Oxford, 1985], 77). Hence, the solid platform towers of period II were introduced to accommodate the new machine. Foss contends that the counterweight trebuchet reached Byzantium by the middle of the twelfth century or earlier, and accordingly places the rebuilding of period II in the middle of the twelfth century (Foss, *Survey*, 83–84). Certainly, sturdier towers are required to support the weight of heavier artillery, but they need not be solid, as the hollow towers of al-ʿĀdil indicate. The purpose behind solid towers may be to create a nearly indestructible platform on which to mount artillery. But the original purpose of such construction may have been limited to preventing rams or mines from breaching the defensive enclosure. Foss's thesis rests upon his dating of the rebuilding of period II, and this has recently been called into question by Robert W. Edwards. Edwards has suggested that the work of period II covers part of period I construction of the mid-ninth century (review of *Survey of Medieval Castles of Anatolia*, I: *Kütahya* by Clive Foss, *Speculum* 62, no. 3 [1987]: 675–80). If Foss's thesis and dating of period II construction prove enduring, then it would be Byzantium, rather than Islam, which was the first to introduce changes in the design of fortifications to utilize the more powerful counterweight trebuchet. Even so, this would not diminish the importance of al-ʿĀdil's system of defensive planning, for his fortifications led to the first systematic attempt to introduce a new defensive scheme over an extensive part of the Ayyūbid empire. If the rebuilding of period II at Kütahya was part of a Byzantine attempt to respond to the challenge of the counterweight trebuchet, such an undertaking does not appear to have been carried out on a very wide scale.

8   Jean Sauvaget, "La citadelle de Damas," *Syria* 11 (1930): 229; A. Abel, "La citadelle eyyubite de Bosra Eski Cham," *Annales archéologiques arabes Syriennes* 6 (1956): 123; Janine Sourdel-Thomine, "Burdj," in *Encyclopedia of Islam, New Edition*, ed. H.A.R. Gibb, J.H. Krammers, E. Lévi-Provençal, J. Schacht, et al., 9 volumes to date (Leidon, 1960–), 1:1316. Hugh Kennedy endorses my interpretation that the introduction of the counterweight trebuchet led to radical changes in the design of fortifications in his *Crusader Castles* (Cambridge, 1994), 9, 107–19, 182.

introduction of a new and devastating piece of artillery, the counterweight trebuchet. This very powerful and extremely accurate weapon revolutionized the defensive-offensive pattern of warfare and stimulated innovations in fortification design that sought to offset the tremendous advantage enjoyed by offensive forces due to the use of gravity-powered artillery.

To determine what a revolutionary impact the counterweight trebuchet had and to understand how al-ʿĀdil's system of defensive planning was designed to counter it, we must first examine the machine. By the end of the sixth century a new class of artillery had replaced the tension and torsion-powered stone-projectors of classical antiquity.[9] This class of artillery, conventionally denoted by the French term "trebuchet," consisted of a beam that pivoted around an axle that divided the beam into a long and short arm. At the end of the longer arm was a sling for hurling the missile, and at the end on the shorter one, pulling ropes were attached, or, in later versions, a counterweight. To launch a projectile, the short arm, positioned aloft, was pulled downward by traction or gravity power, or by a combination of both forces. The impetus applied to the beam propelled the throwing arm of the machine upward and caused the missile to be hurled from the sling.

Three distinct forms of this artillery developed: the traction trebuchet, powered by crews pulling on ropes; the hybrid trebuchet, powered by both a pulling-crew and gravity power; and the counterweight trebuchet, activated solely by the force of gravity obtained by the fall of a large pivoting mass. The traction trebuchet, invented by the Chinese sometime before the fourth century BCE, was superceded at the beginning of the eighth century by the hybrid trebuchet. This machine appears to have originated in the realms of Islam under the impetus of the Islamic conquest movements. By the ninth century the hybrid trebuchet was being used in the Middle East and the Mediterranean world, as well as in northern Europe. The early twelfth century marked a breakthrough in the development of mechanical artillery with the introduction of the counterweight trebuchet. This behemoth of the siege arsenal made its first appearance in the Eastern Mediterranean as the crusader states were being established. During the thirteenth century the Mongols facilitated the diffusion of the counterweight trebuchet across Eurasia when they utilized this machine in their conquest of Sung China.[10]

---

[9] On the artillery of classical antiquity, see Paul E. Chevedden, "Artillery in Late Antiquity: Prelude to the Middle Ages," in *The Medieval City under Siege*, ed. Ivy Corfis and Michael Wolfe (Woodbridge, Suffolk, 1995), 131–73.

[10] Paul E. Chevedden, Les Eigenbrod, Vernard Foley and Werner Soedel, "The Trebuchet: Recent Reconstructions and Computer Simulations Reveal the Operating Principles of the Most Powerful Weapon of its Time," *Scientific American* (July 1995): 66–71; Paul E. Chevedden, "The Artillery of King James I the Conqueror," in *Iberia and the Mediterranean World of the Middle Ages: Essays in Honor of Robert I. Burns, S.J.*, ed. P. E. Chevedden, D.J. Kagay and P.G. Padilla (Leiden, 1996), 179–222; Paul E. Chevedden, "The Hybrid Trebuchet: The Halfway Step to the Counterweight Trebuchet," in *On the Social Origins of Medieval Institutions: Essays in Honor of Joseph F. O'Callaghan*, ed. Donald J. Kagay and Theresa M. Vann (Leiden, 1998), 179–222.

The elaboration of the trebuchet in its three forms advanced the destructive power of mechanical artillery considerably. The most powerful Chinese traction trebuchet with a 250-man pulling-crew was capable of throwing a stone-shot weighing between 54 and 60 kilograms a distance of more than 77 meters.[11] The hybrid trebuchet was far more powerful than its progenitor and easily outstripped the artillery of the classical world. In 1218, crusaders besieging Damietta in the Nile delta utilized a hybrid trebuchet that launched stone-shot weighing 185 kilograms, six times as heavy as that of the most commonly used large ancient catapults.[12] Counterweight trebuchets could do much more. Their projectiles probably reached a common maximum of 300 kilograms, and during the fourteenth century there are reports of counterweight trebuchets which launched stones weighing between 907 and 1,360 kilograms.

The counterweight trebuchet was so far superior to any artillery piece yet invented that its introduction brought about a revolution in siegecraft that rendered existing systems of defense inadequate or obsolete. This gravity-powered siege engine could discharge missiles of far greater weight than the traction or hybrid machines, and it could do so with remarkable accuracy. The machine was thus able to deliver devastating blows against the same spot of masonry time after time, and this made it potentially capable of demolishing the strongest built fortified enclosures.

A counterweight trebuchet (*manjanīq maghribī*) employed by al-Sālih Ayyūb at his siege of Homs in the winter of 646/1248–49 threw a stone-shot weighing 140 Syrian *ratl*s (259 kilograms).[13] The large Frankish trebuchets (*manjanīq al-kibār al-ifranjīyah*) employed by Sultan al-Ashraf Khalīl at the siege of Acre in 690/1291 launched stone-shot weighing more than one Damascus *qintār* (185 kilograms).[14] Rounded stone missiles of trebuchets preserved at Qalʿat Sahyūn

---

11 This quantitative data is taken from the Chinese military treatise, *Wu Ching Tsung Yao* ("Collection of the Most Important Military Techniques"), completed in 1044. For this important data see Yang Hong, ed., *Weapons in Ancient China* (New York, 1992), 266; and Chevedden, "Hybrid Trebuchet," 213–14.

12 Sawīrus ibn al-Muqaffaʿ, *History of the Patriarchs of the Egyptian Church*, ed. and trans. Y. ʿAbd al-Masīh and O.H.E Burmester, 4 vols. (Cairo, 1942–74), 3, pt. 2, 219 (Arabic text); 218.

13 Jamāl al-Dīn Muhammad ibn Sālim ibn Wāsil, *Mufarrij al-kurūb fī akhbār Banī Ayyūb* fol. 61r, MS. 1703, fonds arabe, Bibliothèque Nationale, Paris; Donald R. Hill, "Trebuchets," *Viator* 4 (1973): 106.

14 Qutb al-Dīn Mūsá ibn Muhammad al-Yūnīnī, *Dhayl mirʾāt al-zamān*, in Antranig Melkonian, *Die Jahre 1287–1291 in der Chronik al-Yūnīnīs* (Freiburg, 1975), 86 (Arabic text). Melkonian unfortunately provides the equivalent weight of 45 kilogram for one Damascus *qintār* by considering it to be equal to 100 Egyptian *ratl*s (al-Yūnīnī, *Dhayl*, 162). Little has followed Melkonian in this error (Donald P. Little, "The Fall of ʿAkkā in 690/1291: The Muslim Version," in *Studies in Islamic History and Civilization in Honour of Professor David Ayalon*, ed. Moshe Sharon [Jerusalem–Leiden, 1986], 171). The Damascus *qintār*, composed of 100 *ratl*s, was equal to 185 kilogram or 408 pounds (see Walther Hinz, *Islamische Masse und Gewichte* [Leiden, 1970], 26, 30).

vary in weight from 50 to 300 kilograms.[15] With missiles uniformly calibrated
and with a counterweight set at a fixed amount, this machine was capable of pin-
point accuracy.[16] Huge missiles, of the size mentioned above, launched repeatedly against the same spot of a fortified enclosure would eventually demolish
the best defensive masonry.

The devastating effect of the counterweight trebuchet is exhibited in the following account of al-Kāmil's siege of Harrān and Edessa in 633/1236.

> [T]he Sultan [al-Kāmil] returned to Harran (Harrān), and took up position
> against its fortress, and he besieged it for some days, and it resisted, and he set
> up a Western-Islamic trebuchet [*manjanīq al-maghribī*], and he took it by the
> sword. . . . And he (the Sultan) went to Edessa (al-Ruhā), and he took up
> position against its fortress, and it was more fortified and more impregnable,
> than the fortress of Harran (Harrān), but it did not withstand the Western-
> Islamic trebuchet, for it demolished its curtain walls, the day it was set up
> against it, and it (the fortress) was also taken by the sword.[17]

The ease with which these two well-fortified cities were overrun demonstrates
the effect which the counterweight trebuchet had upon siege warfare.

To avert the danger posed by the counterweight trebuchet al-ʿĀdil devised
new fortifications that utilized gravity-powered artillery for defense. Optimal
use of the new artillery required that the machines be mounted on the platforms
of towers in order to prevent enemy artillery from coming within effective range.
Towers had been used previously as elevated artillery-emplacements, but the
size of the new artillery now necessitated an extensive overhaul in fortification
design. As a result, towers became larger in order to accommodate counterweight trebuchets and taller to enable the artillery to out-range enemy machines
of greater power. Maximum exploitation of the new artillery was achieved by
the proliferation of towers. Fortifications were now transformed from walled
enclosures with small towers into clusters of large towers joined by short
stretches of curtain walls.

The use of artillery on the platforms of towers was not the only element in
al-ʿĀdil's new defensive scheme. Walls were thickened in order to offer more
resistance to bombardment. Strong masonry and stout walls, however, could no
longer be relied upon for protection. The counterweight trebuchet had rendered
the passive system of defense obsolete. Now, an active defense was required.
Consequently, the floors of towers and curtain walls were brought down to
ground level, and postern gates were erected in order to conduct sallies in force
aimed at destroying the enemy's siege machines. If the enemy attack could not

---

[15] Paul Deschamps, *Terre Sainte Romane* (Paris, 1964), 34; Jabrāʾīl Saʿādah, "Taʾrīkh Qalʿat
Salāh al-Dīn," *Annales archéologiques arabes Syriennes* 17 (1967): 66 and fig. 5.

[16] Ibn Urunbughā mentions other adjustments which can be made to the counterweight trebuchet to vary the range of the shot (Ibn Urunbughā al-Zaradkāsh, *al-Anīq fī al-manājanīq*,
ed. Nabīl Muhammad ʿAbd al-ʿAzīz Ahmad [Cairo, 1981], 22–24; idem, *al-Anīq fī al-
manājanīq*, ed. Ihsān Hindī [Aleppo, 1985], 41–44).

[17] Ibn al-Muqaffaʿ, *History*, 4, pt.1, 147.

be stopped by bombardment and sallies, the ditch and the walls, flanked by boldly projecting and closely-spaced towers, provided the last line of defense.

This new system of defensive planning was first realized by al-ʿĀdil in his construction of the citadel of Damascus. Although al-ʿĀdil's rebuilding of the citadel of Bosra had begun nearly a year earlier, activity had abruptly halted following the completion of just one tower. Work on the citadel of Bosra was not resumed until most of the outer defenses of the citadel of Damascus were completed, and the citadel of Bosra did not take its final form, with eight massive towers projecting from its defensive perimeter, until 615/1218.

Al-ʿĀdil's work on the citadel of Cairo amounted to additions to the fortress of Saladin rather than to a thorough revamping of the fortifications, as was the case at Damascus.[18] The citadel of Mt. Tabor, begun by al-ʿĀdil in 607/1211, and completed by his son al-Muʿazzam ʿĪsá in 612/1215, possessed relatively few towers for a fortress of its size. Only thirteen have been located along its vast rectangular enclosure of 250 by 580 meters.[19] The citadel of Damascus, therefore, represents the earliest unambiguous expression of al-ʿĀdil's new defensive scheme and constitutes the first large-scale systematic attempt to thwart the most powerful form of mechanical artillery ever devised. As the forerunner of revolutionary changes in fortification design, the citadel of Damascus stands as one of the finest achievements of Islamic military architecture.

From the early thirteenth century onward, fortifications were steadily overhauled and improved to defend against the devastating counterweight trebuchets. Within the Ayyūbid realm, new towers of massive dimensions were added to castles and citadels, such as those of Shayzar, Qalʿat Mudīq, Baalbek, Qalʿat al-Shaqīf, Qalʿat al-Subaybah, and Qalʿat ʿAjlūn.[20]

Urban defenses were also revamped with the addition of large towers. In

---

18 On al-ʿĀdil's work on the citadel of Bosra, see Abel, "Citadelle," and Salīm ʿĀdil ʿAbd al-Haqq, "Masrah Busrá wa-qalʿatuhā," *Annales archéologiques arabes Syriennes* 14 (1964): 5–22. The work on the defenses of the citadel of Cairo undertaken by al-ʿĀdil's son and successor al-Kāmil comprised the construction of six massive towers (Burj al-Suffah, Burj Kirkyilān, Burj al-Turfah, Burj al-Sahrāʾ, the northwest corner tower, and the square tower immediately to the south of the northwest corner tower), and the rebuilding and enlargement of four semi-circular towers built by Saladin (the two towers flanking Bāb al-Qarāfah, Burj al-Raml and Burj al-Haddād). The large square towers are immense structures: Barj al-Suffah is approximately 25 meters square, Burj Kirkyilān is roughly 21 meters square, Burj al-Turfah is about 30 meters square, the northwest corner tower is approximately 21 meters square, and its southern neighbor is about 25 meters square. On these fortifications, see K.A.C. Creswell, *The Muslim Architecture of Egypt*, 2 vols. (Oxford, 1952), 2:1–40.

19 On this fortress, see A. Battista and B. Bagatti, *La fortezza saracena del Monte Tabor: AH. 609–15/AD. 1212–18* (Jerusalem, 1976), pp. 45–46, pls 1 and 33. The largest tower of the citadel of Mt. Tabor is the rectangular west gate-tower which measures 20 by 15 meters.

20 On the citadel of Shayzar, see Max van Berchem and Edmond Fatio, *Voyage en Syrie*, 2 vols. (Cairo, 1913–15), 1:178–87, 2: pls. 25–27; Kāmil Shahādah, "Qalʿat Shayzar," *Annales archéologiques arabes Syriennes* 31 (1981): 107–28; and Gaston Wiet, Jean Sauvaget, and Etienne Combe, eds., *Répertoire chronologique d'épigraphie arabe [RCEA]*, 17 vols. in progress (Cairo, 1931–), 11:36–37, no. 4057. On Qalʿat al-Mudīq, see Berchem-Fatio, *Voyage*

Jerusalem, a tower erected by al-Muʿazzam ʿĪsá in 609/1212 was recently uncovered along the southern part of the city wall. It measures 23 meters square.[21] The other towers constructed by this prince along the city walls of Jerusalem were probably of similar size, but all trace of them now lies below ground level. The new city walls which al-Muʿazzam ʿĪsá erected in Jerusalem were dismantled in 616/1219 shortly after their construction, and what portions survived were reused in the building of the new city walls constructed by Sultan Sulaymān I between 944/1537 and 947/1541.

The city walls of Aleppo, rebuilt by al-Nāsir Yūsuf in 642/1244–45, were also fortified with massive towers. Some twenty towers of these were erected between Bāb al-ʿArbaʿīn and Bāb al-Qinnasrīn, and Ibn Shaddād states that each resembled a castle (*qalʿah*). According to this author, the towers exceeded 40 *dhirāʿ* (22 meters) in height and were between 40 to 50 *dhirāʿ* (22 to 27 meters) in length. Each tower had galleries to protect the combatants from arrows and the stones of the trebuchets (*majāniq*).[22]

The city wall of Damascus also appears to have been refortified with some large rectangular towers at this time. The northeast corner tower (face, 8.58 meters; east side, 5.14 meters; west side, 5.82 meters) was constructed by al-Sālih Ayyūb in 646/1248–49.[23] In 1967, the foundations of a large rectangular tower dating from the Ayyūbid period were uncovered at the southeast corner of

1:189–94; 2: pl. 27; and *RCEA* 10: 5, no. 3608. On the citadel of Baalbek, see Theodor Wiegand, ed., *Baalbek Ergebnisse der Ausgrabungen und Untersuchungen in dem Jahren 1898–1905*, 3 vols. (Berlin–Leipzig, 1921–25), 3: 15, 16, 62–65, 69–72, pls. 3–4. On Qalʿat al-Shaqīf, see Deschamps, *Châteaux*, 2: 177–208, pls. 53–57. On Qalʿat al-Subaybah, see Deschamps, *Châteaux*, 2: 145–74, pls. 35–52. On Qalʿat ʿAjlūn, see C.N. Johns, "Medieval ʿAjlūn," *Quarterly of the Department of Antiquities in Palestine* 1 (1932): 21–33.

[21] On this tower and the inscription commemorating its construction in Jumādá I 609/29 September–28 October, 1212 by al-Malik al-Muʿazzam ʿĪsá, see Magen Broshi, "Notes and News: Mount Zion," *Israel Exploration Journal* 24 (1974): 285; idem, "Along Jerusalem's Walls," *Biblical Archeologist* 40 (March 1977): 11–17; M. Sharon, "The Ayyūbid Walls of Jerusalem: A New Inscription from the Time of al-Muʿazzam ʿĪsá," in *Studies in Memory of Gaston Wiet*, ed. M. Rosen-Ayalon (Jerusalem, 1977), 182; Nahman Avigad, "News and Notes: Jerusalem, the Jewish Quarter of the Old City, 1977," *Israel Exploration Journal* 28 (1978): 200–201; idem, *Discovering Jerusalem* (Nashville, 1980), 251–55. Both Broshi and Avigad believe that this tower is a gate-tower, which they identify with the Nea Gate, since it is situated in line with the *cardo* of Roman-Byzantine Jerusalem running south from the Damascus Gate. This tower is most likely not a gate-tower. The stones which Broshi ascribes to the gate do not offer convincing proof of the existence of a main gateway on the tower; there are no surviving Ayyūbid or Mamlūk gate-towers like this one, designed with an obtrusive pillar in the center; and the foundation inscription makes no mention of a gate, only of the construction of a tower. The tower may have been provided with a postern, but not a main gate.

[22] ʿIzz al-Dīn Muhammad ibn Shaddād, *al-Aʿlāq al-khatīrah fī dhikr umarāʾ al-Shām wa-al-Jazīrah: [Taʾrīkh madīnat Halab]*, ed. Dominique Sourdel (Damascus, 1953), 19.

[23] Salāh al-Dīn al-Munajjid, *Dimashq al-qadīmah: aswāruhā, abrājuhā, abwābuhā* (Damascus, 1945), 31–33.

the city wall. The tower measured 20 meters along its face and its west flank projected 17 meters from the curtain.[24]

It is very likely that this tower was erected by al-Muʿazzam ʿĪsá in 623/1226, since comtemporary inscriptions of this ruler on Bāb Sharqī, to the north of this tower, and on Bāb al-Saghīr, to the west of this tower, record the rebuilding (*tajdīd*) of the city wall.[25] Sibt ibn al-Jawzī even credits al-Muʿazzam ʿĪsá with the building of the city wall of Damascus (*baná sūr Dimashq*),[26] so it is quite likely that the work of al-Muʿazzam ʿĪsá was extensive and that he erected a number of large rectangular towers along the section of wall stretching from Bāb al-Saghīr to Bāb Sharqī. Stephan von Gumpenberg, who visited Damascus in 1449, records that all of the towers along the city walls were semi-circular, except for every fourth tower, which was a large rectangular tower.[27] These large rectangular towers, which have long since vanished, most probably date from al-Muʿazzam ʿĪsá's rebuilding of the city wall in 623/1226.

In the Islamic realms of Anatolia, towers erected during the thirteenth century took on immense proportions. The enormous circular towers constructed by the Artuqid sultan al-Sālih Nāsir al-Dīn Mahmūd (597–619/1201–22) on the city walls of Diyarbakir – the Ulu Badan and Yedi Kardash – are over 25 meters in diameter.[28] The octagonal Red Tower at Alanya erected in 623/1226 by the sultan of the Seljuqs of Rūm, ʿAlāʾ al-Dīn Kay Qubādh I (613–34/1219–37), is 29 meters in diameter and reaches a maximum height of 33 meters.[29]

At the same time, crusader fortifications were transformed to meet the threat posed by the counterweight trebuchet. During the early thirteenth century, the Krak des Chevaliers (Hisn al-Akrād) was ringed with an outer wall. Once this work was completed, the inner defenses were revamped, and the southern front, which was the side most vulnerable to attack, was provided with three massive towers (towers K, J, and I). These structures surely functioned as artillery-emplacements.[30]

---

24 Nasīb Salībī, "Asbār al-burj al-janūbī al-sharqī li-sūr Dimashq," *Annales archéologiques arabes Syriennes* 32 (1982): 23–34.

25 Nikita Elisséeff has published the inscription at Bāb Sharqī ("A propos d'une inscription d'al-Malik al-Muʿazzam ʿĪsá; contribution à l-étude de son regne," *Annales archéologiques arabes Syriennes* 4–5 [1954–55]: 4), and Salāh al-Dīn al-Munajjid has published the inscription at Bāb al-Saghīr (*Dimashq al-qadīmah*, 50).

26 Shams al-Dīn Yūsuf Sibt ibn al-Jawzī, *Mirʾāt al-zamān fī taʾrīkh al-aʿyān*, ed. J.R. Jewett (Chicago, 1907), 429, and idem, *Mirʾāt al-zamān*, 2 vols. (Hyderabad, 1951–52), 2: 650.

27 Von Gumpenberg's description of the city wall of Damascus is found in Sigmund Feyerabend, *Reyszbuch desz heyligen Lands* (Frankfurt-am-Main, 1584), 242v–43r.

28 The Ulu Badan, which is 25.50 meters in diameter, was constructed, according to its foundation inscription, in 605/1208–09 (Albert Gabriel, *Voyages archéologiques dans la Turquie orientale*, 2 vols. [Paris, 1940], 1:115–21, 323–24). The Yedi Kardash, which is 27.80 meters in diameter, carries a foundation inscription, but it is not dated (Gabriel, *Voyages*, 1:121–25, 324).

29 Seton Lloyd and D. Storm Rice, *Alanya (ʿAlāʾiyya)* (London, 1958), 11–16, 50–54.

30 Deschamps, *Châteaux* 1: pp. 190–92, pls. 25, 32, 38, 40, 41, and 43.

The defenses of the Château Pèlerin at 'Atlīt, begun in 1217, were designed with artillery in mind. Since the castle is surrounded on three sides by the sea, its defensive strength is concentrated on the landward or eastern side. Here the outer wall is fortified with three rectangular gate-towers set approximately 44 meters apart. These towers are composed of two floors and were originally surmounted by a spacious platform enclosed by a parapet. The two southernmost towers are approximately 20 meters long and the northern tower is roughly 16 meters long. All three towers project about 12 meters from the curtain wall. Behind this formidable outer defense is the inner wall which is fortified by two enormous towers which are approximately 28 meters long by 18 meters deep. Both of these towers originally rose to a height of over 34 meters. The reason for the great size and height of these towers is that they were designed primarily as artillery-emplacements.[31]

The fortifications of crusader cities were also transformed during the thirteenth century with the addition of large towers. Acre is a good example of urban fortifications. Its outer defenses consisted of a double line of walls fortified by enormous rectangular towers.[32] Only the most massive bombardment by trebuchets ever mounted was able to break the defenses of this city.[33]

---

[31] C.N. Johns, "Excavations at Pilgrims' Castle, 'Atlit (1932); The Ancient Tell and the Outer Defences of the Castle," *Quarterly of the Department of Antiquities in Palestine*, 3, no. 4 (1933), 145–64.

[32] Wolfgang Müller-Wiener, *Castles of the Crusades* (London, 1966), 72–74; David Jacoby, "Crusader Acre in the Thirteenth Century: Urban Layout and Topography," *Studi Medievali*, 3rd ser., 20, fasc. 1 (1979): 1–45.

[33] According to Abū al-Fidā', more trebuchets were employed in the siege of Acre in 1291 than against any other place (*al-Mukhtasar fī ta'rīkh al-bashar*, 4 vols. [Cairo, 1907–8], 4:24). The very detailed and authoritative accounts of the siege by Shams al-Dīn al-Jazarī and Badr al-Dīn al-'Aynī put the total number of trebuchets employed by the Muslims at seventy-two (al-Jazarī, *Hawādith al-zamān*, fol. 24v, MS. 6739, fonds arabe, Bibliothèque Nationale, Paris; idem, *La Chronique de Damas d'al-Jazarī* [Paris, 1949], 5; al-'Aynī, *'Iqd al-jumān fī ta'rīkh ahl al-zamān*, fol. 144v, MS. 2912/4, Ahmet III Collection, Topkapı Sarayı Müzesi Kütüphanesi, Istanbul). Ibn al-Furāt and al-Maqrīzī set the number of trebuchets at ninety-two, but this figure is most probably a scribal error for seventy-two, since the unpointed *sabʿ* and *tisʿ* are often confused (Ibn al-Furāt, *The History of Ibn al-Furāt*, ed. C. Zurayk and N. Izzedin, vols. 7–9 [Beirut, 1936–42], 8:112; al-Maqrīzī, *Kitāb al-sulūk li-maʿrifat duwal al-mulūk*, 4 vols. [Cairo, 1934–73], 1, pt. 3: 764). Al-Yūnīnī mentions that fifteen of the machines were large Frankish trebuchets (*al-majānīq al-kibār al-ifranjīyah*), and al-'Aynī states that fifty-two were traction Devilish trebuchets (*manjanīq shaytānī*) (al-Yūnīnī, *Dhayl mir'āt al-zamān*, in Antranig Melkonian, *Die Jahre 1287–1291 in der Chronik al-Yūnīnīs* [Freiburg, 1975], 86 [Arabic text]). While al-Jazarī, al-Yūnīnī, and Ibn al-Furāt all state that *qarābughrā* trebuchets were used in the siege, no author specifies how many (al-Jazarī, *Hawādith al-zamān*, fol. 24v; al-Yūnīnī, *Dhayl*, 86 [Arabic text]; Ibn al-Furāt, *History* 8: 112). If the above accounts can be reconciled with one another, a figure of five *qarābughrā* trebuchets is reached by deducting al-Yūnīnī's fifteen large Frankish trebuchets and al-'Aynī's fifty-two Devilish trebuchets from the total number of seventy-two. Although al-Yūnīnī states that the pole-framed traction trebuchet known as the *luʿbah* was employed in great numbers in the siege, this machine is probably included in al-'Aynī's count of Devilish trebuchets. See the excellent article of Donald P. Little, which analyzes the Arabic accounts of the siege of Acre in great detail ("Fall of 'Akkā"). I would like to thank Professor Little for

Contrary to Smail's assessment, fortifications and defensive planning underwent revolutionary changes during the crusader period in order to counter the greater destructive power of the counterweight trebuchet and to exploit this new artillery for use in the defense of strongpoints. This new system of defensive planning revolutionized the construction of fortifications during the latter part of the Middle Ages and constitutes the last transition which fortifications were to undergo prior to the development of the bastion system of defensive planning in the sixteenth century, which arose out of a need to withstand the devastating blows of even more effective gunpowder artillery.

kindly providing me with transcriptions and photocopies of the relevant sections of Arabic chronicles dealing with the siege of Acre which are still unedited. On the various types of trebuchets used at the siege of Acre in 1291, see Chevedden, "Artillery of King James I," 61–63.

THE "AGE OF CAVALRY" REVISITED

Stephen Morillo

AMONG popular images of the Middle Ages, the "knight in shining armor" is certainly one of the most dominant. A warrior heavily armed, chivalrous, and above all on horseback, he rides off to rescue maidens, battle dragons, and trample peasants. The image is suggestive, for the best known military figures from other eras – the Greek hoplite, the Roman legionnaire, the Napoleonic Imperial Guardsman, the Civil War rifleman – all fought on foot.

Military historians have long viewed the Middle Ages in Europe as an "age of cavalry." The limits of this characterization are much more significant than has often been recognized, and the ways in which the Middle Ages were an age of cavalry must be carefully defined. But once this is done, a core of truth remains to the characterization. What accounts for the dominance, within limits, of cavalry in medieval Europe? The most common explanation has been technological: the introduction of the stirrup into European warfare. I contend in this paper that technology played little role in the changing patterns of medieval European warfare. Rather, I see governmental factors as more important in shaping the tactical practices of armies.

I shall examine some aspects of Anglo-Norman warfare in the context of these competing theories. No comprehensive survey of the evidence is possible in a paper this length, but I do propose a theory which may be useful in explaining aspects not only of Anglo-Norman and medieval European warfare, but also of pre-modern warfare generally.

For the military historian, the Middle Ages as an age of cavalry received its most influential expression from Sir Charles Oman in his monumental *Art of War in the Middle Ages*.[1] For Oman, the age of cavalry began, with Victorian precision if not accuracy, in 378 at the battle of Adrianople, "the first great victory won by that heavy cavalry which had now shown its ability to supplant the heavy infantry of Rome as the ruling power of war." The Goth "had become the arbiter of war, the lineal ancestor of all the knights of the Middle Ages, the inaugurator of that ascendancy of the horsemen which was to endure for a thousand years."[2]

It has long been recognized that Oman's picture of an age of cavalry needs

---

[1] Charles Oman, *A History of the Art of War in the Middle Ages*, 2 vols. (Franklin NY, 1924).
[2] Ibid., 1:14.

modification. In the first place, it must be made clear that the picture Oman and those who have followed him draw applies strictly to battle tactics and battle tactics alone. The heavily armored horseman who was "the ruling power in war" is always described as ruling the battlefield, a battlefield from which infantry rarely fully disappeared, though they are portrayed as playing a distinctly secondary role.[3] Even so, infantry could be useful in certain roles on the battlefield,[4] and at times could even defeat cavalry.[5]

Limiting our view to the battlefield creates a very distorted picture of medieval warfare, as recent research has tended to show.[6] Battles were rare, and infantry never disappeared from campaigns, for good reason. They were essential in siege warfare, garrison duty, and engineering, activities which were far more common than battles in medieval war. The usefulness of infantry in siege warfare points out that field forces operated in conjunction with castles in projecting military force onto the countryside; the prominence of castles ensured that infantry would remain vital to medieval warfare.[7]

Geography also placed limits on the dominance of cavalry. It was difficult for cavalry to operate in rough terrain – heavily wooded areas, broken or hilly ground – or in areas lacking sufficient forage.[8] Thus, regions such as Wales, the highlands of Scotland, and the Swiss cantons, were never dominated by mounted elites in the same way that neighboring areas with more hospitable terrain were. Finally, the temporal limits of the dominance of cavalry are subject

---

[3] This reflects the older tradition of military history as the history of "Decisive Battles"; see not only Oman for this emphasis, but, for example, J.F.C. Fuller, *A Military History of the Western World*, 3 vols. (New York, 1954–56). Oman describes the battle of Muret in 1213 as "the most remarkable triumph ever won by a force entirely composed of cavalry over an enemy who used both horse and foot" (*Art of War*, 1:453), emphasizing the anomaly of an all cavalry force.

[4] See below, 5–7, for further discussion of infantry and cavalry roles on the battlefield.

[5] For example at the battles of Brémule and Bourgethérolde. See note 42 below.

[6] See S. Morillo, *Warfare under the Anglo-Norman Kings, 1066–1135* (Woodbridge, Suffolk, 1994) for a full discussion of warfare in this period, including usual patterns of warfare. See also John Gillingham, "Richard I and the Science of War in the Middle Ages," *War and Government in the Middle Ages: Essays in Honour of J.O. Prestwich*, ed. John Gillingham and J.C. Holt (Totowa NJ, 1984), 78–91, for an excellent discussion of patterns of medieval warfare, including the roles of infantry and battles. He builds on the fundamental work of R.C. Smail, *Crusading Warfare 1097–1193* (Cambridge, 1956). Gillingham's article can also be found in the useful collection *Anglo-Norman Warfare*, ed. Matthew Strickland (Woodbridge, Suffolk, 1992).

[7] See Robert Bartlett, "Technique Militaire et Pouvoir Politique, 900–1300," *Annales* 41 (1986): 1135–59, on the combination of heavy cavalry, archers and castles that contributed to western European political expansion, though Bartlett does not distinguish adequately between "knights" as elite warriors and as mounted soldiers in battle: see esp. 1136, 1150.

[8] The necessity for forage also accounts for the tendency for medieval warfare to be concentrated in summer months, when forage was available and when weather was less likely to reduce mobility.

to question. Lynn White, unlike Oman, dated the initial superiority of cavalry to the Frankish kingdom of the mid-eighth century.[9]

So the term "age of cavalry" refers not to absolute dominance of horsemen, or the disappearance of infantry, but to a relative increase in the importance of cavalry in deciding battles within the geographical and temporal limits discussed above. The elite warriors of the Middle Ages, in short, tended to be mounted – the "knight in shining armor." The implicit comparison is to the warfare of Greece and Rome, when heavy infantry decided most battles, and to European warfare from the mid-fifteenth century onward, when infantry again tended to dominate. Medieval Europe is again, in this view, a "middle age" between classical and early modern.

Given this definition and these restriction there does seem to be a core of truth to the characterization of the Middle Ages as an age of cavalry. Why was this so? Answering this question requires a careful definition of terms. What do we mean by "cavalry" and "infantry"?

I use for this paper a tactical, functional definition of cavalry and infantry: cavalry are soldiers fighting on horseback *on the battlefield*; infantry are soldiers fighting on foot *on the battlefield*. In this view, it does not matter how the soldiers got to the battlefield. There were a number of reasons for a soldier to use a horse, and fighting on the battlefield was only one of them. Mobility on campaign favored the use of horses, for example, as did display of social status. My definitions maintain the important but much neglected distinction between horses as strategic transport and horses as battlefield "weapons," and in fact follows the common medieval usage.[10] Thus, soldiers who rode to battle but fought on foot fought as infantry, not as "dismounted cavalry" or as "mounted infantry," anachronistic terms which can only confuse our picture of medieval warfare.[11]

These definitions allow a further distinction. To ask why the Middle Ages was tactically an age of cavalry is to ask why soldiers on horseback had a relative advantage on the battlefield in medieval warfare. It is not the same as asking why medieval Europe was dominated by a rural warrior elite who happened, most of the time, to ride horses.[12] The two questions are connected, and I shall return to the connection later. But the questions are not the same, and it is with the former that we are concerned here. What gave mounted soldiers their advantage on the battlefield?

The usual explanation for cavalry's relative advantage in the Middle Ages is simple and technological: the introduction of the stirrup into European warfare.

---

9 Lynn White, *Medieval Technology and Social Change* (Oxford, 1962), chap. 1.

10 For example Orderic Vitalis, *Ecclesiastical History* [OV], ed. and trans. M. Chibnall (Oxford, 1969–72), 6:350; see note 43 below.

11 Anglo-Saxon and Norman soldiers frequently rode to battle and fought on foot. There seems no reason to refer to the former as mounted infantry and the latter as dismounted cavalry, as some authorities have done. Functionally, they were identical.

12 It is this distinction, I believe, that Bartlett's otherwise insightful article does not make sufficiently clear.

The basic idea is that the stirrup made the horse a much more stable fighting platform, therby unifying horse and rider into one massive attacking force directed through the rider's couched lance. This made cavalry so much more efficient that infantry could no longer stand a chance against it.

Lynn White, drawing on nineteenth century German histories of the stirrup, stated the case most completely in the first chapter of his *Medieval Technology and Social Change*, a chapter called "Stirrup, Mounted Shock Combat, Feudalism, and Chivalry."[13] This work has become the fountainhead for the spread of the "stirrup theory." Though much criticized in detail, particularly on the dating of the introduction of the stirrup and the conversion of Frankish armies to mounted combat,[14] White's account in broad outline seems to have passed into the realm of accepted textbook canon. It is in the major studies of medieval warfare which have succeeded Oman: J.F. Verbruggen places the stirrup at the heart of knightly dominance; Philippe Contamine notes some of the problems associated with dating the stirrup, but accepts its eventual impact.[15] The stirrup has been used to explain aspects of Anglo-Norman warfare; in particular, it has been cited to explain the result of Hastings and thus the Norman conquest, though this interpretation is disputed.[16] McKay, Hill and Buckler's *History of World Societies* is but one example of the theory's spread to introductory textbooks, while the first chapter of Michael Howard's *War in European History*, entitled "The Wars of the Knights," demonstrates the acceptance of the theory in a scholarly synthesis of European military history.[17] Martin van Creveld, in his recent survey *Technology and War from 2000 B.C. to the Present* sums up the case: "Modern authors, however much they may differ in detail, are united in their opinion that, sometime between 500 and 1000 A.D., the stirrup and the high saddle . . . spread to Europe. Add the horseshoe, the origin of which is

---

[13] White, chap. 1; the title of the chapter shows that for White, social dominance for a mounted warrior elite flowed from military advantage. Oman, interestingly, did not really explain the rise of cavalry except by vague references to "changes in military science" and the reliance of Rome on "untrustworthy and greedy Teutonic *Foederati*": Oman, 18–19.

[14] For example Bernard Bachrach, "Charles Martel, Shock Combat, the Stirrup and Feudalism," *Studies in Medieval and Renaissance History* 7 (1970): 47–75; see K. DeVries, *Medieval Military Technology* (Lewiston NY, 1992), 95–110, for a good summary of the historiography of the stirrup debate.

[15] Verbruggen, 5; Philippe Contamine, *War in the Middle Ages*, trans. M. Jones (Oxford, 1984), 179–84.

[16] On the supposed impact of the stirrup, especially at Hastings, see R. Allen Brown, *The Normans and the Norman Conquest* (London, 1969), 95–99, 166; F.M. Stenton, *Anglo-Saxon England* (Oxford, 1971), 585–8; *1042–1189*, vol. 2 of *English Historical Documents*, ed. D.C. Douglas and G.W. Greenaway (London, 1981), 2:19 (editors' introduction). For a different view of Hastings, arguing that the stirrup had little or no effect on its outcome, see S. Morillo, "Hastings: An Unusual Battle," *The Haskins Society Journal* 2 (1990): 95–104.

[17] John P. McKay, Bennett D. Hill and John Buckler, *A History of World Societies*, 2 vols. (Boston, 1988), 1:335; Michael Howard, *War in European History* (Oxford, 1976), chap. 1.

simply unknown, and the ascent of cavalry over ancient infantry becomes at least understandable."[18]

By contrast, it is my contention that while the stirrup may indeed have appeared in Europe sometime between 500 and 1000, it explains almost nothing about the ascent of cavalry over infantry.

There is, to begin with, a purely logical problem with this theory: it leaves no room for infantry to return to dominance as it did in the fifteenth century. If the combination of horse and rider was so irresistible in 1100, how was it so well resisted in 1500? The usual answer has been to extend the technological argument. In this view, new weapons for the infantry – the longbow and, more importantly, gunpowder – turned the tide again.[19] But such a response must ignore the fact that the Swiss pikemen, with weapons and tactics essentially identical with those of a Macedonian phalanx, could beat any stirrup-wearing cavalry in Europe.[20] Indeed, it was not until the invention of the bayonet that missile troops, whether they carried bows or guns, could stand against cavalry without the support of pikemen. The bayonet, of course, made every musketeer his own pikeman. The "stirrup theory" must also ignore or dismiss as anomalous those victories that medieval infantry did win over stirruped cavalry. The Anglo-Norman experience of battles discussed below indicates that such victories were not anomalies.

But the more fundamental problem with the technological argument is that it is based on a misunderstanding of the mechanics of infantry and cavalry combat. A reexamination of these will provide the basis for a new general theory of the patterns of infantry and cavalry dominance.

The basic difference between infantry and cavalry on the battlefield was the superior mobility of the horseman. Mobility made cavalry the natural arm of attack and pursuit, and also made its retreat easier. Cavalry was not good in static defense. Low mobility made infantry the natural arm of defense, though infantry, if it were experienced and well led, was capable of attack.[21] It should

---

18 Martin van Creveld, *Technology and War from 2000 BC to the Present* (New York, 1989), 18.

19 Especially with respect to gunpowder weapons, this line of argument is one explanation for the so-called "military revolution": see Geoffrey Parker, *The Military Revolution. Military Innovation and the Rise of the West, 1500–1800* (Cambridge, 1988), for the clearest statement of this technological determinist argument. See Bert Hall and Kelly DeVries, "Essay Review – the 'Military Revolution' Revisited," *Technology and Culture* 31 (1990): 500–7, for a critique of Parker's book that raises many of the issues discussed below. See John Lynn, ed., *Tools of War: Instruments, Ideas, and Institutions of Warfare, 1445–1871* (Urbana IL, 1990), for a set of essays which "challenge the concept of technological determinism in military history" (vii) from a number of angles. And see below for further discussion of the end of the age of cavalry.

20 As Oman himself recognized: *Art of War*, 2:233–80, on the Swiss pike armies.

21 Infantry could also often make better use of missile weapons than cavalry, due to their greater concentration of fire from denser formations and their ability to wield longer range weapons.

be noted that these strengths are complementary, and tactics which combine the arms are in fact historically the most successful.

The classic cavalry attack, and the maneuver where the stirrup was supposed to have made such a difference, was the charge in line. A charge could be launched against either cavalry or infantry. We are concerned here with the latter.[22]

The key point is that against a solid infantry formation, a cavalry charge was a psychological weapon, not a physical one. Its success had to depend on frightening at least some of the foot-soldiers into breaking ranks or fleeing. Otherwise, cavalry horses would balk in the face of an obstacle they could neither jump over nor go around – the solid wall of foot-soldiers. Individual horses and riders might accidentally crash into an unfortunate foot-soldier in rank, but on the whole the charge would be brought up short of a mass collision.[23] Clearly, the presence or absence of stirrups would have had little effect on the psychological impact of a charge.

If a charge failed to break a line of infantry, the cavalry could then either retreat and renew its charge, or advance the last few yards to engage in single combat. When cavalryman and infantryman met in single combat, the superior height of the horseman could give him an advantage, but this height advantage existed with or without stirrups, and the added stability stirrups conveyed was not decisive in the context of individual combat along the front of an infantry formation.

Given some familiarity with the usual close range tactics of horsemen and

---

[22] Against opposing cavalry, a charge could result in the two lines meeting head on, in the style of a mass joust or tournament. At the moment of impact in such a collision, some riders were thrown from their horses by enemy lances; many lances undoubtedly shattered under the stress of blows. But the crashing together of two lines of cavalry can be overdramatized. Depending on the density and depth of the formations, many of the horsemen were likely to pass through each other's lines. If the lines were too deep or tightly packed to allow this result, the charging lines had to slow before impact, and the soldiers then came together into a series of single combats (John Keegan, *The Face of Battle* [London, 1976], 148–50). It was in cavalry against cavalry combat that the introduction of the stirrup may have made some difference in combat techniques. The stirrup allowed (but did not require) the lance to be carried couched, or underarm, with the weight of man and horse behind it. Stirruped cavalry would have had some advantage over cavalry without stirrups. But even in the general history of warfare, the effect of the stirrup on cavalry technique may be exaggerated. Alexander's Companion Cavalry, who did not have stirrups, formed a superb heavy cavalry force. Robin Lane Fox's claim that "What writing has done to the memory, stirrups have done to riding; without them, men simply had to grip harder and ride better than they mostly do nowadays" (Robin Lane Fox, *Alexander the Great* [New York, 1974], 75), may be exaggerated, but the effectiveness of Macedonian cavalry shock tactics is widely accepted: see A. Jones, *The Art of War in the Western World* (Oxford, 1987), 21. And see Fox, 72–80 generally for an excellent discussion of the Macedonian army of Philip and Alexander; many of the points of tactics presented there bear directly on this argument. Finally, the lance was not always (or even often?) the preferred weapon for serious combat; the sword was the killing weapon. See below, for the cavalry action at Lincoln in 1141.

[23] Keegan, 95–6, 156.

given similar armor, professional infantry could more than hold its own against professional cavalry. Henry I's instructions to his English infantry in 1101 are revealing on this point: William of Malmesbury tells how Henry, preparing his troops for his brother Robert's invasion, "frequently circulating through the ranks, . . . taught them how to elude the ferocity of the *milites*, to obstruct with their shields and return strokes."[24] We should remember in this context William of Poitiers' comments about the effectiveness of Saxon axes at Hastings, said to be able "easily to cut a way through shields or other armor."[25] Instructive too is the dismounting of knights in the first rank of infantry: as experienced cavalry-men, the knights would have had a good idea how to counter a mounted attacker.[26]

On the other hand, if cavalry caught infantry scattered in the open field, or got in among infantry in a broken or disordered formation, the superior mobility and attacking height of the horseman could be put to full use. The success of the Norman counter-attacks against those Saxons who left the shield wall at Hast-ings testifies to this.[27] A similar though less decisive advantage fell to cavalry which attacked infantry formations on the flank or rear before they had time to reface. The decisive blow in Henry I's victory at Tinchebrai in 1106 – a battle for the most part between two infantry forces – came from a hidden flanking force of cavalry under Helias of La Fleche, who swept onto Duke Robert's army from the rear after the battle had been joined.[28] The important point here is that the stirrup made little or no difference to this type of encounter, either: height and mobility were the keys to the cavalryman's advantage in such situations, as they had been since long before the stirrup. In any case, this is not the sort of encounter envisioned by the "stirrup theory."

Opening up the infantry formation was thus the psychological goal of a frontal charge. For infantry to stand up to a cavalry charge its formation had to be sufficiently deep and dense to force horses to refuse, and it had to have the morale and courage to stand in the face of the terrifying sight of charging cavalry. For infantry to attack cavalry required even greater cohesion, because it was difficult for troops not trained in formation marching to keep close order in

---

24 William of Malmesbury, *Gesta Regum Anglorum*, ed. W. Stubbs, 2:472. The term *miles* may mean either "soldier" in its classical sense, and especially with the overtones of "well armed, elite soldier," or may mean "cavalryman," as in the phrase *milites peditesque*. The latter meaning followed and derived from the former. The meaning in 1100 is by no means set, but assuming cavalry in this case seems safe, given the context of Norman baronial dis-loyalty.

25 William of Poitiers, *Histoire de Guillaume le Conquerant*, ed. R. Foreville (Paris, 1952), 188. And see Frank Barlow, *The Feudal Kingdom of England 1042–1216* (London, 1972), 79, on Harold's familiarity with continental tactics.

26 I shall discuss dismounting further below.

27 William of Poitiers, 190. But those Saxons who maintained their formation in their advance fared much better: *The Carmen de Hastingae Proelio of Bishop Guy of Amiens*, ed. C. Morton and H. Muntz (Oxford, 1972), lines 429–35.

28 OV, 6:88–90.

an advance; if close order were lost, the infantry were open to counter-attack by
the cavalry.

There were very few medieval infantry forces which even had the confidence, discipline and cohesion to stand in defense, much less the cohesion to
attack. Why was this so? What does it take to produce good infantry?

The answer is deceptively simple: trust. Each man in the formation must trust
his neighbor not to run away. How is trust achieved? It may be a result of the
social origins of the formation: neighbors, either from a *polis*, a canton, or some
other small polity, may know and trust each other from long association on and
off the battlefield. But practice and experience is crucial even for such naturally
cohesive groups; it is far more necessary for formations drawn from more het-
erogeneous backgrounds. Normally, an infantry unit gains cohesion through
drill, and through experience.

We may now come back to the social and institutional setting of good infantry. Drill may only be instituted where there is a central authority strong enough
to gather sufficient numbers of men together, and rich enough to maintain them
while they are trained. Administrative and financial capacity will also keep a
formation together long enough to gain joint experience, which can substitute
for drill to some extent in creating cohesion. In effect, strong infantry depends
on strong government.

The same is not true of cavalry, because the bases of cavalry effectiveness are
not quite the same as infantry's. As I have noted, mobility is cavalry's great
advantage, and mobility makes cavalry the natural arm of attack, pursuit, and
flight. Cavalry may be effective in smaller numbers than infantry, and so may
require less training in large groups. On the other hand, making a horseman
requires much more individual training from an earlier age,[29] and an individual
horseman is much more expensive to maintain than an individual footsoldier.

As a result, cavalry in the traditional world was very often the product – the
natural arm – of social elites.[30] Rural warrior elites were in fact a common
feature of many traditional civilizations. Sons of such classes were raised to the
military lifestyle, trained in small groups built from the social connections
among the class, and exercised military force in the interest of maintaining their
own position in the hierarchy of power. While a central authority could often
harness the skills and energies of this elite to its own military and policy ends, it
could just as easily find itself at odds with the same class, especially over the
form and distribution of power. Consequently, such an elite (and the effective

---

[29] "He who has stayed at school till the age of twelve and never ridden a horse, is fit only to
be a priest" claims the old Carolingian proverb: cited in Marc Bloch, *Feudal Society*, trans.
L.A. Manyon, 2 vols. (Chicago, 1961), 2:293–94; cf. the similar Japanese injunction to practice riding in Hojo Soun's Articles: Carl Steenstrup, "Hojo Soun's Twenty-One Articles. The
Code of Conduct of the Odawara Hojo," *Monumenta Nipponica* 29 (1974): 297, no. XVI.

[30] Horses, expensive to raise and maintain, were thus often seen as "noble" animals, and
display of social status was another reason for warrior elites to adopt riding as a mode of
transport, fighting, and lifestyle. Roman armies initially drew their cavalry from the upper
classes.

cavalry which it formed) could easily exist outside the context of a strong central authority.

Here we have the key to the problem of the dominance of cavalry. Cavalry was not better from the fourth to the fourteenth centuries: infantry was worse. Why? Because medieval governments did not have the capacity, in general, to create good infantry. The breakdown of the western Roman empire left no central authority in Europe capable of maintaining and training infantry forces in peacetime. The decline of infantry standards comes well before the final collapse of the Roman state: it is one of the things Vegetius frequently complains about.[31] With less training, infantry lost the ability to attack, which it surrendered to cavalry; with no training, it became unreliable even for standing in defense.[32]

Only in areas where drill and training were partially replaced by institutionalized experience, that is group continuity and either professionalism (i.e. money) or regular community service, did effective infantry forces appear between the fourth and fourteenth centuries. The independent and rich city-states of Italy and to a lesser extent those of Flanders were virtually the only governments capable of putting battle-worthy infantry in the field in the Middle Ages. Cavalry, therefore, gained its battlefield dominance almost by default.

Government strength also connects the question of battlefield dominance by mounted soldiers to the larger question of social structure and dominance by a mounted warrior elite. The decline of central, public authorities left governance, such as it was, to rural warrior chieftains and their followers. This class virtually monopolized society's surplus resources[33] – including the wealth to buy the best arms, armor, and horses, and the leisure to make military training a lifestyle. That such a class then dominated warfare should not be surprising; they dominated virtually every aspect of society. But they did so because they were elite, trained warriors, not because they were mounted; they dominated battlefields whether they fought on horseback or on foot.[34] A peasant levy was no more likely to defeat a force of Anglo-Saxon housecarls than one of Norman knights.

Returning to the battlefield, this theory also explains the eventual re-emergence of infantry. In this view, it was the rise of stronger governments in late medieval Europe[35] that caused the reappearance of effective infantry formations such as had not been seen since the decline of the imperial Roman government and its legions. Stronger governments built infantry initially on the use of weapons like the pike that had always been available. As gunpowder technology spread, it could then be taken up by armies already developing

31 Flavius Vegetius Renatus, *Epitoma Rei Militaris*, ed. C. Lang (Stuttgart 1967), *passim*.
32 Cf. Jones, 93–95, 144.
33 I am intentionally excluding the religious elite from this military discussion, admittedly something of an oversimplification.
34 Cf. Jones, 119.
35 J.R. Strayer, *On the Medieval Origins of the Modern State* (Princeton, 1970), is a classic account of this process, emphasizing developments in justice and finance in the context of warfare that was present throughout the medieval period.

along organizational lines compatible with its use. It is no coincidence that the first infantry forces to attack and defeat horsemen in the open field since the Roman legions, the pikemen of the Swiss cantons, were the first since the Romans to march in time to music.[36] Drill had returned to European warfare, and with it the dominance of infantry. The resurgence of central authority, the rise of the early modern state, made that dominance permanent.

An examination of some important aspects of Anglo-Norman warfare provides partial evidence for the contention that institutional factors were more important than technological ones in shaping patterns of dominance on the battlefield.

There is little argument that the Anglo-Norman government was one of the richest and most centralized in medieval Europe.[37] This is reflected in its military system. The _familia regis_ of the Anglo-Norman kings, a professional permanent force of soldiers who were the heart of the Anglo-Norman military system, provided the essential prerequisites for sustaining a tradition of infantry tactics.[38] Grafted onto the strong infantry tradition of Anglo-Saxon England, especially the select _fyrd_, of which the Norman kings made regular use, the _familia_ supported by the Anglo-Norman administration made for a military system which outperformed continental rivals.

Specifically, Anglo-Norman knights consistently dismounted to fight their battles. At Tinchebrai in 1106, the Battle of the Standard in 1138, and Lincoln in 1141, dismounted knights joined other infantry forces to defeat armies which were also of mixed cavalry and infantry. At Brémule in 1119 and Bourgethérolde in 1124, infantry forces made up exclusively of dismounted knights defeated forces of heavy stirruped cavalry.[39]

Why did Anglo-Norman knights fight as infantry? The theory I am proposing suggests that the strength of central authority played an important role. I

[36] R.E. Dupuy and T.N. Dupuy, _The Encyclopedia of Military History from 3500 B.C. to the Present_ (New York, 1986), 407; cf. Jones, 176–77.

[37] See for example Marjorie Chibnall, _Anglo-Norman England 1066–1166_ (Oxford, 1986), 105ff.; William of Poitiers, 156; J.O. Prestwich, "War and Finance in the Anglo-Norman State," _TRHS_, 5th series, 4 (1954): 35–36; D.J.A. Matthew, _The Norman Conquest_ (London, 1966), 18–20; Barlow, 192.

[38] On the _familia regis_, see J.O. Prestwich, "The Military Household of the Norman Kings," _EHR_ 96 (1981): 1–35.

[39] Tinchebrai: OV, 6:88–90; Priest of Fécamp's letter, _EHR_ 25 (1910): 296; Henry of Huntingdon, _Historia Anglorum_, ed. T. Arnold, 235; Eadmer, _Historia Novorum in Anglia_, ed. M. Rule, 184. _The Standard: Henry of Huntingdon_, 263–64; John of Hexham, in _Symeonis Monachi Opera Omnia_, ed. T. Arnold, 2:293–95; Florence of Worcester, _Chronicon ex Chronicis_, ed. B. Thorpe (London, 1848–49), 2:111–12. _Lincoln: Henry of Huntingdon_, 271–74; William of Malmesbury, 47–49; John of Hexham, 2:307–10. Brémule: OV, 6:236–42; Henry of Huntingdon, 241–42; Suger, _Vita Ludovici grossi regis_, ed. H. Waquet (Paris, 1929), xxvi, 196–98; _Liber Monasterii de Hyda_, ed. E. Edwards (London, 1886), 317–18. Bourgethérolde: OV, 6:348. It is interesting to note that in actions at Dol in 1076, Gerberoy in 1079 and Alençon in 1118, where Anglo-Norman troops seem not to have dismounted, the Anglo-Norman army was defeated. Dol: _ASC_ (E) 1076; OV, 2:352. Gerberoy: _ASC_ (E) 1079; OV, 3:110. Alençon: OV, 6:206–8.

believe the Anglo-Norman practice of dismounting shows the influence of strong central authority in two ways. First, the Anglo-Norman kings could raise fairly large numbers of infantry of enough quality that casting the knights in with them was both possible and beneficial. A front line of elite soldiers stiffened the morale of the less experienced masses behind them, making the whole formation more effective.

But this does not fully explain the dismounting of knights, for at Brémule and Bourgthérolde there was no infantry to stiffen. Nor does it explain how the knights were convinced to dismount, for there were conflicting group and individual motives at work in this process. It was to the advantage of the force as a whole that at least some of the knights dismount. But it was to the advantage of any individual knight to fight mounted: it was more prestigious and glorious, there was a greater possibility of successful pursuit with the chance of prisoners and ransoms, and perhaps above all it was easier to run away safely. Only a leader with enough authority to impose dismounting on his troops could overcome this individual tendency and reap the benefits of this tactic. Dismounting made the army as a whole more effective, and stiffened the resolve of the knights themselves, for it effectively removed flight as a safe alternative for them. As Amaury of Montfort told his fellow rebels before Bourgthérolde:

> See, Odo Borleng has dismounted with his men, so you know he will fight tenaciously to win. When a warlike horseman becomes a foot-soldier with his men, he will not flee; rather, he will die or conquer.[40]

Cavalry employed by King Stephen proved the point in a less glorious way at Lincoln: those who dismounted fought to the end and were captured with the king; those who remained mounted fled at the first enemy charge, contributing mightily to the defeat. Tellingly, the cavalry who fled prepared to fight the battle with lances, as if for a joust, but fled at the sight of cavalry wielding swords, the real killing weapon.[41] So much for the stirrup and the lance as a military revolution.

Given that dismounting regularly performed such important functions in Anglo-Norman battles, it does not seem to me that it has been over-stressed, as R.A. Brown has claimed.[42] In fact the change in Norman attitudes between 1066, when a knight dismounting was a matter for laughter and ridicule,[43] and Bourgthérolde, where the king's men dismounted on their own, indicates a minor revolution in the Norman approach to battle. The importance of infantry tactics in part probably reflects the influence of the Anglo-Saxon tradition on

---

40 OV, 6:350: "Ecce Odo Borlengus cum suis descendit, scitote quia superare pertinaciter contendit. Bellicosus eques iam cum suis pedes factus non fugiet, sed morietur aut vincet."
41 William of Malmesbury, *Historia Novella*, ed. K.R. Potter (London, 1955), 47–49.
42 R. Allen Brown, *Origins of English Feudalism* (New York, 1973), p. 35, n. 10. I believe Brown tended to conflate knightly dominance with cavalry dominance; the two were not necessarily the same.
43 William of Poitiers, 168.

Anglo-Norman combat.[44] Crucially, an infantry tradition resulted from this effectiveness on the part of the *familia regis*.

In fact, the infantry tradition survived in English forces until English infantry took up the longbow, stood beside dismounted knights, and heralded the end of the age of cavalry at Crécy.[45] The tactical expression of this tradition is most clearly visible in a comparison of the English tactics at Crécy with the tactics of the *familia* at Bourgthérolde. In both cases an army made up of soldiers all of whom were mounted for strategic mobility dismounted when faced by a hostile cavalry force. In both cases, knights formed a shield and lance wall in the center of the line, and archers covered the flanks of the knights. The combination of firepower and defensive impenetrability based on cohesion and trust proved as effective in 1346 as it had in 1124. With or without stirrups, a cavalry charge against such a force stood little chance of success; all it took to create such a force was a military administration strong enough to produce good infantry.

I have suggested the connection between strong central authority and good infantry as an explanation of some of the features of Anglo-Norman warfare specifically and medieval warfare generally. I would now further suggest that this connection can explain patterns of infantry and cavalry battlefield dominance throughout the pre-modern world. To cite only two revealing examples, let me turn to the Far East.

China under the Western Chou (c.770 to 480 B.C.) saw the decline of unified central authority; the country was divided into many small provinces (essentially independent states) whose political and military spheres were dominated by an aristocratic warrior elite who used horses and chariots in their battles. China's "age of cavalry" therefore preceded the invention of the stirrup, but came in an age of political weakness. New developments in government would radically alter this political and military pattern.

In the warring states period of Chinese history, from about 480 to 220 B.C., competing governments were transformed from "something resembling a large household" into "an autocratic state run on behalf of a despotic prince by a salaried bureaucracy." The armies raised by these states grew tremendously in size and were transformed from forces of aristocratic charioteers and horsemen into masses of spear-bearing conscript infantry.[46] The basic framework of this military system lasted well into the eighteenth century. The stirrup did not create the

---

[44] The influence of effective infantry tactics on the Anglo-Norman knights may be guessed at as early as 1075, when royal forces under William of Warenne defeated Earl Ralph's rebel army at Fagaduna: "obstantes", they won the field: OV, 2:316. Is it pushing the term *obstantes* too far to suggest that the *familia* knights and their *fyrd* support formed a shield wall at this engagement? The term certainly could not describe a cavalry charge.

[45] See M. Powicke, *Military Obligation in Medieval England* (Oxford, 1962) for the administrative arrangements behind medieval English armies.

[46] Parker, 2–3; see also Hsu Cho-yun, *Ancient China in Transition: An Analysis of Social Mobility 722–222 B.C.* (Stanford, 1965). The governmental reforms followed a path that came to be formulated in the Legalist political philosophy of Han Fei Tzu; Confucian principles later dressed this Legalist political structure in more humane clothing.

dominance of horse-owning Chinese aristocrats, nor did gunpowder (or other new technologies) bring about the supremacy of Chinese infantry.

Medieval Japan provides a comparative case study even closer to the European experience.[47] The Japan of the Kamakura and Ashikaga shogunates was increasingly dominated by a provincial warrior elite,[48] the *bushi*, whose similarities to medieval European warriors politically and militarily have prompted numerous comparative studies of "feudalism."[49] The use of the term indicates that weakness of the central political structures was a prominent feature of Japan during its age of cavalry. In the Onin War (1467–77), all vestiges of central control broke down.

But in the Sengoku (Warring States) period, from 1477 to around 1600, regional leaders built new political structures, and the dominance of the horse-riding class of *bushi* came to an end. The *daimyo*, rulers of the effectively independent states into which Japan had split, established firm control over their military followers. They also erected effective systems of local administration, law, and taxation and harnessed forces of social mobility emerging from village militancy.[50] On these foundations *daimyo* began to build larger, more organized armies whose tactics shifted from "hand to hand combat in which the armored [and mounted] *samurai* predominated" to "large bodies of men . . . [deployed as] lines of pike-wielding footsoldiers."[51] These developments are all visible well before the introduction of gunpowder into Japan in 1543. Although gunpowder has sometimes been seen as the force behind the changes, in fact a close examination of the evidence shows that administrative improvements preceded military change, and that military change preceded the introduction of any new military technology.[52]

[47] I have explored this Japanese case in detail elsewhere: see S. Morillo, "Guns and Government: A Comparative Study of Europe and Japan," *The Journal of World History* 6 (1995): 75–106.

[48] Jeffrey P. Mass, *Warrior Government in Early Medieval Japan. A Study of the Kamakura Bakufu, Shugo, and Jito* (New Haven CT, 1974); Karl Friday, *Hired Swords. The Rise of Private Warrior Power in Early Japan* (Stanford, 1992).

[49] See, e.g., Archibald Lewis, *Knights and Samurai. Feudalism in Northern France and Japan* (London, 1974); also J.R. Strayer, "The Tokugawa Period and Japanese Feudalism," and John W. Hall, "Feudalism in Japan – a Reassessment," both in Hall and Jansen, *Studies in the Institutional History of Early Modern Japan* (Princeton, 1968); and Peter Duus, *Feudalism in Japan* (New York, 1993). On the question of "feudalism" generally, I tend to follow Elizabeth A.R. Brown, "The Tyranny of a Construct: Feudalism and Historians of Medieval Europe," *AHR* 79 (1974): 1063–88 – that is I tend to think the term obscures more than it reveals unless defined very carefully.

[50] See the fundamental account of the province of Bizen during this age in John W. Hall, *Government and Local Power in Japan 500 to 1700* (Princeton NJ, 1966), 238–70, and the important article by Michael P. Birt, "Samurai in Passage: Transformation of the Sixteenth Century Kanto," *Journal of Japanese Studies* 11 (1985): 369–400.

[51] John W. Hall, *Japan from Prehistory to Modern Times* (New York, 1970), 131.

[52] See Delmer M. Brown, "The Impact of Firearms on Japanese Warfare, 1543–98," *Far Eastern Quarterly* 7 (1947): 236–53, for the argument that gunpowder changed Japanese warfare; cf. Morillo, "Guns and Government."

In Europe between 1450 and 1800, a period which is not usually called a "Warring States period" but clearly was one, governments improved their financial and administrative abilities, armies got bigger, and infantry came to predominate, bringing the European age of cavalry to an end. The Japanese case, offering as it does a close parallel with the European experience, but with one critical variable – the introduction of gunpowder weapons – is further evidence that interpretations of the military revolution in Europe and of the age of cavalry that preceded it should probably look more to administrative and governmental factors than to technological ones for explanations of changing military practices.

In sum, I do not think there is much role for the stirrup, gunpowder, or other technologies, in explaining any of these patterns. The age of cavalry was really the age of bad infantry, and was a political, not a technological, phenomenon.

FREEDOM AND MILITARY REFORM
IN TENTH-CENTURY SAXONY

Edward J. Schoenfeld

IN May, 919, the magnates of *Francia Orientalis* convened at Fritzlar, where they chose Henry, the Saxon duke, to be their new king.[1] In the same year, the Magyars, a nomadic people from the Eurasian steppe who had occupied the Danube basin, staged a massive raid that penetrated all the way across East *Francia* into Lotharingia. That raid was only the latest in a series of attacks during which the Magyars had plundered west central Europe from Verona in the south to Bremen in the north; and the Magyar attacks were only one in a group of military threats, including Danish "piracy" and Slav "brigandage," against which the fighting men of East Francia had not enjoyed a notable success since the battle of the Dyle in 891, a generation earlier. It seemed that Henry had been chosen to lead a kingdom unable to defend itself.

Yet, during his reign of less than two decades (919–936), Henry was able to gain the upper hand over the Slavs, contain the Danes behind the dyke which they had built across the Jutland peninsula, and challenge the Magyars to a battle at Riade in 933 from which they ran without fighting. His son and successor, Otto the Great (936–972), ended the Magyar threat at the battle of the Lech in 955 and, seven years later, received the imperial crown from the pope at Rome. The resulting polity, the medieval *Reich*, remained arguably the premier military and political power in Western Christendom until the mid-thirteenth century. It is little wonder that, down to the present day, historians and medievalists have given attention to what it was that Henry and Otto did to secure that pre-eminence.

Henry's military reforms – the king is usually thought of as having built the machine that Otto used, in a sort of Philip and Alexander *topos* – as presented by the writers of his time, consisted mainly in founding and garrisoning defensive structures, in Latin, *urbes*, in German, *burgen*.[2] The key passage regarding Henry's so-called fortification order, or *Burgenordnung*, is found in Book I,

---

1 Timothy Reuter, *Germany in the Early Middle Ages, 800–1056* (London, 1991), 137ff.
2 Carl Erdmann, "Die Burgenordnung Heinrichs I," *Deutsches Archiv für Geschichte des Mittelalters*, n.s. 6 (1943): 59–101; G. Baaken, "Königtum, Burgen, und Königsfreie," in *Vorträge und Forschungen* (Constance/Stuttgart, n.d.), and Erich Sander, "Die Heeresorganisation Heinrichs I," *Historisches Jahrbuch* (1939): 1–26 give representative modern views, with

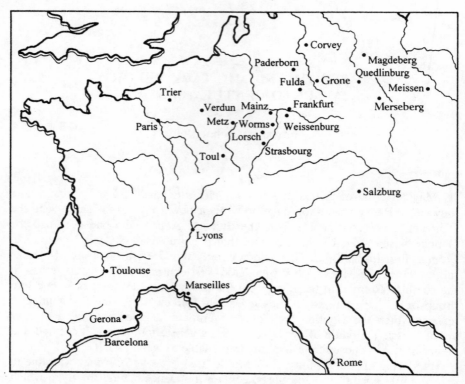

The later Carolingian empire

section 35 of the *Res Gestae Saxonicae* written by a tenth-century monk, Widukind of Corvey:

> Therefore King Henry, accepting peace from the Hungarians for nine years, watched over defending the fatherland and battling the barbarian nations with such prudence as is above our ability to express, yet by no means is it permissible to be silent. And first he chose one from each nine among the *agrarii milites* whom he made to live in fortifications, so that he might construct habitations for the remaining eight of his fellows and receive and store the third part of all the produce. The remaining eight, indeed, were to sow and reap and collect the ninth's produce and remain living in their places.[3]

a broadly comparative study by Kurt-Ulrich Jäschke, *Burgenbau und Landesverteidigung um 900. Überlegungen zu Beispielen aus Deutschland* (Sigmaringen, 1975), 18–33.

[3] *Die Sachsengeschichte des Widukind von Korvei*, ed. H.-E. Lohmann and P. Hirsch (Hannover, 1935), 48ff.: "Igitur Henricus Rex, accepta pax ab Ungariis ad novem annos, quanta prudentia vigilaverit in munienda patria et in expugnando barbaras nationes, supra nostram est virtutem edicere, licet onmimodos non oporteat taceri. Et primum quidem ex agrariis militibus nonum quemque eligens in urbibus habitare fecit, ut ceteris confamiliaribus suis octo habiticula extrueret, frugum omnium tertiam partem exciperet servaretque. Caeteri vero

One of the main difficulties with this passage has been to decipher exactly whom Widukind meant when he referred to *agrarii milites* (literally "farmer-warriors"). Modern scholarship, unfortunately, has not been able to clarify the question very much at all, and the purpose here is to make another attempt, first by examining the question's historiography and second by looking at some of the instruments, specifically royal charters, which reflect the institution as it was intended to operate.

The extent of the confusion can be illustrated by beginning with Rolf Köpke, who, in his edition of and commentary on Widukind, rendered *agrarii milites* as *ministeriales* – a class of warriors and administrators who, though legally unfree and sometimes classed as serfs, were responsible for many of the military and administrative functions of the medieval *Reich*.[4] This interpretation, which still has a significant voice in the debate, originally rested solidly on theories of royal authority in which the king's legislative and executive powers were limited by the so-called traditional constitution or *Verfassung*, as expressed in various codes of customary law dealing with the definition of privileges for freemen against royal interference.

Specifically, this view held that the king had no coercive power (*Heerbann*) over the military service of freemen except in case of direct national defense or formally declared general warfare against a designated foe. These latter actions were thought, instead, to be part of a so-called national defense requirement (*Landesverteidigungspflicht*), as opposed to a requirement to undertake military service at the royal command, which was called the *Heerbannpflicht*. The invocation of the national defense requirement could not be done by the king acting alone, but instead required the consent of the governed as expressed by the principal men of the realm, preferably given in a formally convened imperial diet, or *Reichstag*.[5] Since Henry's fortification order was, as far as Widukind tells us, undertaken without any such consultation, those affected, it was thought, had to be men on whom Henry could rely to carry out orders given on the king's own authority, hence dependent on the king, and hence his *ministeriales*.

Yet the origin of the *ministeriales* was itself a matter of dispute, with no unequivocal reference to them before the eleventh century. Georg Waitz, the great constitutional historian, took the words *agrarii milites* to indicate merely dependent people of the king.[6] W. Giesebrecht, who wrote the nineteenth century's standard narrative history of the medieval *Reich*, thought that the *agrarii*

---

octo seminarent et meterent frugesque colligerent nono et suis eas locis reconderent." For modern commentary see H. Beumann, *Widukind von Korvei* (Weimar, 1950) and K. Hauck, "Widukind von Korvei," in *Die Deutsche Literatur des Mittelalters, Verfasserlexikon*, ed. Karl Langosch, 13 vols. (Berlin, 1953), 40:946–58.

4 Ralf Köpke, *Widukind von Korvei*, Ottonische Studien (Berlin, 1867), 95, 156.

5 Georg Waitz, *Deutsche Verfassungsgeschichte*, 4 vols. (1880–85; Darmstadt, 1953–55), 2:205ff.; and H. Fehr, "Das Waffenrecht der Bauern im Mittelalter," *Zeitschrift der Savigny – Stiftung für Rechtsgeschichte (germanistische Abteilung)* 35 (1914): 118ff.

6 Georg Waitz, *Jahrbücher des deutschen Reiches unter König Heinrich I* (1885; Darmstadt, 1963), 92–98.

milites were limited to the eastern marches of the king's own duchy, Saxony, and his opinion framed the view of the question in standard works such as Geb-hardt's *Handbuch der deutschen Geschichte*, in which Widukind's farmer-warriors are described as dependents of Henry in his capacity as Saxon duke, not as king.[7] While Waitz's formulation neatly sidestepped the question of the origin of the *ministeriales*, the seeming retreat from a broad definition of the *agrarii milites* as ministerials, or at least their forerunners, seems to have been inspired by a strong belief that developments in Saxony were peculiar to that stem-duchy and not generally shared with other regions of Germany.

Later, James Westfall Thompson would wed Giesebrecht's Saxon particular-ism to the Turnerian frontier thesis he had absorbed as a graduate student and maintain that Saxon institutions were unique because Saxony was situated on the frontier of both the Empire and Latin Christendom.[8] While this was techni-cally a misapplication of Turner's frontier thesis, which is supposed to apply to the entire society and not just the immediate frontier district, Thompson's ideas were largely adopted in Geoffrey Barraclough's discussion of the Ottonian period and the beginning of Germany's so-called *Drang nach Osten*.[9]

The progress of scholarly discussion was, of course, not quite so neat as this simplified scheme makes out. For instance, Hans Delbrück, the "father" of ana-lytic military history, dismissed the entire passage concerning the *agrarii milites* as a complete fiction, designed to glorify the hero of Widukind's narrative work.[10] Leopold von Ranke, the father of nineteenth-century "scientific" history, held that Widukind's farmer-warriors were actually the larger land-holders of the region, thus implying a connection to his contemporaries, the Junkers, on whom the burden of defending Germany fell during the so-called second *Reich*. Friedrich Keutgen and Carl Rodenberg argued that the duty of defending Henry's *urbes* fell to the inhabitants of each region in which one was established. The *agrarii milites*, thus, were free peasants in the old Germanic tradition, presumably worthy predecessors to the "nation-in-arms" of the late nineteenth century.[11] Taking another approach, Karl Koehne, a specialist in urban origins, focused on the connection between Latin *urbs*, German *burg*, and

---

[7] W. Giesebrecht, *Geschichte der deutschen Kaiserzeit* (Leipzig, 1881), 222–24 and notes on 811ff.; B. Gebhardt, *Handbuch der deutschen Geschichte* (Stuttgart, 1954), 1:169ff.

[8] James Westfall Thompson, *Feudal Germany* (New York, 1928), 167–84.

[9] Geoffrey Barraclough, *The Origins of Modern Germany* (Oxford, 1947), 37–43. For dis-cussion of the Turner thesis and medieval history, see R.I. Burns, S.J. "The Significance of the Frontier in the Middle Ages," in *Medieval Frontier Societies*, ed. Robert Bartlett and Angus MacKay (Oxford, 1989), 307–30.

[10] Hans Delbrück, *Geschichte der Kriegskunst im Rahmen der politische Geschichte* 6 vols. (1921; Berlin, 1964), 3:112.

[11] Leopold von Ranke, *Weltgeschichte*, 6 vols. (Berlin, 1885), 6, pt. 2: 133; Friedrich Keut-gens, *Untersuchungen über der Ursprung der deutschen Stadtverfassung* (Berlin, 1895), 45; and Carl Rodenberg, "Die Stadtgründungen Heinrichs I," *Mitteilungen des Instituts für Österreichische Geschichte* 17 (1896): 161ff.

the development of cities, and made the tenth-century "farmer-warriors" into the earliest forerunners of a German *bourgeoisie*.[12]

None of these arguments were accepted by the mainstream of professional historical opinion. Delbrück was simply ignored; Von Ranke dismissed as not having done enough work with the documents (he was, after all, not a medievalist); Koehne likewise; and Keutgen and Rodenberg were refuted by an appeal to authority of Köpke. As Dietrich Schäfer proclaimed in 1905, if the translator and editor of Widukind's history said that the *agrarii milites* were *ministeriales*, then *ministeriales* they were and no more questions needed to be asked about the matter. The very most that Schäfer was willing to concede was that the farmer-warriors were, in fact, the institutional forerunners of the ministerials, since they did not yet bear the name.[13] Keutgen would later amend his position by limiting the *agrarii milites* to a class of trained soldiers, but at the same time he would continue to maintain that they were not simply *ministeriales*.[14]

The identification of *agrarii milites* with *ministeriales*, or their forerunners, was soon questioned on more fundamental grounds. That identification rested primarily on the understanding that the medieval German constitution was the product of a society of common free men (*Gemeinfreie*), whose rights and liberties, based upon traditional Germanic customs, were expressed in various law codes. In turn, this view of Germany's medieval military and political constitution was founded on an interpretation of Germanic economic and social organization called the *Markverfassung*. This held that the rights contained in both written law and ancient customs had survived the civilizing influence of Rome and the development of state power. As a result of the survival, they had come to form the organizing principle of German society in the late medieval and early modern periods.[15]

In spite of a vigorous debate, the *Markverfassung* theory did not become untenable until after World War I, when researchers, primarily Alfons Dopsch, established that it turned on the historical anachronism of reading evidence from one century back into another.[16] Further research confirmed that the rights and

---

12 Karl Koehne, "Burgen, Burgmannen, and Städte. Ein Beitrag zur Frage der Bedeutung der ländlichen Grundrenten für die mittelalterliche Stadtentwicklung," *Historische Zeitschrift* 133 (1926): 1–19.

13 Dietrich Schäfer, "Die *agrarii milites* des Widukind," *Sitzungsberichte des königlichen preussischen Akademie der Wissenschaften* 27 (1905): 569–77. But see Albert Bauer and Reinhold Rau, *Quellen zur Geschichte der Sächsischen Kaiserzeit* (Darmstadt, 1971), who replace Lohmann and Hirsch's "*ministerialen*" with "*bauerlichen krieger*" (peasant warriors) when translating Widukind 1.35.

14 Frederich. Keutgens, "Untersuchungen über der Ursprung der deutschen Stadtverfassung," *Neues Archiv für den klassischen Altertumswissenschaft* (1900): 287ff.

15 Franz Staab, "A Reconsideration of the Ancestry of Modern Political Liberty: The Problem of the so-called 'King's Freemen' (*Königsfreie*)," *Viator* 11 (1980): 51–69; and Johannes Schmitt, *Untersuchungen zu den Liberi Homines der Karolingerzeit, Europäische Hochschulschriften Reihe III: Geschichte und ihre Hifswissenschaften Bd. 83* (Frankfurt/M, 1977), 5–26.

16 Alfons Dopsch, *Die Wirtschaftsentwicklung der Karolingerzeit vornehmlich in*

privileges of free peasants in late medieval Germany owed far more to the need of late medieval territorial lords to attract settlers to unused land than they owed to any underlying structure of Germanic liberties. As a result, it became possible, even necessary, to question the received interpretation of Widukind's *agrarii milites* as forerunners of the medieval Reich's royal *ministeriales*. Research and argument proceeded along two distinct but interrelated lines.

The first line of research concerned the physical evidence for the activities of Henry I in regard to the construction of *burgen* and the defense of the realm. Historians had accepted at face value the assertions of various chroniclers that Henry had built fortifications and cities throughout Germany. They had then expected that archeologists would find numerous so-called "Henry castles" if only they looked. Yet, by the 1930s, archaeologists had been looking assiduously for at least a generation and the results were disappointing.[17] At best, the various remains of early medieval fortifications which had been found could only be dated to a vague period (850–1050), roughly the time of Henry I; at worst, there was simply no positive evidence for Henry's construction of *urbes*, outside one or two examples already known from his charters. It seemed therefore the reputation of Henry I as a builder of castles and the genius behind Germany's medieval defensive organization had fallen for lack of sufficient concrete evidence.

Yet, it was the very loss of Henry's reputation as a builder that provided an opportunity to reinterpret the status of the *agrarii milites* and, with them, Henry's military reform. Walther Schlesinger responded by showing that even if Henry had not built physical defenses from scratch, he had reorganized military administration. According to Schlesinger, Henry extended the organization of regional defense around centrally located strong-points, the so-called *Burgbannverfassung*, inherited from the Carolingians in the western regions of Germany, to the eastern frontier of his native Saxony. In Schlesinger's view, the *agrarii milites*, therefore, were the inhabitants of the new military districts, whether dependent or not, reorganized for the purpose of common defense by the king.[18] The actual fortifications, at least in their surviving form as constructions of stone around which the burghal districts (*burgwardia*) were organized, could have been built either at the time the districts were established or later. Indeed, the precise moment at which any specific fortification was constructed really had little to do with Henry's achievement.

Deutschland, 2 vols. (1912–13; Darmstadt, 1962) and idem, *Wirtschaftliche und soziale Grundlagen der europäischen Kulturentwicklung aus der zeit von Cäsar bis auf Karl den Grossen*, 2 vols. (1918–20; Aalen, 1961).

17 Carl Schuchhardt, *Die Burg im Wandel der Weltgeschichte* (1931), 188; Herbert Jahnkuhn, " 'Heinrichsburgen' und Königspfalzen," *Deutsche Königspfalzen*, 2 vols. (Göttingen, 1965), 2:61–69; and S. Krüger, "Einige Bemerkungen zur Werla-Forschung," *Deutsch Königspfalzen*, 235–37.

18 Walther Schlesinger, "Burgen und Burgbezirke: Beobachtungen im mitteldeutschen Osten," in *Mitteldeutsche Beiträge zur Verfassungsgeschichte des Mittelalters* (Göttingen, 1961), 165–76 and map.

Schlesinger's research coincided with the work of Heinrich Dannenbaur, who took up Thompson's ideas about Saxony as the German frontier. Dannenbaur maintained that Henry's activities constituted a continuing effort at colonization east of the Elbe, where most of the burghal districts Schlesinger attributes to Henry are to be found. Apparently latching onto Thompson's adaptation of the "frontier thesis," Dannenbaur also argued that the inhabitants of the newly established districts had to be given the incentive of personal freedom to settle areas under threat from the Slavs. In return for the freedom they were granted by the king, these so-called "royal free men" (*Königsfreie*) had to perform certain duties, among them the building and maintaining of fortresses. It was they who formed the class of *agrarii milites* to which Widukind referred.[19]

In any case, one can view both Dannenbaur and Schlesinger as attempting to preserve the idea of Germanic liberty as it had been expressed in the concept of *Markverfassung*: Schlesinger by linking the burghal districts to the hundred (*centena*), the basic subunit of the old Germanic *Mark*, and Dannenbaur by deriving the *agrarii milites* from that class of freemen which supposedly had always existed in Germanic society and to which the royal free men were at least partially elevated.[20] There was, however, one very significant difference between the new and old interpretations. According to the former, the *agrarii milites*, like the *ministeriales*, had to be individuals of a servile status because the king was unable to coerce free men into mandatory military service. By contrast, the new interpretation depicted them as free men (or at least freed-men) because the king actively had to recruit individuals to serve in districts under perpetual threat of invasion and brigandage. The later interpretation of Henry's military reform turned the earlier one on its head.

During these developments older positions were not without their defenders. Maintaining the cause of Saxon particularism, Martin Lintzel asserted that Saxon resistance to Charlemagne in the late eighth and early ninth centuries had been a truly national movement, resulting in a tenth-century Saxon duchy far less influenced by Carolingian ways than the rest of Germany.[21] Because of this, the exceptional freedom enjoyed by the *agrarii milites* and other Saxon classes arose from conditions that were peculiar to Saxony and the Saxon way of doing things, rather than from the accident of Saxony's location on a frontier or from any widespread adoption of Carolingian institutions.

On the other hand, Erich Sander and Robert Holtzmann changed the focus of the argument. In their view, the real achievement of Henry I was the introduction into Saxony of large numbers of heavily armored mounted warriors, or *milites armati*. These troops replaced the Saxon levee which had fought as *inermes*, that is unarmored or lightly armored.[22] Conceptually, the theory espoused by Sander

19 H. Dannenbaur, *Grundlagen der mittelalterlichen Welt* (Stuttgart, 1958), 321.
20 Staab, 60.
21 Martin Lintzel, "Die Unterwerfung Sachsens durch Karl den Grossen und der Sächsische Adel," in his *Ausgewöhlten Schriften* (Berlin, 1936).
22 Robert Holtzmann, *Geschichte der Sächsische Kaiserzeit* (Munich, 1943), 89; Sander, "*Heeresorganisation*," 7.

and Holtzmann put Henry's reform as well as Saxon military development squarely within the paradigm of feudalism as constructed by Heinrich Brunner in 1887.[23] It should be noted that all these schools, including the one associating the *agrarii milites* with the *Königsfreie*, retained the idea that Henry could command directly only people who were somehow dependent on him, whether they were his *ministeriales*, his vassals, or his free men.

More recently, Karl Leyser tried to solve the dilemma presented by Widukind's farmer-warriors.[24] Following Holtzmann and Sander in thinking that Henry's real achievement was the introduction of heavily-armored cavalry to the Saxon host, Leyser went on to separate that change from Henry's fortification order and the *agrarii milites* in Widukind.[25] Indeed, he observed that while Henry and Otto could rely on the armored warriors in open battle, the farmer-warriors were given duties, including fortress work, such as those expected in Carolingian times of free men who could not afford to ride with the host.[26] Thus Leyser concluded that those *milites* who were not wealthy enough to make the transition to the new and very expensive kind of warfare continued to fight unarmored, and that it was from such low-wealth, low-status individuals that Henry drew the *agrarii milites*. Since low status and dependency went hand in hand, Widukind's farmer-warriors must, therefore, have been dependent or unfree individuals, as maintained all along by the school of Köpke and Waitz. Leyser had successfully, it seemed, accomplished three goals. He had asserted the identification of Henry's military reform as the introduction of feudal institutions, overturned the thesis that special privileges were required to attract new settlers to Germany's eastern frontier, and denied the peculiar condition of Saxony maintained by Lintzel. By altogether removing the idea of fortification from Henry's military reform, he had also severed completely the debate over the *agrarii milites* from its original heuristic moorings.

Leyser's argument, which has dominated since its appearance, relies on two fundamentally interrelated premises.[27] The first is the idea that Henry and Otto were able to command only their own direct dependents, in accord with either the institutions of early Germanic liberty or medieval lordship, the choice between the two depending on whether one wishes to hold that the *agrarii milites* were *ministeriales* or *Königsfreie*. Second is the identification of those individuals subject to the *burgbannum*, namely the *agrarii milites*, not only as unarmored, but also as of low socio-economic status – dependent or at least not wholly free. Leyser supports this position by reference to various charters granted by Henry I and Otto I which deal with the establishment and confirma-

---

[23] Heinrich Brunner, "Der Reiterdienst und die Anfönge des Lehenwesens," *Zeitschrift der Savigny Stiftung für Rechtsgeschichte, Germanistische Abteilung* 8 (1887): 1–38, especially as revised by Lynn T. White, Jr., *Medieval Technology and Social Change* (Oxford, 1962).

[24] Karl Leyser, "Henry I and the Beginnings of the Saxon Empire," *EHR* 83 (1968): 1–32.

[25] Ibid., 6.

[26] Ibid., 9 citing *Edictum Pistense*, chap. 27, *MGH, Capitularia Regum Francorum* (Hannover, 1897), 2:321ff.

[27] See for example Reuter, 143–44.

tion of burghal districts. He also examines the narrative sources, particularly Widukind, to show that Henry and Otto introduced a new element into the fighting style of the Saxons. Lastly, as the historiographic discussion has shown, the silence of archaeology underlies the entire project to show that Henry introduced heavily armored mounted troops to Saxony.

Fortunately, we are able to test Leyser's premises by examining the evidence. To begin with, just what kind of people were under the obligation of defending fortifications in tenth-century Saxony? Or, rather, a question that is easier to answer, what sort of people appeared in the charters of Henry I and Otto I, which established burghal districts or otherwise defined military jurisdictions?

The key documents are several of Otto I's charters which confirm the burghal districts of Corvey, Weissenburg, and Magdeburg. In the charter pertaining to Magdeburg, Otto "hands over the *bannum* and the work of gathering to the *urbs* the *incoles circummanentes*" to the church of St. Maurice and forbids anyone "whether a *comes, vicarius, judex, tribunus*, or *exactor*" from exercising the *bannum*, with the exception of the head of that church or his appointed *advocatus*.[28] The *bannum* here is simply the power of command, and *incoles circummanentes* means "the inhabitants dwelling around," a sufficiently general term to include anyone who might be living in the district, whether dependent or not. In this document, at least, Otto seemed unconcerned with the possible jurisdiction or lordship that other persons – and he names a whole hierarchy, from count (*comes*) down to tax gatherer (*exactor*) – may have possessed over them. With regard to the *bannum*, these people belonged to Magdeburg and that was that. Likewise, the charter took no cognizance of differences in wealth or status among the people living around the city. Whoever they may have been, they were to go the Magdeburg for defense.

Similarly, in a charter for Weissenburg Abbey, Otto ordered the *"servi, lidi,* or *coloni,* or those who are called *fiscales* or *censuales"* to go for defense to the monastery and "to no other *civitas* or *castella*."[29] *Servi, lidi* and *coloni* were all dependent classes of one type or another, although *lidi* and *coloni* might be considered partially free. *Fiscales* were people who paid tribute to the royal fisc; it was from such individuals that Dannenbaur got his royal free men. *Censuales* were rent paying tenants, people who, like the *fiscales,* had a status somewhere

---

28 *MGH, Urkunden der Deutschen Könige und Kaiser, Diplomatum Ottonis [DOI]*, I, no. 300: "opus consturndae urbis a circummanentibus illarum partium incolis nostro regio vel imperatorio iuri debitum ecclesiae in eadem civitate constructe sanctoque Mauricio in ius perpetuum liberaliter offerimus; . . . Proscripti vero nostri banni deo sanctoque Mauricio a nobis oblati nullus vel comes vel vicarius vel vel iudex vel tribunus exactor vel alia aliqua persona in eadem civitate sibi usurpandi vel aliam aliquam in prescriptis legem aut disciplinam exercendi potestam habeat, nisi ipse qui eidem loco vel aecclesiae prefuerit, vel advocatus quem nostro consensu sibi et eidem ecclesie preficiendum elegerit."
29 *MGH, Urkunden, DOI,* no. 287: "statuimus et jubemus ut servi vel lidi vel coloni vel qui dicuntur fiscales vel censuales qui in proprietate beati Petri apostolorum principis Uuizinburg vel ubicumque commorantur et habitant, seu ad opus monachorum deserviant seu fidelibus nostri beneficiales existant, ad nullam aliam civitatem vel castellum muniendum ab aliquo cogantur vel distringantur . . ."

between servile and free. Otto also specifically stated that this order applied to both those "devoted to the work of the monastery" or who existed as "*beneficiales* to our *fideles*." By specifically stating that the order applied to *beneficiales*, the holders of benefices, of his *fideles*, the retainers or vassals of the king, thus including the magnates, Otto again ignores any theoretical limitation on his authority over men holding from another lord. The charter also indicates that individuals with partially free status, like *fiscales* or *censuales*, were liable to the *bannum*. It is important also to note that Weissenburg was in Alsatia and thus outside Saxony proper. The institution being examined here was not relegated to a frontier district or a single stem-land.

The charter concerning Corvey is important because Corvey's immunity was derived from grants made in the Carolingian era and had long-standing connections with the Saxon house. In that charter, Otto gave the "*bannum* over the *homines*" who ought to take refuge in the monastery and "the *civitas* around it" to the abbots of Corvey. The king went on to specify that the *bannum* he means is called the *burgbannum*, the power to command a fortification, its garrison, and its supernumerary population, and that the men he meant were those in

> the *pagus* Auga in the *comitatus* of Rethardus; and the *pagus* Netga in the *comitatus* of Dendus and Hamponus; and the *pagus* Huetigo in the *comitatus* of Herimannus.

Here Otto named specific districts (*pagi*) over which the abbot of Corvey's *burgbannum* was valid and forbade those magnates who held other kinds of jurisdiction from exercising the *burgbannum* over those men.[30] Again, Otto appeared unconcerned by the thought that he might have been interfering in the jurisdictions of his magnates, in this case magnates whom he specifically names. Further, the order applied to all the men in the affected *pagi*.

The documents examined so far suggest two things. First, the coercive power of the king in military affairs was not greatly limited by the so-called rights of free individuals or of lords. Otto appears to have created military districts (*burgwardia*) as needed, for the purpose of organizing defense, and ordered men to garrison them as that defense required, regardless of any other jurisdiction to which such men might be subject. Otto seems to be maintaining a military administration that relied on royal policy and the king's authority rather than on ties of dependence between individuals, and one that based defensive organization on geography rather than lordship *per se*.

The second observation suggested by the study of these three key documents

---

[30] Ibid., no. 27: "ut omnes abbates qui super monachos in Noua Corbeia deo sanctoque Stephano protomartiri et Vito famulantes constituentur, et nunc qui eis preest Folcmarus abbas, bannum habeant super homines qui ad prefatum coenobium et ad civitatem circa illud debent constructam confugere et in ea operari, hoc est in pago Auga in comitatu Rethardi et in pago Netga in comitatu Dendi et Hamponis et in pago Huetigo in comitatu Herimanni; nulus horum aut aliqua iudiciaria potestas super prefatos homines potestatem [habeat exercendi] ullius banni quem burgban voccant . . ." Compare Leyser, "Henry I," 6–10, who ignores this aspect of the charter.

is that the status of individuals as freemen or dependents had little to do with their liability for military service in fortifications. The people affected by the *burgbannum* are designated in general terms – the *incoles circummanentes* or *homines* of the affected districts. Where more specific indications of status are used, several types of people are affected – not just *servi, laeti,* and *coloni,* but *fiscales* and *censuales* as well. It might be suggested that Otto nowhere named men of high status, *nobiles,* as subject to the *burgbannum*; except for the fact that, by addressing the charters to great men such as bishops and abbots, he obviously meant those magnates to organize and lead the defense, which was their proper role in tenth-century society. That this consideration applied to secular as well as clerical magnates is demonstrated by the fact that counts like Rethardus, Dendus, Hamponus, and Herimannus were also expected to lead people in defense of fortified places by exercising the *Burgbannum.*

This second impression is reinforced by examining a charter that establishes the immunity of the archbishop of Hamburg.[31] While this document did not directly describe the creation of a *burgwardium,* it did require that no public official (*judex publicus*), or official power (*judicaria potestas*) should interfere in the affairs of the archbishopric. Nor could such officials prevent anyone, free or dependent, from pledging himself to the archbishopric so long as that individual's co-heirs consented. Further, while the activities covered by the parts of the charter discussed so far were not essentially military in nature, Otto went on to give the archbishop the same right and privilege which the abbot of Corvey had exercised since the time of Charlemagne, the right to command the men (*homines*) from his archbishopric while in attendance in the royal palace (*palatium*) or on expedition (*expeditio*). This provision again used a general term, *homines,* to indicate all the men of the archbishopric, whether free or unfree, and specifically stated that the military authority of the archbishop extended to both *liberti* and *iamundlingi.* It appears from this that the liability to military service did not depend on the legal status of the individual, and that the service of dependent individuals was required even when on campaign, not just within fortifications.

Further, the charter regarding Hamburg suggests that the condition of dependency may have had little to do with economic status. Indeed, the connection, if any, between legal caste – freedom or unfreedom – and economic status – wealth – appears to be far more complex than can be rendered by a simple equation between low wealth and low status. The tenth century knew many

---

31 *MGH, Urkunden, DOI,* no. 11: "ut nullus iudex publicus vel quaelibet iudicaria potestas aliquam sibi vindicet potestam in supradictorum hominibus monasterioirum, litis videlicet et colonis, vel eos aliquis capitis banno ob capitis furtum vel quocumque banno constringat aut aliquam iusticiam facere cogat nisi advocatus archepiscopi . . . Si vero aliquis ex libertis voluerit iamundling vel litus fieri aut etiam colonus ad monasteria supradicta cum consensu coheredum suorum, non prohibeatur a qualibet potestate, sed habeat licentiam nostra auctoritate, habeat quoque potestatem praedictus Adalag successoresque eius Hammaburgensis ecclesie archiepiscopi super libertos et iamundlingos monasteriorum supradictorum in expeditionem sive ad palatium regis."

strata of free or partially free individuals below the magnates, some of whom had difficulty maintaining the obligations of their freedom and were thus classed as poor (*pauperes*). The terms used to describe freemen, *liberi* and *ingenui*, could be applied even to the possessors of estates. On the other hand, even the magnates fit into a hierarchy of a kind and could be thought of as the vassals (*fideles*) of the king – persons technically unfree who might have other people as dependents below them.[32] Even individuals who clearly fought as armored warriors found it difficult to maintain their status. The *miles armatus* required great resources in order to possess horses, weapons and, armor. For example, Widukind reports that Otto I rewarded one *miles*, a certain Hosed, with revenues of twenty *manses* after Hosed killed a Slav leader.[33] Even if Widukind gave special mention to Hosed because of a connection to Corvey, the example shows that heavily-armored *milites* relied on the king or other lords for the resources to act as warriors.

Indeed, throughout the *Res Gestae Saxonicae*, Widukind used the term *miles* to indicate a warrior in a magnate's following; the only apparent exception is the so-called Merseburg legion, which he states was made up of robbers and thieves settled on the frontier because they could be useful there.[34] Yet the epithet *latrones* may not necessarily indicate that the individuals that made up this peculiar unit were of ignoble or servile origin as Leyser suggests.[35] Charges of brigandage and robbery were normally made against participants in a feud, especially the side that lost. Feuds and rebellions were very common in tenth-century Saxony, the most famous, perhaps, being those against Otto in 936 by his brother, Henry the Quarrelsome, and in 951 by his son, Luidolf. As can be seen from these examples, participation in feuds was not limited to persons of low status and the epithet *latrones*, alone, is not enough to show that the members of the Merseburg legion came from a lower socio-economic groups than that which provided most armored warriors.

Discussion of this item provides one more sidelight. Widukind states that the legion marched to defend one of Henry's Slavic clients against the Bohemians. Even if the Merseburgers were not the armed following of a lord, Widukind still portrayed them as taking the field against an enemy – to him, then, *milites* are men who fight. This has interesting implications for the question of the *agrarii milites*. If the farmer-warriors are to be connected to the provisions of the Edict of Pîtres, in which poor but free men were called upon to provide noncombatant services, then why did Widukind describe them with a word that he uses everywhere else to indicate combatants?[36]

---

[32] Heinrich Fichtenau, *Living in the Tenth Century: Mentalities and Social Orders*, trans Patrick G. Geary (Chicago, 1991), 359–69; and Schmitt, 240–46.

[33] Widukind, p. 135, 3:55: "Merces tam famosi gesti donativum imperiale cum reditu viginti mansuus."

[34] Ibid., pp. 68ff., 2.3, See also the discussion in Leyser, p. 14, n. 5.

[35] Leyser, 12.

[36] See n. 26 above.

While the introduction of heavy cavalry or at least the expansion of that branch of the military may have constituted one of Henry's reforms, mentioning only this change would not do justice to Widukind's account of the king's achievements. After the chapters of the *Res Gestae Saxonicae* which tell of Henry's fortification order and his battles against the Slavs, Widukind informs us that the monarch now possessed and army "proven in battle" (*probatus*).[37] This passage suggests that Henry's real aim had been the establishment of a highly reliable military force, rather than one which simply wielded new weapons or fought in an unfamiliar fashion. As part of the process of increasing the army's reliability, Henry seems to have considerably expanded his own following, now that his possession of the royal fisc provided him the resources to do so. By the time of the Lechfeld in 955, the royal contingent was twice the size of all others.[38] Similarly, Widukind's description of the battle of Riade in 933, where Henry sent out the Thuringian contingent "with few heavily armored warriors" in order to lure the Magyars into a decisive battle, may describe a tactical maneuver or a ruse, rather than indicate that the Saxons had not fought as *milites armati* before Henry's reform.[39] Widukind, who wrote only a generation after the battle of Riade, needed to state that the force set out as bait had few heavily armored warriors with it in order to clearly describe Henry's ruse. This passage description does not require us to believe that under normal circumstances the Thuringians only provided the host with a few heavily armored warriors.

In fact, the assertion that Henry introduced *milites armati* to Saxony on a large scale may push the narrative material farther than it reasonably can go. Recent archaeological findings also serve to cast light on the debate over the true nature of Henry's military reforms. It is fairly well accepted that Henry did, in fact, engage in some building activity, especially in places that had long associations with the Saxon house, such as Merseburg, Meissen, and Quedlinburg.[40] While only forty-one authentic charters have survived from Henry's reign, a few other potential *burgen* can be located using them. Defensive walls (*muri*), are mentioned for the *civitates* of Toul and Trier; and charters identify further *civitates* at Worms, Mainz, Quedlinburg, Pöhlde, Grone, Duderstadt and Nordhausen.[41] To this short list, narrative sources allow us to add the monasteries of Hersfeld and Corvey, the episcopal seats of Regensburg and Augsburg, and the royal *palatium* at Werla where Henry took refuge from Magyar attacks in 924.[42] It is important to note that Toul, Trier, Regensburg, and Augsburg are all outside

---

37 Widukind, pp. 57ff., 1:38.
38 Ibid., pp. 123ff., 3:44,
39 Ibid., p. 57, 1:38, with discussion at Leyser, 5, 23.
40 Reuter, 143.
41 *MGH, Diplomatum Henrici I* [*DHI*], no. 11 for Worms; *DHI*, no. 15 for Mainz; *DHI*, no. 20 for Quedlinburg, Pöhlde, Grone, Duderstadt and Nordhausen; *DHI*, no. 21 for Toul; and *DHI*, no. 24 for Trier.
42 Widukind, 1:32 for Werla and 1:35 for Corvey; and Erdmann, "*Burgenordnung*," for Hersfeld, Regensburg, and Augsburg.

the boundaries of the Saxon stem-duchy. Henry's activity was apparently applied, or imitated, throughout Germany.

Thus, the widely-held contention that (1) Henry's fortifications were manned by low status, low wealth individuals and (2) that the real improvement he made in Saxon military organization was the introduction of heavy of cavalry has been called into serious question. The archaeological evidence and its associated documentary and literary remains do, in fact, indicate that considerable fortification building activity was going on during the early tenth century, much of it outside the boundaries of Saxony proper. The narrative passages in Widukind do not necessarily support the idea that the Saxons were unaccustomed to fighting from horseback in heavy armor before Henry's time. The charters applicable to service in fortifications indicate that the king (or emperor) seemed to have been well able to demand military service in the *burgwardia* in spite of the jurisdiction of magnates and other lords, who were in any case the ruler's *fideles*.

Further, the status of individuals as free men or dependents (a key for identifying who the *agrarii milites* actually were) seems to have had little bearing on anyone's liability for military service in tenth-century Saxony. Some of the farmer-warriors may have worked their own land and perhaps even owed servile duties to others. The language of the charters, however, leaves open the possibility that other members of this class did not engage in agriculture and were either landowners in their own right or warriors in the retinue of some other magnate.

In conclusion, some type of military service was required from all individuals regardless of status, and both Henry and Otto were concerned with organizing the defense of the *Reich* on the broadest possible social and geographic bases. In any case, it seems that Leyser's identification of the *agrarii milites* as being drawn from those warriors who still fought as *inermes* because they were poor and therefore dependent, and his position, shared with Sander and Holtzmann, that Henry's actual reform mainly concerned the introduction of *milites armati* to Saxony, deserves a thorough re-examination.

Part II

MEDIEVAL WARFARE AS A DIVINE TOOL

APPARITIONS AND WAR IN ANGLO-SAXON ENGLAND

Kent G. Hare

IN his seminal 1935 work on the *Origin of the Idea of Crusade*, Carl Erdmann noted that tales of divine intervention in military affairs were common in Eastern Christendom even before the First Crusade at the end of the eleventh century. Erdmann saw this participation by heavenly beings in earthly war as pre-Crusade evidence that "the contradiction between war and Christianity was no longer felt in the East."[1] Such a celestial dimension to warfare was not, however, limited to the East. In the Latin West, there was a similar accommodation between war and Christianity. By examining a series of apparition stories emanating from Anglo-Saxon and Norman England in the period between roughly 700 and 1150, one discovers a pattern interesting for several reasons: first, because of a marked increase in martial activity attributed to the denizens of heaven; second, because Erdmann overlooked this evidence in formulating his thesis.[2] Considering the Carolingian ninth century as a critical prelude to the calling of the First Crusade, Erdmann concentrated his study on Francia, Germany, and Italy. With the exception of brief treatment by Christopher Tyerman as preamble to his 1988 investigation of *England and the Crusades*,[3] historians since Erdmann have also neglected early medieval English antecedents to crusading ideology. Nevertheless, the increasingly bellicose apparitions which appear in English sources point to a growing acceptance of the active role heaven played in medieval warfare.[4]

A major source for any investigation of religion and society in the Middle Ages must be the hagiographical works most commonly characterized by the "*Lives*" of the saints. These made up the most widespread genre of medieval

---

[1] Carl Erdmann, *The Origin of the Idea of Crusade*, trans. Marshall W. Baldwin and Walter Goffart (Princeton, 1977), 6.

[2] Ibid., p. 97, n. 3.

[3] Christopher Tyerman, *England and the Crusades, 1095–1588* (Chicago, 1988), 8–14.

[4] The "apparitions" with which this study is concerned are limited to supernatural appearances of heavenly beings normally hidden from man's sight. Other "signs and wonders" connected with battle, such as the famous vision of Constantine before the Milvian Bridge, which do not include some sort of apparitional being, are not here examined, but would doubtless yield valuable insights. Christopher Holdsworth, " 'An Airier Aristocracy': The Saints at War," *Transactions of the Royal Historical Society*, 6th ser., 6 (1996): 103–22, briefly considers battlefield appearances by martial saints, pp. 117–19.

literature, and are sometimes the only texts surviving from a given age and region. While these *Lives* have never been neglected as historical sources, their study has nevertheless undergone something of a renaissance in recent years. New methods and approaches have forced open a window not so much on the saints themselves as on the attitudes and perceptions of the society from which they sprang and in which the hagiographers lived and wrote.[5] In addition, hagiographical elements appear in other works. For example, histories and chronicles, while not in the strictest meaning of the term "hagiographical," nevertheless contain much material which may be treated similarly.

Hagiography was increasingly modeled on the gospel accounts of Christ Himself.[6] Four early saints' *Lives* – Athanasius's *Life of St. Antony*, Jerome's *Life of St. Paul the First Hermit*, Sulpicius Severus's *Life of St. Martin*, and Gregory the Great's *Life of St. Benedict* (all dating from before 600) – established plot line and narrative structures which later hagiographers adapted wholesale, sometimes changing only the names of the protagonists.[7] In fact, any drastic break with previous convention by a later author may be interpreted as showing how much the world in which he wrote had changed from that of his predecessors. Such changes had made necessary his new conception of the nature of the holy and its role in this world.

In the following discussion, we shall examine in detail the degree to which visions reported by later authors depart as a result of their increasing militarism from the models established by the four prototypical saints' *Lives*.[8] From a selection of sources, I have constructed a typology of eighty-eight representative holy apparitions (see table and index at end of text). The apparitions are divided into five categories.

"Benign" apparitions are mainly characterized by healings and saintly defense of threatened cults, shrines, or putative relics. As an example of the

---

[5]   Paul Fouracre, "Merovingian History and Merovingian Hagiography," *Past & Present* 127 (1990): 3–38. Stephen Wilson, *Saints and their Cults* (Cambridge, 1983), 1. See also Peter Brown, *The Cult of the Saints: Its Rise and Function in Latin Christianity* (Chicago, 1981); idem, *Society and the Holy in Late Antiquity* (Berkeley, 1982); Alexander Murray, *Reason and Society in the Middle Ages* (1978; Oxford, 1985), 317–404; Donald Weinstein and Rudolph M. Bell, *Saints and Society* (Chicago, 1982).

[6]   Fouracre, 3–33; Susan J. Ridyard, *The Royal Saints of Anglo-Saxon England: A Study of West Saxon and East Anglian Cults*, ed. J.C. Holt (Cambridge, 1988), 10.

[7]   Bertram Colgrave's introduction to Felix, *The Life of St. Guthlac*, ed. and trans. Colgrave (1956; Cambridge, 1985), 16–17. The *Life* by Felix, for example, depends heavily on both Bede's *Life of St. Cuthbert* and Evagrius's Latin translation of Athanasius's *Life of St. Antony*. See Benjamin P. Kurtz, "From St. Antony to St. Guthlac: A Study in Biography," *University of California Publications in Modern Philology* 12 (1926): 103–46.

[8]   Michael E. Jones, "The Historicity of the Alleluja Victory," *Albion* 18 (1986): 363–73, esp. 373 applies a similar method in examining the miraculous military victory recounted in Constantius's fifth-century *Life of St. Germanus*. Against those dismissing the tale as a pious invention, Jones concludes "that the Alleluja victory rests on historical fact," partly because of "the sheer implausibility of such an invention in the context of ascetic thought and hagiographic precedent."

latter, Raymond d'Aguilers recounts many apparitions verifying the authenticity of the Holy Lance of the Crucifixion, miraculously rediscovered by the First Crusaders at Antioch.[9] The earlier authors of the four prototypes had portrayed heavenly visitors as having relatively peaceful purposes. These visitors were in no way envisioned as taking an active role in warfare. This was in keeping with the absence of an established theory of holy war in the early Church. While the just war theory as set down in the early fifth century by St. Augustine of Hippo did allow that one's participation in war might not be sinful, the more extreme notion that warfare could be not only meritorious but even redemptive was alien to the thoughts of early Christians.[10] Since these prototypes provided conventions for later medieval authors to follow, their benign portrayal of apparitions serves as a standard against which to compare the later and more belligerent assessment of the role of the saints.

A trend toward what may be termed individual violence on the part of apparitional beings manifested itself early on. Readers of Gregory of Tours' late-sixth-century *History of the Franks* will recall his vengeful St. Martin as a heavenly being who severely chastised sinners, even striking them dead on occasion.[11] The saint presented by Gregory as administering divine "Chastisement" (my second category) is barely recognizable as the same gentle, Christ-like holy man of the earlier *Life* by Sulpicius Severus.[12] The disparity between the two views of Martin helps to illustrate the extent to which the authors' attitudes and the worlds in which they lived influenced their writings. The very late fourth century, the time of Martin and Sulpicius, was the twilight of the Western Roman Empire, before the massive movement of barbarians had swept across Roman Gaul in the fifth century.[13] By contrast, the late sixth century, during which Gregory wrote, was marked by incessantly brutal, fratricidal war among the Frankish successors of Clovis, who now controlled the former Gallic provinces.[14] As described by Gregory, Francia found itself in the midst of an endless blood feud. The more violent times shaped the chronicler's whole outlook.[15]

---

9   Raymond d'Aguilers, *Historia Francorum Qui Ceperunt Iherusalem* [*HFI*], trans. John Hugh Hill and Laurita L. Hill (Philadelphia, 1968), pp. 66–70, 96–8, chaps. 9, 12.

10 James A. Brundage, "Holy War and the Medieval Lawyers," in *The Holy War*, ed. Thomas Patrick Murphy (Columbus, 1976), 102–3; Frederick H. Russell, *The Just War in the Middle Ages* (Cambridge, 1975).

11 Gregory of Tours, *The History of the Franks* [*HF*], trans. Lewis Thorpe (London, 1974), pp. 137, 230–2, 262; bk. 2, chap. 23; bk. 4, chap. 36; bk. 5, chap. 5.

12 See especially Sulpicius Severus, *The Life of St. Martin*, trans. F.R. Hoare in *The Western Fathers*, ed. Christopher Dawson (New York, 1954), p. 43, chap. 27.

13 Ralph H.C. Davis, *A History of Medieval Europe* (London, 1988), 21–24; Edward James, *The Franks* (Oxford, 1988), 1.

14 Davis, 105; Edward James, *The Origins of France: From Clovis to the Capetians, 500–1000*, ed. Maurice Keen (London, 1982), 127–44.

15 See Thorpe's introduction to Gregory of Tours, *HF*, 15. Another consideration is that, while Sulpicius was a contemporary of Martin, Gregory lived two centuries later, long after the holy man had passed out of living memory. He was thus not as constrained by the character of the "real" Martin. Fouracre, 11–13, addresses the problem of temporal as well as spatial

Such punitive apparitions form a type which remained a constant in the hagiographic and narrative sources throughout the early medieval period. In the Venerable Bede's eighth-century *Ecclesiastical History of the English Nation*, a severe beating administered by St. Peter convinced the early-seventh-century archbishop Laurence not to abandon his English mission in frustration over Anglo-Saxon backsliding.[16]

The other three categories in my typology – military counsel, military defense and military offense – most clearly establish a direct connection between heaven and war. Heavenly beings were seen by medieval authors to give "Military Counsel" including advice, encouragement, and prediction of victory, to take an active role in "Military Defense," and even at times to participate aggressively in "Military Offense." This portrayal of apparitional beings as participants in earthly warfare was increasingly common and it is to these more militaristic apparitions that we shall now turn.

The earlier Anglo-Saxon sources, from roughly the time of Bede, portray celestial beings as acting with both benign and chastising intents. Several works from the tenth and early eleventh centuries exhibit them taking an even more direct role in war. Recent scholarship has restored to the main text of the anonymous *History of Saint Cuthbert* (c.945) a sequence long considered an eleventh-century interpolation.[17] In this passage, Cuthbert of Lindisfarne, a seventh-century English saint, is said to have appeared to King Alfred the Great during the 870s and to have advised him how to proceed in his struggle against the Viking invaders.[18] A remarkably similar story in the anonymous *Life of Saint Neot* (c.990),[19] tells how that saint while living had castigated King Alfred but promised God's mercy if the king would change his ways. The king did so, and later, when the Vikings invaded after the death of Neot, the saint appeared to Alfred pledging help in the forthcoming battle. Neot appeared again on the eve

---

proximity of author to subject as it relates to conformity to medieval hagiographic convention.

[16] Bede, *Ecclesiastical History of the English People [EH]*, trans. and ed. Bertram Colgrave and R.A.B. Mynors (Oxford, 1969), pp. 154–55, bk. 2, chap. 6. Examples of saintly chastisement besides those already cited include: *The Earliest Life of Gregory the Great by an Anonymous Monk of Whitby*, ed. and trans. Bertram Colgrave (Lawrence KS, 1968), pp. 102–5, chap. 19; Aelfric, *Life of St. Aethelwold*, in *English Historical Documents [EHD]* 1, ed. David C. Douglas (1955; reprint, New York, 1968), p. 838, doc. 235, par. 24; *Gesta Francorum et aliorum Hierosolimitanorum [GFH]*, ed. and trans. Rosalind Hill (London, 1962), pp. 57–8, bk. 9, chap. 24; Simeon of Durham, *Historia Regum [HR]*, ed. Thomas Arnold, *Symeonis Monachi Opera Omnia*, 2 vols. (London, 1882–1885), 2:146, 225, *s.a.* 1014, 1095; William of Malmesbury, *De Gestis Regum Anglorum [GR]*, ed. William Stubbs, 2 vols. (London, 1887–1889), 1:212; 2: 296, 323, 345–6, bk. 2, par. 179; bk. 3, pars. 237, 264, 293–4.

[17] See Luisella Simpson, "The King Alfred/St. Cuthbert Episode in the *Historia de sancto Cuthberto*: Its Significance for Mid-tenth-century English History," in *St. Cuthbert, His Cult and His Community to AD 1200*, ed. Gerald Bonner et al. (Woodbridge, 1989), 397–411.

[18] *Historia de Sancto Cuthberto*, ed. Thomas Arnold in *Symeonis Monachi Opera Omnia*, 1:204–6, pars. 15–18.

[19] Simon Keynes and Michael Lapidge, *Alfred the Great: Asser's "Life of King Alfred" and Other Contemporary Sources* (London, 1983), 197, 255.

of the battle, guaranteeing even more explicitly that the English would prevail. Speaking to his men before battle, Alfred pointed to the saint's visit as a sign of divine support for their struggle. Naturally, events developed as Neot had foretold: Alfred fought the Vikings to a standstill, and their leader Guthrum was baptized.[20] In the earlier story, involving Cuthbert of Lindisfarne, the saint not only encouraged the king and assured him of victory, but also advised him on how to gain the victory.[21]

The tenth-century monastic reform in England witnessed the composition of a number of homilies for the religious education and edification of the laity. The *Blickling Homiliary*, possibly written as early as 971, contains eighteen sermons to be delivered on Sundays and certain saints' days.[22] The homily for Michaelmas (the feast of the warrior archangel St. Michael) relates a traditional story which is found in its fullest form earlier, in an eighth- or ninth-century Lombardic account.[23] According to the Blickling Homilist's version, when the people of Sepontus and Benevento in Italy were harassed by the still-pagan Neapolitans, St. Michael appeared in a vision to the bishop of Sepontus and promised victory for his people. The archangel instructed the bishop when his forces

---

[20] *Vita Prima Sancti Neoti et Translatio*, ed. Michael Lapidge in *The Annals of St. Neots with Vita Prima Sancti Neoti*, ed. David Dumville and Michael Lapidge, *The Anglo-Saxon Chronicle: A Collaborative Edition* 17 (Cambridge, 1983), pp. 120–22, 126–28, 130–32, secs. 8, 9, 13, 16.

[21] Keynes' and Lapidge's introduction to *Alfred the Great*, 21–22, 211–12; Bertram Colgrave's introduction to *Two "Lives" of St. Cuthbert: A "Life" by an Anonymous Monk of Lindisfarne and Bede's Prose "Life"* (Cambridge, 1940), 2; Edmund Craster, "The Patrimony of St. Cuthbert," *EHR* 69 (1954): 177–99. It should be noted also that both the Cuthbert and Neot stories are strikingly similar to one told c.700 by Adamnan wherein St. Columba is said to have appeared to Oswald of Northumbria in a dream on the night before his battle with Cadwallon of Gwynedd and assured him of victory and prosperity in his rule. See Adamnan, *Life of St. Columba*, in *EHD*, 1:691, no. 153, bk. 1, chap. 1. I would speculate that Adamnan's story is the ultimate inspiration for both later tales in the King Alfred tradition, the later Neot version possibly depending on the Cuthbert story. Neither version appears in Asser's *Life of King Alfred*, written c.893, despite Matthew Parker's interpolation of the Neot story into his sixteenth-century edition of Asser along with the story of "Alfred and the Cakes." See Keynes and Lapidge, 197–202.

[22] Michael Swanton, *Anglo-Saxon Prose [ASP]* (London, 1975), 63. The entire set of homilies are written in but two hands, alternating, and in the homily for Ascension Day (Homily 11, fol. 72r, line 10) it is stated that "the year 971 A.D. [*sic*] had been reached 'this very year' " – Rudolph Willard, *The Blickling Homilies*, ed. Bertram Colgrave et al. (Copenhagen, 1960), 14. Willard, 13, follows Neil R. Ker, *Catalogue of Manuscripts Containing Anglo-Saxon* (Oxford, 1957), in assigning the Homiliary manuscript itself to the early eleventh century.

[23] Swanton, 70. Veneration of St. Michael in England certainly predated the mid-eleventh century, as witnessed by the eighth-century story of the archangel's apparition, albeit in a non-military capacity, to St. Wilfrid (Eddius Stephanus, *The Life of Bishop Wilfrid*, ed. and trans. Bertram Colgrave [1927; Cambridge, 1985], pp. 120–23, chap. 56) as well as a number of church dedications (David Hugh Farmer, *The Oxford Dictionary of Saints* [Oxford, 1987], 301). Indeed, Aelfric of Eynsham recounted in his *Catholic Homilies* of c.990 the same story as did the Blickling Homilist (Swanton, 70; regarding date of Aelfric, see Dorothy Whitelock, *EHD*, 1:849).

should attack the Neapolitans. He also promised to watch over and to aid them in the battle. During the attack, storm and lightning shrouded Monte Gargano, the site of the battle, engulfing the pagan Neapolitans and bringing victory to the Christians. The people of Benevento and Sepontus counted six hundred Neapolitans slain "by the lightning and by the fiery arrows alone, beside those whom they had destroyed and slain with their own weapons."[24]

The Blickling Homily for Michaelmas is an important development in the idea of celestial participation in war. Even though the text does not refer explicitly to the archangel's reappearance in visible form during the battle, his presence was plainly perceived in the "lightning and . . . fiery arrows" that devastated the enemy. The significance here is not whether the events happened as the sermon recounts them, but instead that the battle, as presented by an Anglo-Saxon homilist of the late tenth century, had a supernatural dimension and protagonist. A similar but even more explicit instance of angelic intervention derived from a traditional source is found in another Old English homily from the very end of the tenth century.

In about the year 995, Aelfric of Eynsham composed a set of homilies for the feasts of the liturgical year known collectively as his *Lives of Saints*. Three of Aelfric's homilies are important for pre-Crusade holy war ideology.[25] Of the three, only that entitled "Of the Machabees" contains an apparition. This homily is a paraphrased rendition into Old English verse of the Old Testament Books of Maccabees. According to the tale depending specifically on II Maccabees, chapter ten, the apparition occurred during the Jewish campaign led by Judas Maccabeus against the Seleucid general Timothy in 164 BC:

> Lo! then wonderfully came five angels from heaven,
> riding on horses with golden apparel
> and twain of the angels on both sides of Judas
> were fighting, and eke defended him;
> and they all five fought on the side of Judas,
> shooting their arrows and fiery lightnings
> on the heathen people, till they, lying down, died,
> twenty thousand men, and six hundred [horsemen] slain.[26]

In this homily, the angels are clearly portrayed as participating in battle on the Jewish side. Defending Judas, they pressed the attack and wrought havoc on the Seleucids.

As in the case of the Blickling Homily on Michaelmas, Aelfric's work deals not with events of relatively recent Anglo-Saxon history, but instead retells a story from the remote past, in this case from the Bible. But Aelfric chose his

---

[24] Blickling Homilist, *A Michaelmas Sermon*, in *ASP*, 72–73.

[25] Tyerman, 11. In addition to the homily for August 1 ("Of the Machabees"), Tyerman also cites those for August 5 ("Of Saint Oswold") and November 20 ("Of Saint Edmund").

[26] Aelfric, "Of the Machabees," ed. W.W. Skeat in *Aelfric's "Lives of Saints"*, 2 vols. (London, 1881–1900), 2:99, lines 490–97. Brackets in translation.

material and wrote for the lay aristocracy of late Anglo-Saxon England. Such direct participation in earthly warfare by beings from heaven was evidently considered appropriate by both Aelfric and his audience. Aelfric's source is in itself significant. Crusade propagandists of the twelfth century considered Maccabees to be an inspired account of a war in the Holy Land which was clearly sanctioned by God. The scriptural tale provided them with many biblical analogies.[27] Aelfric drew upon the story a full century before the First Crusade. Considering the similarity of the pyrotechnic imagery, it seems likely that the Blickling Homilist (or his Lombardic source) also drew inspiration from this episode in II Maccabees.

After such clear examples of celestial participation in earthly war, tales of apparitions found in three sources from eleventh-century England (the *Life of St. Dunstan*, Aelfric's *Life of St. Aethelwold*, and the anonymous *Life of King Edward*) seem almost anticlimactic. They are, however, important in confirming the persistence of the benign hagiographical prototypes in the later sources. Thereafter, the First Crusade brought a radical transformation in how the heavens were seen to participate in war.

Accounts of the First Crusade record many events perceived as miraculous by the crusaders and their contemporaries throughout western Europe. Jonathan Riley-Smith considers these events to be crucial in the development of a crusading ideology. Even during the course of the journey the crusaders considered themselves to be on an expedition endorsed by Almighty God. The various holy apparitions which aided and supported the crusaders were critical in formulating this attitude.[28] Besides the series of visions surrounding the Holy Lance,[29] almost half of the twenty-six apparitions recorded in the three original accounts of the First Crusade are overtly military.

Both Raymond d'Aguilers and the unknown author of the *Gesta Francorum* recorded the active participation of saints in battles of the First Crusade. During the battle at Antioch against the besieging Turks, the Christians carrying the Lance before them as a standard were said to have been aided by three soldier saints – George, Mercurius, and Demetrius – leading a host of men on white horses.[30] The crusaders themselves did not see, but rather learned from captured Turks that their array had been led into battle at Dorylaeum by "two handsome

---

27 Tyerman, 11–12. See also E.O. Blake, "The Formation of the 'Crusade Idea'," *JEH* 21 (1970): 23, 25, 27; Jonathan Riley-Smith, "Crusading as an Act of Love," *History* 65 (1980): 182–83.
28 Jonathan Riley-Smith, *The First Crusade and the Idea of Crusading* (London, 1986), 99–107.
29 *GFH*, pp. 59–60, 65–66, bk. 9, chaps. 25, 28; Raymond d'Aguilers, *HFI*, pp. 51–58, 65–72, 93–103, chaps. 7, 9, 12; Fulcher of Chartres, *A History of the Expedition to Jerusalem, 1095–1127*, trans. Frances Rita Ryan (Knoxville, 1969), pp. 99–101, bk. 1, chap. 18, pars. 1–5; Colin Morris, "Policy and Visions: The Case of the Holy Lance at Antioch," in *War and Government in the Middle Ages: Essays in Honour of J.G. Prestwich*, ed. John Gillingham and J.C. Holt (Cambridge, 1984), 33–34.
30 *GFH*, p. 69, bk. 9, chap. 31.

knights in flashing armor" who were "seemingly invulnerable to the thrusts of the Turkish lances."[31] After the crusaders took Jerusalem, many swore that they had seen the late bishop Adhémar, the papal legate who had died previously at Antioch, now leading the final assault and urging the Christians on to victory.[32]

No English author left a first-hand account of the First Crusade. However, with the conquest of Jerusalem on July 15, 1099, a wave of exultation swept across Western Europe. From early twelfth-century Francia issued forth the crusading *apologiae* of Robert the Monk, Guibert of Nogent, and Baldric of Bourgueil. Nor were the Anglo-Norman historians of twelfth-century England immune to this enthusiasm. Writing in about 1140, William of Malmesbury demonstrated his interest in the Crusade and its aftermath by an extended treatment in his *Chronicle of the Kings of England*.[33]

In the vision tales recounted by both William of Malmesbury and his near-contemporary Simeon of Durham (c.1130), we see a synthesis of the apparitional types from all the earlier sources. Celestial beings heal, console, protect, and chastise; they also provide military counsel and aid in attacks. In their histories, both Simeon and William recount the events of the First Crusade, including the apparitions said to have graced the siege of Antioch.[34] Besides dealing with the apparition accounts emanating from the First Crusade, however, both authors also recorded the occurrence of heavenly intervention in earlier centuries. The most bellicose of these past episodes are set two-and-a-half centuries earlier during the Viking wars. Simeon records explicitly that angelic spirits aided the English against the Vikings.[35] Both Simeon and William tell once more of St. Cuthbert's appearance to Alfred the Great.[36] And both recount an episode (here classified as a chastisement) involving revenge exacted by St. Edmund the Martyr on the Danish invader Swein. The Dane not only mocked St. Edmund, but also threatened and exacted tribute from the town in which the saint's sacred remains lay buried. The royal saint, who as king of East Anglia had been tor-

---

[31] Raymond d'Aguilers, *HF*, p. 28, chap. 3.

[32] Ibid., p. 128, chap. 14.

[33] William of Malmesbury, *GR*, 2:390–463, bk. 4, pars. 343–389.

[34] Simeon of Durham, *HR*, *s.a.* 1098, 2:229, records the visions surrounding the unearthing of the Lance; William of Malmesbury, *GR*, 2:420, bk. 4, par. 365, reports the appearance of the military saints aiding the Christians against the Turks at Antioch.

[35] Simeon of Durham, *HR*, *s.a.* 860, 2:73. (Note that *HR* is in two parts, the first comprising the years 731–957, the second 848–1129. It is therefore useful, for the annals 848–957 recorded twice, to specify the part – 1 or 2 – which I will henceforth place in parentheses after the year where appropriate; the preceding was from part 1.) Simeon (*HR*, *s.a.* 740, 2:37–38), also records – out of sequence – an incident during the invasion of England by the Scots under King Malcolm (probably in 1079 or 1091), when St. Acca and the other saints of the church of Hexham appeared to a priest, promising aid against the approaching enemy and providing that aid by swelling a river and causing a great mist, preventing Malcolm's progress and causing him to turn back.

[36] Simeon of Durham, *HR*, *s.a.* 877, 2:83, 111 (pts. 1 and 2). William of Malmesbury, *GR*, 1:125, bk. 2, par. 121. Simeon's monastery at Durham held the relics of Cuthbert, the promotion of whose cult became a strong theme in the *Historia Regum*.

tured to death for refusing either to submit to or take up arms against an earlier Viking warlord,[37] is said to have transfixed Swein with a javelin, striking him dead.[38]

From the earliest period, when the four prototypical hagiographical texts were written, to the age of the First Crusade, authors expanded on the activities in which apparitions were featured. The prototypes contain only the benign apparitions which would continue to predominate in strictly hagiographical works. They fail to record any instances of apparitional beings administering punishment or participating in war. On the other hand, by the end of the tenth century, there did exist English sources which depicted saints as active parties in warfare. Saints Cuthbert and Neot counselled and encouraged Alfred the Great before battle; the archangel Michael advised the people of Monte Gargano and hurled fiery lightning against their enemies; angels accompanied Judas Maccabeus into battle with similar pyrotechnics. As innovations in an otherwise traditional genre, these later tales take on a significance they would not otherwise have.

According to Erdmann, the Christian idea of "Holy War" underwent a prolonged development, one which culminated in the First Crusade. While Erdmann situated the crucial coalescing of ideas in Carolingian Francia of the ninth century, the same period witnessed the emergence of a "Holy War" ethic in Anglo-Saxon England. This fits well with Christopher Tyerman's assertion that the Viking invasions were critical.[39] Two of the three militaristic apparitions documented in late tenth-century Anglo-Saxon sources were set during Alfred's ninth-century conflict with the Vikings. By the twelfth century, the Viking wars were perceived even more explicitly as having evoked instances of direct offensive aid from heaven. The early twelfth century witnessed a flowering of medieval historiography in England which, despite a dearth of sources, attempted to retrieve England's pre-Norman history.[40] The tales of the First Crusade, with their spectacular and well-publicized militaristic apparitions, may well have exerted a heavy influence on the writings of both William of Malmesbury and Simeon of Durham. Like Gregory of Tours interpreting St. Martin in the terms of his own violent times, these two twelfth-century historians viewed their Anglo-Saxon past through a window stained with the martial apparitions of the First Crusade.

---

37 See Abbo, *Life of St. Edmund* (from MS Cotton Tiberius B.ii), ed. Michael Winterbottom in *Three Lives of English Saints*, ed. A.G. Rigg (Toronto, 1972), 65–87; also Aelfric, *The Passion of St. Edmund, King and Martyr*, trans. Swanton in *ASP*, 97–102.
38 Simeon of Durham, *HR*, s.a. 1014, 2:146; William of Malmesbury, *GR*, 1:212, bk. 2, par. 179.
39 Tyerman, 10–11.
40 James Campbell, "Some Twelfth-Century Views of the Anglo-Saxon Past," in *Essays in Anglo-Saxon History* (London, 1986), 209–28.

Summary Typology of Holy Apparitions

The following summary represents not an exhaustive quantitative study but rather an indication of the types of apparitions in the sources examined. An index follows with citations.

Sources in chronological order	Benign	Chastisement	Military counsel	Military defense	Military offense
Prototypical Hagiographies					
Athanasius, *Life of St. Antony*	1				
Jerome, *Life of St. Paul**					
Sulpicius, *Life of St. Martin*	3				
Gregory the Great, *Life of St. Benedict*	4				
Anglo-Saxon Sources					
(Anonymous), *Life of St. Cuthbert*	2				
Earliest Life of Gregory the Great	3	1			
Eddius, *Life of Bishop Wilfrid*	2				
Bede, *Life of St. Cuthbert*	2				
Felix, *Life of St. Guthlac*	5				
Bede, *Ecclesiastical History*	5	1			
Asser, *Life of King Alfred**					
Historia de sancto Cuthberto	1		1		
Blickling Homilist, *Michaelmas Sermon*	2		1		

* No apparitions

Sources in chronological order	Benign	Chastisement	Military counsel	Military defense	Military offense
Vita Sancti Neoti			2		
Aelfric, "Of the Machabees"					1
"B," *Life of St. Dunstan*	1				
Aelfric, *Life of St. Aethelwold*	1	1			
Life of King Edward	1				
First Crusade Accounts					
Gesta Francorum		2	4		1
Raymond d'Aguilers, *Historia Francorum*	10	2	2		2
Fulcher of Chartres, *History*			3		
Anglo-Norman Historians					
Simeon of Durham, *Historia Regum*	2	2	3	1	1
William of Malmesbury, *De Gestis Regum*	8	4	1		1

Index of Holy Apparitions, with Citations

Aelfric, *Life of St. Aethelwold* (1006) [trans *EHD* 1]. 1 benign: par. 28; 1 chastising: par. 24

Aelfric, "Of the Machabees" (995). 1 military offense: lines 490–97

(Anonymous), *Life of St. Cuthbert* (700). 2 benign: bk. 1, chap. 4; bk. 2, chap. 2

Asser, *Life of King Alfred* (893).   No apparitions

Athanasius, *Life of St. Antony* (A.D. 357). 1 benign: chap. 10

"B," *Life of St. Dunstan* (1004) [trans *EHD* 1]. 1 benign: chap. 15 (referring back to chap. 3)

Bede, *Ecclesiastical History* (731). 5 benign: bk. 1, chap. 19; bk. 2 chap. 12 (repeat of *Gregory the Great* chap. 16), bk. 4, chap. 25; bk. 5, chaps. 9, 19 (repeat of Eddius, chap. 56)

Bede, *Life of St. Cuthbert* (720). 2 benign: chaps. 2, 7 (repeats of [Anonymous] bk. 1, chap. 4; bk. 2, chap. 2)

Blickling Homilist, *A Michaelmas Sermon* (971?) [trans M. Swanton, *Anglo-Saxon Prose*]. 2 benign: 71–2, 74; 1 military counsel: 72–3

Earliest Life of Gregory the Great (714). 3 benign: chaps. 16, 18; 1 chastising: chap. 19

Eddius Stephanus, *Life of Bishop Wilfrid* (715). 2 benign: chaps. 56, 67

Felix, *Life of St. Guthlac* (725). 5 benign: chaps. 29, 32–3 (1), 50 (2), 52; 1 chastising: bk. 2, chap. 6

Fulcher of Chartres, *A History of the Expedition to Jerusalem* (1100). 3 military counsel: bk. 1, chap. 7, pars. 2–4; bk. 1, chap. 20, pars. 1–3 (2)

Gesta Francorum (1100). 2 chastising: bk. 9, chap. 24 (2); 4 military counsel: bk. 9, chaps. 24 (2), 25, 28; 1 military offense: bk. 9, chap. 31

Gregory the Great, *Life of St. Benedict* (593) [*Dialogues* bk. 2]. 4 benign: chaps. 1, 23, 35, 37

Historia de Sancto Cuthberto (945) [*RS* 75 vol. 1]. 1 benign: par. 13; 1 military counsel: pars. 15–18

Jerome, *Life of St. Paul the First Hermit* (376). No apparitions

Life of King Edward who rests at Westminster (1067). 1 benign: bk. 1, chap. 1

Raymond d'Aguilers, *Historia Francorum* (1100). 10 benign: chaps. 7 (3), 9 (3), 12 (3), 13; 2 chastising: chaps. 10, 12–13; 2 military counsel: chaps. 12, 14; 2 military offense: chaps. 3, 14

Simeon of Durham, *Historia Regum* (1130). 2 benign: *s.a.* 781, 1117; 2 chastising: *s.a.* 1014, 1095; 3 military counsel: *s.a.* 877, 883, 1098; 1 military defense: *s.a.* 740; 1 military offense: *s.a.* 860

Sulpicius Severus, *Life of St. Martin* (400). 3 benign: chaps. 14, 19, 21

Vita Sancti Neoti (990). 2 military counsel: bk. 4, chaps. 54–6, 60

William of Malmesbury, *De Gestis Regum Anglorum* (1140). 8 benign: bk. 1, chap. 2 (2); bk. 2, chap. 13 (2); bk. 3 (3); bk. 4, chap. 1; 4 chastising: bk. 2, chap. 10, bk. 3 (3); 1 military counsel: bk. 2, chap. 4; 1 military offense: bk. 4, chap. 2

GOD AND DEFEAT IN MEDIEVAL WARFARE: SOME PRELIMINARY THOUGHTS

Kelly DeVries

THE most basic principle learned by a military historian is that in every battle there must be a loser. A second principle follows close behind: the defeated in said battle must then rationalize their defeat so that they might not lose royal or popular support. For the medieval military historian, one other principle must be considered when studying a battle lost; the medieval commentator writing about that loss must also demonstrate that God had not abandoned his side despite its lack of success on the battlefield. This is therefore the basis from which I wish to approach the subject: medieval writers and apologists rationalizing military defeat had to explain that God was still with them even though they had lost in battle; also, these rationalizations did not differ whether they were applied to losses suffered at the hands of non-Christian or Christian opponents.

The problem takes form as early as the fourth century with a simple epistle attributed to St. Augustine and known as *Gravi de pugna*. It states:

> You complain about harsh battles. Do not doubt for I will give useful advise to you and yours – Take up arms! Let the words of the Creator echo in your ears; since when there is a battle, God looks down from the open heavens and the side which he sees to be just he gives victory.[1]

Although short, this epistle was used to justify wars by a long list of later canonists and preachers, among them Hincmar of Reims, Hrabanus Maurus, Sedulius Scotus, Ivo of Chartres, and Bernard of Clairvaux.[2] It even appears word for word in a battlefield oration delivered at the 1147 conquest of Lisbon.[3]

Naturally the *Gravi de pugna* was only valid until the first Christian army lost. Then questions began to arise: Were we the most just army on the field? If not, why did we undertake the fight? And, if so, why did God allow us to lose, especially if we were fighting non-Christians?

---

[1] Pseudo-Augustine, *Epistola 13*, in *Patrialogia latina* [*PL*] 33:1098: "Gravi de pugna conqueris: dubites nolo, utile tibi tuisque dabo consilium: arripe manibus arma, oratio aures pulset Auctoris; quia quando pugnatur, Deus apertis caelis prospectat, et partem quam inspicit justam, ibi dat palmam."

[2] For Hincmar of Reims, Hrabanus Maurus and Sedulius Scotus see Frederick H. Russell, *The Just War in the Middle Ages* (Cambridge, 1975), 29. For Bernard of Clairvaux, see Russell, 37. And for Ivo of Chartres, see Russell, 38.

[3] *De expurgatione Lyxbonensi*, ed. and trans. Cook W. David (New York, 1936), 82.

This problem is made even more complex by the statements of popes Leo IV (853)[4] and John VIII (876)[5] which promised salvific indulgences to anyone who died defending the church, even while preferring that the troops not have to die in the endeavor. (The point of war after all, to paraphrase Patton, is not to die for your Church, but to make someone else die for his.) Later, perhaps understanding the difficulty that such indulgences posed, they simply granted them to anyone participating on a Crusade whether they died or not.[6]

It is easy for the victor to claim that his victory came from God. "Victories come from heaven," states Philippe de Mezières,[7] while Ordericus Vitalis writes concerning the victory at Falaise, gained in 1106:

> All pious men were overjoyed when they heard the news of the king's victory; outlaws and evil-doers, on the other hand, were filled with grief and sorrow because they had no doubt that a yoke had been laid on their hitherto unconquered necks by God's will. When these seditious predators discovered that the monarch whose effective justice they had already experienced had conquered his enemies in battle by God's help, they acknowledged his greatness and fled at once in all directions, abandoning their habitual oppressions solely out of fear of him.[8]

Even chroniclers who minimize God's role in connection with a victory often allude to some divine acceptance of the victor. Lodewijk van Velthem, for example, writing on the victory of the Flemings over the French at the battle of Courtrai in 1302 records the appearance of a star over the heads of the victorious forces, the host of the communion disappearing when about to be given to the French general, Robert of Artois, the spectre of St. George appearing among the Flemish ranks and the flight of black birds above the French while above the Flemings there flew white birds.[9] Others attribute victory to divinely-given prophecies or divinely-sent omens or comets.

Thomas Bradwardine, in his *Sermo epinicus*, not only claims that God alone is the author of victory, but also refutes seven "erroneous" attributions of victory: victory due to the stars, to the constellations, to blind fortune, to the fates, to human prowess, to sexual virility, or to women.[10]

We know from Symeon the Monk's description of Alfred the Great's battles against the Vikings that God can promise victory before a battle and then grant

4   Leo IV, *Epistola* 28, in *MGH, Epp*, 5, ed. A. de Hirsch-Gereuth (Berlin, 1899), 601.

5   John VIII, *Epistola* 22, 36, in *MGH, Epp*, 7, ed. Erich Casper (Berlin, 1928), 20, 36.

6   See Russell, 203–4, 253–55 for a list of canonists permitting indulgences for merely serving on a Crusade.

7   Philippe de Mezières, *Le songe du vieil*, ed. G.W. Coopland, 2 vols. (Cambridge, 1969), 2:382.

8   OV, 6:92–93.

9   Lodewijk van Velthem, *Spiegel historiaal of rymspiegel*, ed. Isaac Long, 4 vols. (Amsterdam, 1727), 4:22, 24, 29.

10 See Heiko A. Oberman and T.A. Weisheipl, "The *Sermo epinicus* Ascribed to Thomas Bradwardine," *Archives d'histoire doctrinale et litteraire du moyen âge* 35 (1958): 295–327 for the best edition of this sermon.

it.[11] We know from Fredegar's account of Emperor Heraclius in the seventh century that God can even grant victory by trickery.[12] We can see where a victory "from God" can give legitimacy to a reign, such as that of Edward IV of England.[13] We know from the *Chronicle* of Pere III of Catalonia that the fear of God's punishment can keep a king from waging an unjust war.[14] And, finally, from Eusebius's account of Constantine's victory over Maxentius at the battle of Milvian Bridge, fought in 312, we can see where a divine victory leads an entire empire to seek the Christian God.[15]

Other medieval writers were not so sure about the presence of God on the victor's side. Without directing their thoughts to any particular defeat, some simply "hedged their bets" when it came to warfare. War must be just and, according to Anselm of Lucca (later Pope Alexander II), must be accompanied by constant prayers for victory.[16] Some, such as John Wyclif, believe that God sanctions no warfare. His statement, that "wise men of the world hold their strengths, and thus vanquish their enemies without any stroke," shows a surprisingly modern Christian pacifism.[17] While still others, like the fifteenth-century monk Philippe de Vilette, recognize that God "according to the Holy Scriptures . . . sometimes gives victory to the good, sometimes to the wicked, not by chance or hazard, but for reasons and causes which are very good, even though they may not seem constant or intelligible to men."[18]

However, more often than not, medieval writers were less able to look at defeat in battle in such open-minded terms. It was the general's responsibility to ensure that the battle was fought justly. It was the Church's responsibility to see that it was fought for righteous purposes.

There was no question of God's allegiance when wars were fought against pagans or infidels. But Christian forces did not always triumph. Thus medieval Christian writers needed to explain why the obviously just failed to defeat the obviously unjust. In rationalizing these defeats the writers are often extremely clever. One way of rationalizing the defeat of Christian armies was to blame the comfort and complacency of the people. For example, the Venerable Bede

---

11 See Symeon the Monk, *Historia de sancto Cuthberto*, in *Opera omnia*, ed. Thomas Arnold, 2 vols. (London, 1885), 1:205.

12 Fredegar, *The Fourth Book of Fredegar and Continuations*, ed. and trans. J.M. Wallace-Hadrill (London, 1960), 52–53.

13 See C.T. Allmand, ed., *Society at War: The Experience of England and France during the Hundred Years War* (Edinburgh, 1972), 40–41.

14 Pere III of Catalonia, *Chronicle*, trans. Mary Hillgarth, ed. Jocelyn M. Hillgarth, 2 vols. (Toronto, 1980), 2:514.

15 Eusebius, *Life of Constantine*, trans. E.C. Richardson, 2 vols. (New York, 1890), 1:489–91.

16 Anselm of Lucca, *Collectio canonum*, in *PL* 149:533–34.

17 John Wyclif, "On the Seven Deadly Sins," in *Select English Works of John Wyclif*, ed. Thomas Arnold, 3 vols. (Oxford, 1871), 3:137–38.

18 Charles J. Liebman, "Une sermon de Philippe de Vilette, abbé de Saint-Denis, pour la levée de l'Oriflamme (1414)," *Romania* 68 (1944–45): 463–65.

claims that this was the cause of the victories of the Saxons over the Romano-British people in the fifth century. He writes:

> there was so great an abundance of corn in the island as had never before been known. With this affluence came an increase of luxury, followed by every kind of foul crime; in particular, cruelty and hatred of the truth and love of lying increased so that if anyone appeared to be milder than the rest and somewhat more inclined to the truth, the rest, without consideration, rained excretions and missiles upon him as if he had been an enemy of Britain. Not only were the laymen guilty of these offenses but even the Lord's own flock and their pastors. They cast off Christ's easy yoke and thrust their necks under the burden of drunkenness, hatred, quarrelling, strife, envy and other similar crimes.

This abundance led to constant attacks by enemies to the north, and the Saxons were called in to protect the inhabitants of England. Bede continues: "As events plainly showed, this was ordained by the will of God so that evil might fall upon the miscreants."[19]

The same rationale is used by the battlefield preacher at the conquest of Lisbon to explain the initial loss of Spain to the Moslems: "We believe it has already become well enough known in the countries from which you come that through the presence of the Moors and Moabites divine vengeance has smitten all Spain with the edge of the sword."[20]

But these authors were looking back in hindsight and thus were allowed to harshly indict those who had lost before. Authors more contemporary to military defeats take a different view. A few even play somewhat with traditional theology. For example, the anonymous eyewitness of the *Vita Hiltrudis* writes that God simply had "the disposition to whip his people" and therefore allowed the Hungarians to ravage the countryside of the tenth-century Low Countries.[21]

However, these writers are in the minority. More often, medieval authors choose more routine reasons for their military losses, even though God was supposed to be on their side. A major explanation for defeat is that the overweening pride of individual leaders gave victory to their opponents. For example, the Old English poem "The Battle of Maldon" recognizes that the Viking defeat of the Anglo-Saxons came not from God, but from the *ofermode* (pride) of the Anglo-Saxon duke, Byrhtnoth, who "yielded to the invaders too much land."[22]

King Alfred the Great, in the preface to his translation of Gregory the Great's *Pastoral Care*, attributes the failure of the Anglo-Saxons to defeat the Vikings to a sin of omission rather than commission – the sin of not learning. He writes:

---

[19] Bede, *Historia ecclesiastica gentis Anglorum*, ed. and trans. Bertram Colgrave and R.A.B. Mynors (Oxford, 1969), 48–49.

[20] *De expurgatione Lyxbonensi*, 76–77.

[21] Albert d'Haenens, "Les incursions hongroises dans l'epace belge (954/955). Histoire ou historiographie?" *Cahiers de civilisation médiévale Xe–XIIe siècle* 4 (1961): 435.

[22] "Battle of Maldon," in *A Choice of Anglo Saxon Verse*, ed. and trans. R. Hamer (London, 1970), 54–55.

"Remember what temporal punishments came upon us, when we neither loved wisdom nor allowed it to other men; we possessed only the name of Christians, and very few possessed the virtues."[23]

The failure of the Crusades sparked even more controversy. Here were wars called for from the pulpit, righteous and just; yet after the first victories, the armies of the Christian God generally met with resounding defeat.[24] Some writers attribute the defeats in the Holy Land simply to natural perils and difficulties which the Crusaders faced.[25] Other writers are more critical. They allege as the principal reason for defeat sins committed by the Christians themselves, sins which made possible the victory of Islam, despite the "injustice" of its cause. Roger of Wendover claims that God even used the non-Christian Saladin to punish these sins:

> there was much evil among men on earth, so that "all flesh almost had corrupted its way before the Lord;" for the practice of sin had burst forth among the people to such a degree, that all, casting aside the veil of shame, everywhere inclined to wickedness openly. Too tedious is it to enumerate the slaughters, robberies, adultery, obscenities, lies, treason, and other crimes, especially so to us, who design to write of the events which occurred. . . . For this reason therefore the Lord and Saviour of the world, seeing that the land of his nativity, suffering, and resurrection had fallen into depths of wickedness, scorned his inheritance, and allowed the rod of his anger, namely Saladin, to vent His anger to the extermination of that obstinate race; for He preferred that the Holy Land should for a short time be a slave to profane rites of nations, than those people should any longer flourish, who were not restrained from unlawful actions by any regard to probity.[26]

Others echo Roger of Wendover's words, insisting that the fall of the Holy Land to the Saracens was the judgement of God. Ralph Niger, for example, avers that the Crusaders should have fought the rise of Catharism prospering in their own countries, before venturing into the Holy Land, adding that it is far better to bring the Saracens voluntarily to the faith, for God was not pleased by forced service.[27]

Some blame the leaders of the crusading armies for their defeats, due either to their sins or to their lack of experience or discretion. For example, in commenting on the losses of the Second Crusade, John of Salisbury and Bernard of Clairvaux blame all of the leaders – especially the German emperor, Conrad II,

23 *EHD*, no. 226.
24 For example, on the reaction to the defeat of the Second Crusade see Giles Constable, "The Second Crusade as Seen by Contemporaries," *Traditio* 9 (1953): 213–79.
25 A long list of these sources include the *Historia Welforum Weingartensis* in *MGH SS*, 21:468; Lambert of Ardres, *Historia*, in *MGH SS* 24:633–34; the *Annales Magdeburgenses* in *MGH SS* 16:188; and the *Annales Palidenses* in *MGH SS* 16:83.
26 Roger of Wendover, *Chronicon*, in *Christian Society and the Crusades, 1198–1229*, ed. and trans. Edward Peters (Philadelphia, 1971), 154.
27 Ralph Niger, *De re militari et triplici via peregrinationis Ierosolitane (1187/88)*, ed. Ludwig Schmugge (Berlin, 1977), 187–88.

and the French king, Louis VII – for their continual bickering and politicking. The author of the German *Chronicon Mauriniacense* excuses the German Emperor from blame while accusing the French king alone for the defeat.[28]

After the crusade undertaken by Frederick II, Gerold, the Patriarch of Jerusalem sent a harsh letter to all the faithful accusing the emperor of conduct unbecoming a crusader. Gerold begins the letter: "If it should be fully known how astonishing, nay rather, deplorable, the conduct of the emperor has been in the eastern lands from the beginning to the end, to the great detriment of the cause of Jesus Christ and to the great injury of the Christian faith, from the sole of his foot to the top of his head no common sense would be found." The patriarch then goes on to explain at length how the emperor lied to the people, hated the Templars ("you may be sure that he never showed as much animosity and hatred against the Saracens"), and finally attacked his own people because they questioned his tactics.[29]

Other writers denounce the crusading soldiers and their sinful behavior as the cause of the defeats in the Holy Land. Such was the case with Fulcher of Chartres, who in trying to explain why members of the First Crusade had failed in their attempt to take Tyre writes: "Already our people were distributing the booty they expected to get . . . men trust in their own strength not considering what they owe to God."[30] This is echoed by Henry of Huntingdon who comments on the defeats of the Second Crusade:

> The armies of the emperor of Germany and the king of France who, accompanied by the greatest leaders, walking with the highest pride, arrived at nothing, because God spurned them. For their incontinence which they practiced in unhidden fornications, even in adulteries (which displeased God greatly), and finally in rapes and all kinds of crimes, rose in the sight of God.[31]

Still others accuse the Latin inhabitants of Jerusalem, remnants of the successful First Crusade, for the defeats which followed. For example, in the Second Crusade the German emperor, Conrad II, blames them for the failure of the siege of Damascus, although he leaves doubt about whether the treason was committed by the king of Jerusalem, the Templars or the princes of Syria.[32] Later, in the Third Crusade, Ralph Niger lays the defeat at the feet of Heraclius, the patriarch of Jerusalem, and the other great magnates of Palestine who came forth with their "pomp of riches and abundance," to meet the European princes, but fled when Saladin came near. Niger adds: "Whence it happened that by the

---

[28] John of Salisbury, *Historia pontificalis*, ed. R.L. Poole (Oxford, 1927), 4; Bernard of Clairvaux, *De consideratione*, in *Opera omnia*, 3:410–13; and the *Chronicon Mauriniacense*, in *RHF,* 12:88.

[29] *Christian Society and the Crusades*, 165–66.

[30] Fulcher of Chartres, *A History of the Expedition to Jerusalem, 1095–1127*, trans. F.R. Ryan, ed. H.S. Fink (New York, 1973), 204.

[31] Henry of Huntingdon, *Historia Anglorum*, ed. Thomas Arnold (London, 1879), 280–81.

[32] Constable, 273.

judgement of God the land was taken and the princes captured and those who in some way were able to flee went in dispersion."[33]

There are also threads of a harsh anti-crusading spirit among some critics. Several feel that the Crusades were frivolous ventures. This is perhaps shown best in the rather cynical "Crusader's Song" first unearthed by H. Pflaum and later translated by Colin Morris:

> If you go to hear the preachers,
> Do beware of clever teachers,
> Who can (with their style and gloss)
> Make you captive to the Cross.
>
> Would you give me your attention?
> There is something I should mention.
> If you want a cross to carry
> And are not inclined to tarry,
>
> You must check the real position:
> Are the roads in good condition?
> Or you'll start with courage burning
> And the next day you'll be returning.
>
> Country roads have rocks and cracks;
> They are really cul-de-sacs.[34]

Gerhoch of Reichersberg and the anonymous author of the *Annales Herbipolenses* go further in their criticism of the Crusades; they believe that the whole endeavor was the work of the devil. The annalist writes:

> God permitted that the Western Church be afflicted, since its sins required that punishment. Thereupon, certain pseudo-prophets, sons of Belail, heads of the anti-Christ, were in power, who by stupid words misled the Christians and by empty preaching induced all sorts of men to go against the Saracens for the freeing of Jerusalem.[35]

In turning to war against other Christian realms, the allegiance of God is less easy to discern. Whereas godliness versus non-godliness was easily determined when fighting pagans, the Christian apologist of wars who fought against other Christians had a much more difficult task in rationalizing his kingdom's defeat.

In some places where Christians fought each other little blood was shed and chivalric rules of war were followed simply because the armies were Christian.

---

[33] Ralph Niger, 187–88.
[34] H. Pflaum, "A Strange Crusader's Song," *Speculum* 10 (1935): 337–39. Translation in Colin Morris, "Propaganda for War: The Dissemination of the Crusading Ideal in the Twelfth Century," *Studies in Church History* 20 (1983): 86–87.
[35] *Annales Herbipolenses*, in *MGH SS*, 16:3 and Gerhoch of Reichersberg, *Libri III de investigatione antichristi* in *MGH Libelli de lite*, 3:374–84.

For example, concerning the battle of Bremule, fought in 1119, Ordericus Vitalis writes:

> I have been told that in the battle of the two kings, in which about nine hundred knights were engaged, only three were killed. They were clad in mail and spared each other on both sides, out of fear of God and fellowship in arms; they were more concerned to capture than to kill the fugitives. As Christian soldiers they did not thirst for the blood of their brothers, but rejoiced in just victory given by God for the good of the holy Church and the peace of the faithful.[36]

Other authors, such as Bernard Gui commenting on the French defeat at Courtrai and John of Trokelowe commenting on the English defeat at Bannock-burn, simply dismiss them as turns of the Wheel of Fortune. Tokelowe puts it most elegantly: "But let this outcome destroy no one; for the fates of battles are unknown. For the sword consumes now these and now those, and thus with fortune turning its wheel, the victory remained in this one turn to the Scots."[37]

Still other writers are determined to rationalize these defeats more carefully by blaming someone or something for their occurrence. Several believe that defeat came to Christians because they fought each other instead of fighting jointly against the Saracens. Gerald of Wales, for example, writing in the early twelfth century, attributes King John of England's defeats by the Irish to the fact that "this man . . . went not into the East but into the West, not against the Saracens but against Christians."[38] And, commenting on the battle of Courtrai, fought nearly a century later, the *Kronyk van Vlaenderen* insists that the French failed to defeat the Flemings there because they went against other Christians rather than against the Saracens who had just recaptured Majorca.[39]

John Gower echoes this sentiment during the Hundred Years War, as he wishes to end the Christian versus Christian conflict in order to make another, combined Anglo-French Crusade to the Holy Land:

> The world's situation is weighed down./ There are wars everywhere/ except for Christ's own cause/ in which the swords and spears are dull,/ and the Church is turned from its true path,/ with the sentence of the pope's bull/ as if to obey the pagans.
> And if men should nevertheless wax wroth,/ let them be armed to fight/ against the Saracens who are hateful to Christ./ Thus a knight may rightfully perform his deed of arms.[40]

---

36 OV, 6:240–41.
37 John of Trokelowe, *Annales*, ed. H.T. Riley (London, 1866), 87 and Bernard Gui, *Flos chronicorum necnon chronico regum Francorum*, ed. Guignant de Wailly (Paris, 1855), 713.
38 Gerald of Wales, *Expugnatio Hibernica*, ed. J.F. Dimock (London, 1867), 388–89.
39 *Kronyk van Vlaenderen van 580 tot 1467*, ed. P. Blommaert and C.P. Serrière, 2 vols. (Ghent, 1839), 1: 156.
40 John Gower, in *Political Poems and Songs*, ed. Thomas Wright, 2 vols. (London, 1861), 2:10–11.

Other reasons for defeat parallel more closely the excuses given for losses suffered to the pagans. An anonymous fifteenth-century poem entitled "Now England is Perished" is the perfect example of this. It explains that the losses in the war against France were due to the sins of the people:

> Many beads and few prayers/ Many debtors and few good payers
> Small feasting and little penance/ Thus all is turned to mischance.
> Extortion and much simony/ False covetousness and perjury
> With lechery and adultery/ Pretended friendship and hypocrisy.
> Also guile on every side/ With murder and much pride
> Great envy and willfulness/ Without mercy or righteousness.
> The cause is because of the lack of light/ Which should be in the church of right.[41]

Other writers target the sins of the soldiers who lost in battle as the reason for defeat. For example, in the *Vita Edwardi secundi* the anonymous author writes, "perchance some one will ask why the Lord smote us this day, why we succumbed to the Scots, when for the last twenty years we have always had the better of them." He then answers his own question by charging the English troops and their "proud arrogance" with causing their own defeat at Bannockburn.[42] A further, more curious, example of this excuse for defeat comes from the continuation of the fourteenth-century *Eulogium historiarum*. Describing the Bishop of Norwich's loss at the siege of Ypres in 1383, the anonymous author of this chronicle reports that the defeat came because "God hit them in the 'derrieres' " (*percussitque eos Deus in posteriora*), indicating that God had punished the English with dysentery because of their sins.[43]

A final example of this comes from John Bromyard who writes (c.1390) that the wrong motives of the English soldiers had led to defeat in France:

> For victory in battle is not achieved by the size of one's army, but by the help of God. Yet, nowadays, alas, princes and knights and soldiers go to war in a different spirit; with their cruel actions and desire for gain, they incline themselves more to the ways of the devil than to those of God; for they set out for war not with prayers, but rather oaths and curses in their mouths; nor do they fight at the expense of the king or themselves but at that of the Church and the poor, despoiling both . . . And if they obtain victory, it is more frequently because of their opponents' lack of ability than because of their own merits, although they attribute it more to themselves than to God.[44]

The sins of the military leader was another explanation for loss in battle against other Christians. Giovanni Villani, for example, claims that the troops of Manfred, the king of Sicily, were defeated at the battle of Benevento in 1266

---

[41] "Now is England Perished," in *Historical Poems of the XIVth and XVth Centuries*, ed. Robin H. Robbins (New York, 1959), 149–50.
[42] *Vita Edwardi secundi*, ed. and trans. Noel Denholm-Young (London, 1957), 56.
[43] *Eulogium historiarum sive temporis*, ed. F.S. Hayden, 3 vols. (London, 1863), 3:357.
[44] Allmand, 38–39.

because of their king's heresy and persecutions.[45] And the annalist of the *Annales Gandenses* believes that the ultimate Flemish loss in their 1302–05 insurrection against the French was the result of their leader William of Jülich's loss of righteousness:

> Ungrateful for the graces bountifully bestowed on him by God (for he was a handsome youth, high-spirited and eloquent and sagacious in many respects), and forgetful of the honor conferred on him by God in victory over his enemies, he abjured and consulted evil spirits, spent his time in wantonness, made use of service, advice and friendship of magicians, enchanters and the wickedest of men, and expended untold amounts of money and riches, lavishly and heedlessly, not caring from whom he seized or extorted them. Wherefore it seems that it was by the just judgement of God that he was never after the battle of Courtrai fortunate in any battle or other business.[46]

Finally, the continuator of Guillaume de Nangis' *Chronicon* blames both the king of England and the king of France for the battles fought in 1340 which opened the conflict later to be known as the Hundred Years War. He writes:

> In this year of calamity and misery, of ignominy and confusion, nothing laudable was achieved between the two kings of France and England, because whatever was done during this year was not from the Holy Spirit, but ought to be supposed to have proceeded from the angel of Satan. . . . in this year the highest confusion prevailed; however it occurred not in any way for the utility of the republics of the aforementioned kings, but, alas, for the degradation and confusion of all Christianity, and of the holy and universal Mother Church, for whom the said princes ought to be the sustenance and the support.[47]

Ultimately, some writers simply recognize God's absence from their army and hope, in almost a prayerful way, that He will soon return. In April 1471, shortly after suffering a defeat in the War of the Roses, John Paston writes home: "The people here are very afraid. God has shown himself in a marvelous way, as Creator of All who can undo the world again when it pleases Him: and I think in all likelihood that He will show himself as marvelously again within a short while, and perhaps more than once in such cases."[48]

While this look at God and war during the Middle Ages has been brief, there are a few conclusions to be drawn. The first is the distinct lack of difference found in the rationalizations of defeat when suffered at the hands of pagans or of other Christians. Second, in determining why an army lost in battle, the question of justice or of God's presence disappears. Few writers question the justice of their army's participation in a war, and no one admits that God was actually

---

[45] Giovanni Villani, *Chroniche Fiorentine*, ed. and trans. P. Wicksteed (London, 1906), 127–28.

[46] *Annales Gandenses*, ed. and trans. Hilda Johnstone (London, 1951), 41.

[47] Guillaume de Nangis, *Chronicon et continuationes*, ed. H. Geraud, 2 vols. (Paris, 1843), 2:166.

[48] Richard Barber, *The Pastons: The Letters of a Family in the War of the Roses* (Woodbridge, 1986), 169.

fighting with the other side against his kingdom's forces. Finally, there are a few archetypical explanations for defeat; the sins of the people, of the army, or of the leaders all are used to explain why an otherwise just and "godly" military adventure failed. There is also the belief that the enemy targeted for war is wrong; the Crusaders should have been fighting the heretics of their own lands and the Christian kings should have been fighting the Saracens rather than each other.

Part III

THE ORDERS OF SOCIETY AT WAR

THE PROBLEM WITH MERCENARIES

Steven Isaac

WHEN Henry I of England died in 1135 after over-indulging in his favorite dish of lampreys, his lack of a direct male heir set the stage for a contested throne. Stephen of Blois appeared to settle the issue with his quick dash across the channel and subsequent coronation. By 1139, however, Henry's daughter and former Holy Roman Empress, Matilda, began to oppose Stephen's position vigorously. Her arrival in England that same year signaled the start of the longest sustained conflict northwest Europe would see between the end of the investiture conflict and the start of the Capetian-Plantagenet struggles. Militarily, Stephen's troubled reign has caught scholars' attention with its explosive burst of castle-building and questions of baronial independence. But the conflict between Stephen and Matilda was important for another development in medieval warfare: the widespread use of mercenaries. With vassalic loyalty proving all too fluid, both sides collected additional warriors from varied sources and with whatever resources they could muster. If contemporary chroniclers agree on anything, it is that England was inundated with these men and that their presence only served to intensify the violence wracking the land. What the chroniclers were not aware of, naturally enough, was that they were witnessing a transitional period in the development of hired fighters.

The primary problem with mercenaries in the twelfth century has lain in the historiographical assumption that their willingness to fight in return for financial compensation somehow violated the tenets of feudalism, that currency-driven service made them into immediate pariahs. A better understanding of Anglo-Norman military and administrative structures has clarified this picture, however. Articles by Marjorie Chibnall and J.O. Prestwich made it abundantly clear that paid warriors were not only no aberration, but rather an integral component of the period's armies and governments.[1] Chibnall's analysis in particular, relying on a sermon of St. Anselm's, accentuated the complementary role money played with other motivations. Instead of being perceived as antagonistic elements, fealty and financial ties have together been recognized as the "twin

---

[1] J.O. Prestwich, "War and Finance in the Anglo-Norman State," *Transactions of the Royal Historical Society,* 5th ser., 4 (1954): 19–43; and "The Military Household of the Norman Kings," *English Historical Review* 96 (January 1981): 1–35; Marjorie Chibnall, "Mercenaries and the *Familia Regis* Under Henry I," *History* 62 (1977): 15–23.

pillars" underlying Anglo-Norman governmental precocity.[2] Such a symbiosis makes the traditionally pejorative sense of the term harder to place within the confines of the twelfth century's first half.[3] An examination of the sources makes it apparent that in the period before the Plantagenet kings, mercenaries had yet to emerge as a fully distinct component within medieval armies. Admittedly, the chroniclers eagerly pointed out the misdeeds of hired warriors of either side during Stephen's and Matilda's struggle – men like William of Ypres and Robert fitz Hubert – but they did not do so on the basis of their paid service. Thus we need to ask how applicable the term mercenary really is to these particular men. And the answer to that lies in whether medieval observers perceived that these warriors fulfilled a function, or operated in a fashion, noticeably different from their fellow knights.

Besides the supposed tension with feudalism, the other drawback inherent to the mercenary label is its purely negative connotation. Stephen Brown neatly summed up the accretion of judgments implicit in the term recently, enjoining scholars to adopt a more laboratory-style approach to the phenomenon of mercenaries and their label.[4] Stripping the term of its pejorative sense, however, may not only prove impossible but counter-productive. The condemnation is too long-rooted in Western culture and expresses a value which is hardly in jeopardy of changing. The problem with mercenaries in the Middle Ages, according to C.W. Oman, actually consists of a number of problems. In that historian's words, the mercenary was "A stranger to all the nobler incentives to valor, an enemy to his God and his neighbor, the most deservedly hated man in Europe."[5] Oman cast his shadow over the medieval portions of Hans Delbrück's *The History of the Art of War*, although Delbrück avoided making any overt judgements about mercenaries. Even as he showed through detailed exposition that mercenaries proliferated throughout the Middle Ages, he betrayed, however, a continued suspicion of such combatants. In England, especially, they led to feudalism's devolution into a "mercenary system."[6] The condemnation of the twelfth century's hired soldiers has thus carried the imprint of Machiavelli's

---

[2]   Stephen Morillo, *Warfare under the Anglo-Norman Kings* (Woodbridge, 1992), 13.
[3]   In addition, the whole edifice of feudalism has been more effectively called into question of late. Elizabeth Brown, "The Tyranny of a Construct: Feudalism and Historians of Medieval Europe," *American Historical Review* 79 (1974): 1063–88, opened the debate, which has been covered much more fully by Susan Reynolds, *Fiefs and Vassals* (Oxford, 1994).
[4]   Stephen D. Brown, "Military Service and Monetary Reward in the Eleventh and Twelfth Centuries," *History* 74 (1989): 20–38, but especially 22: "In truth, any unease felt upon this subject is of our own creation, rooted in the fact that in current usage the adjective 'mercenary' is employed above all to condemn." And later, 37: "Commentators on the mercenary would be well advised to adopt the pragmatic approach and avoid the temptation of a moralistic stance."
[5]   C.W. Oman, *The Art of War in the Middle Ages*, ed. and rev. John H. Beeler (Ithaca, 1953), 65–66.
[6]   Hans Delbrück, *Medieval Warfare*, vol. III of *History of the Art of War*, trans. Walter J. Renfroe, Jr. (Lincoln, 1982), 169, 172, 313. Originally published as *Geschichte der Kriegskunst im Rahmen der Politischen Geschichte* in 1924.

even stronger denunciations in *The Prince* and *The Art of War*, which described the Renaissance *condottieri* as treacherous, cowardly, ungodly and always hungry for power.[7] The rapid proliferation of mercenary bands in the latter twelfth century, however, would seem to justify such comparisons, since it produced similar condemnation from contemporaries. Walter Map attended the Third Lateran Council of 1179 which banned the employment of those warriors commonly called *routiers* or *Brabançons*. Map agreed that these bands were heretical; according to his description, they confessed to a faith in Christ, but their activities indicated no true faith in God. They were simply ruffians who, by their numbers and weapons, had "made for themselves a law against all law."[8]

We cannot make the assumption, however, that Map's portrayal is applicable in its entirety to Stephen's time, especially since Map did little more than retell as narrative "fact" the litany of charges assembled by the Third Lateran Council. Some of those who flocked to England undoubtedly were forerunners of the loathed infantry which intruded onto the field of battle in the latter twelfth century. There were the "wolves" and "kites" – to use contemporary metaphors – whose depredations could only be explained by the fact that Christ and the saints must be asleep.[9] But other salaried warriors, especially among Stephen's forces, do not fit this profile. Foremost among this other group was William of Ypres, commander of the king's Flemish troops and, for a time, of all the royal household forces. All too often, though, historians have conveniently pigeon-holed William of Ypres as a "mercenary captain" and a precursor of the *condottieri* to come, meaning both the *routiers* of the 1100s and the bands of the late Middle Ages.[10] Deeper analysis, however, shows that William occupies a much more complex position right amid the development of political and military structures in the twelfth century.

William's father was Philip of Loo, younger son of Robert the Frisian, the count of Flanders from 1071–1093. Although William was undoubtedly considered an illegitimate offspring, there is some question whether this determination arose from an illicit relationship or just the lowly status of his mother. Louis VI of France denied William the countship in 1127 ostensibly on these grounds, elaborating on the point that William's mother not only carded wool for a living, but never rose above that station.[11] The conditions of William's birth were merely excuses in this instance, and not a real barrier. He continued to play an

---

[7] Niccolo Machiavelli, *Machiavelli: The Chief Works and Others*, ed. and trans. Allan Gilbert (Durham, 1965), vol. I, 46–54.

[8] Walter Map, *De Nugis Curialium*, ed. M.R. James (Oxford, 1914), 56–7.

[9] *Anglo-Saxon Chronicle [ASC]*, trans. G.N. Garmonsway (London, 1990), 154; and William of Malmesbury, *Historia Novella [HN]*, ed. and trans. K.R. Potter (London, 1955), 17.

[10] Delbrück, III: 316; also, John Schlight, *Monarchs and Mercenaries* (Bridgeport, 1968), 43.

[11] Galbert of Bruges, *The Murder of Charles the Good*, trans. James Bruce Ross (New York, 1960), 187.

influential role in Flemish affairs and the count's office was never really considered out of his reach. In order to solidify his own hold on the county, Thierry of
Alsace found it necessary to exile William in 1133.[12] Until 1137 the details of
William's life remain hidden. R.H.C. Davis in his study of Stephen's reign supposed that William went straight from his wife's holdings at Sluys to Stephen's
fief of Boulogne, but he gave no indications of why he reached this conclusion.[13] William of Malmesbury recorded that Stephen began hiring soldiers
from Flanders before Robert of Gloucester's return from Normandy in 1136.[14]
Since William would eventually command this force, he may well have been
present to play an instrumental role in its employment, especially if he was
already familiar with those being recruited.

In any case, William had definitely entered Stephen's service by 1137 when
Orderic notes that the king brought him and the Flemish troops into the duchy to
help repel Geoffrey of Anjou's invasion.[15] William continued to render valuable
military service to Stephen, the best examples of which come from 1141. Stephen's capture at the Battle of Lincoln early in that year would have seemed to
signal the end of his cause. But while most of Stephen's supporters in the civil
strife, including his own brother, either threw their support to the empress or at
least stayed carefully neutral, William joined the queen, Matilda of Boulogne, in
Kent where they maintained the king's cause. With the queen's naval resources,
Kent was a natural base into which more troops from Flanders could easily be
imported. At this point William apparently moved from being the commander of
Flemish stipendiaries to a position of overall command of the military forces
still loyal to the imprisoned king. John of Hexham relates that William assumed
leadership of the king's household troops – the *familia regis Stephani* – along
with Pharamus of Boulogne, a nephew to the queen.[16]

Once Henry of Blois decided he would be better advised to return to his
brother's cause, William of Ypres is the only warrior mentioned by name among
the many the bishop asked for help. And once William and the queen, along with
a well-equipped force from London, arrived at Winchester, a siege of the
empress and her party began in earnest. William conducted a pragmatic, harshly
efficient blockade; besides other operations, he burnt the town of Andover, and
thwarted an attempt by John Marshal at Wherwell to break the encirclement.
In the engagement that ensued, the empress's men retreated into the nunnery
there, which William did not hesitate to torch. Most contemporaries agree that
the defeat at Wherwell broke the resolve of the empress's party. Unfortunately

12 *Flandria Generosa*, in *MGH SS* 9:324; also see E. Warlop, *The Flemish Nobility Before
1300*, trans. J.B. Ross and H. Vandermoere (Kortrijk, Belgium, 1975), 213.
13 R.H.C. Davis, *King Stephen* (New York, 1967), 66.
14 *HN*, 17.
15 Orderic Vitalis, *The Ecclesiastical History of Orderic Vitalis* [*OV*], ed. and trans. Marjorie
Chibnall, 6 vols. (Oxford, 1978), 6:481–83; *HN*, 21.
16 John of Hexham, *Symeonis Historia Regum Continuata per Johannem Hagustaldensem*,
ed. Thomas Arnold (London, 1885), 310: "Rexit autem familiam regis Stephani Willelmus
d'Ipre, home Flandrensis, et Pharamus, nepos reginae Matildae, et iste Boloniensis."

for her cause, the retreat from Winchester turned into a disastrous flight and saw the capture of Robert, earl of Gloucester, by Stephen's Flemings at Stockbridge. Significantly, William of Ypres was not leading the stipendiaries, but rather William de Warenne, earl of Surrey.[17]

Once Stephen gained his freedom, he made plain to whom he felt he owed his release. Davis notes that when the king held his first Christmas court at Canterbury, it was a "polite compliment to William of Ypres and his Kentish vassals."[18] Unfortunately, Davis is unclear at this point whether the vassals of which he speaks are those of the king or William. A contemporary of William's later days back in Flanders recounted that Stephen granted Kent to William after his release. The Christmas court was the likely occasion since the writer wrote of William receiving the honor before "the first men of the kingdom."[19]

This Flemish account is the only one to make William's acquisition of Kent a seemingly formal feudal investment. Gervase merely credits him with "abusing" the county.[20] Typically, however, writers admitted his lordship over the county even though he never held the title of earl. The Battle Abbey chronicle relates that he "held the county of Kent"; Gervase himself, in a less disparaging moment, notes that Stephen gave the county into William's keeping. The most telling evidence, as Round pointed out, is that William himself never added the title *comes* to his name on official documents.[21] Nonetheless, William did well enough without a formal title; the Pipe Roll of 2 Henry II shows that William was receiving £261 *blanch* and over £178 *ad numerum*, or roughly three-fourths of the revenues the king expected from Kent when it remained within the royal demesne.[22] Besides revenues William also controlled lands and vassals in Kent. John of Salisbury's correspondence shows that William felt the church at Chilham was his to give to the Abbey of St. Bertin. Moreover the gift of Chilham also involved a certain Odo, described as "attached" to William of Ypres. St. Bertin's also received the church at Throwley, courtesy of William; in

---

[17] *Gesta Stephani [GS]*, trans. K.R. Potter, ed. R.H.C. Davis (Oxford, 1976), 113; OV 6:541–543; Henry of Huntingdon, *Historia Anglorum* (London) 268–75; Davis, 54; also Marjorie Chibnall, *The Empress Matilda* (Oxford, 1991), 113.

[18] Davis, 70.

[19] *Flandria Generosa* in *MGH SS*, 9:325: "Rex vero non immemor beneficiorum, liberatori suo totam provinciam que dicitur Cantia possidendum concessit, et inter primos regni, dum vixit, honoravit."

[20] Gervase of Canterbury, *Historical Works*, ed. William Stubbs, 2 vols. (London, 1879), 1:121: "Willelmo Yprensi qui Cantia abutebatur. . . ." and 2:73: "Quorum unus erat Willelmus de Ipre, cui rex totam Cantiam commisit custodiendam."

[21] *The Chronicle of Battle Abbey*, ed. and trans. Eleanor Searle (Oxford, 1980), 145: "Cantia comitatum tunc possidebat." For Gervase, see n. 14. John Horace Round, *Geoffrey de Mandeville* (London, 1892), 146, 270–71; and *Regesta Regum Anglo-Normannorum: 1066–1154*, ed. H.A. Cronne and R.H.C. Davis, 3 vols. (Oxford, 1968), *passim*.

[22] Davis, 140. Round, 275, calls Stephen's generosity to William "enormous for the time at which it was made." *Blanch* refers to coinage that was paid by its actual weight while *ad numerum* was rendered by a simple tally, regardless of whether the coins might have been "clipped."

another instance he gave a bequest of 100 shillings *per annum* to Holy Trinity Aldgate from his property at Queenhithe.[23]

Not everything that William of Ypres did in the years after 1141 benefitted the Church. His willingness to burn down the Wherwell convent has already been noted, but other religious houses suffered at his hands without the justification of direct military necessity. Sometime between 1139 and 1146 William joined the earls of Surrey and Arundel plus William Martel in threatening to burn down St. Albans. They were bought off with a skillfully wrought table made of gold, silver, and jewels.[24] In another case Stephen heard of a large cache of coins being held at Abingdon Abbey. He sent William to secure a "donation." The monks at first barred the door to William, but then let him in when he expressed a need to pray. Once in, he strode to the money chest, broke it open with an axe, and requisitioned 50 marks of gold and 500 marks of silver.[25]

It is evident then that William of Ypres moved comfortably among the magnates of the Anglo-Norman realm; perhaps he was not liked, but he and they understood one another. The same can be said of the troops William led. No more than their leader were these men heretical upstarts waging war alongside and against their social superiors. Contemporaries agree that the force was a highly trained cavalry unit. Writing of William during his attempt to become count of Flanders, Galbert of Bruges gave a figure of three hundred knights, plus an undetermined number of foot-soldiers and auxiliary personnel.[26]

E. Warlop's study of the Flemish nobility has provided the name and background of at least one mounted warrior serving under William. Following Thierry of Alsace's victory in the struggle for the countship of Flanders, he began weeding out those who had opposed him in 1127–28. This process picked up speed as it became apparent in the early 1130s that William of Ypres was not going to accept peacefully exclusion from his grandfather's title. Part of Thierry's effort included removing from influential positions men in William's former center of power. Thus the Bailleul family replaced the hereditary castellans of Ypres probably in 1132, only a year before William himself was exiled. Fromold I had held the castellany as late as 1126, although the date is unknown at which his son, Fromold II, inherited the office. Charter evidence from 1148

---

[23] John of Salisbury, *The Letters of John of Salisbury*, ed. W.J. Millor and H.E. Butler (London, 1955), 37–39, 258; and Davis, 66, n.7.

[24] Round, 206, dates this event to 1143 and makes it part of the confusion surrounding Geoffrey de Mandeville's arrest by the king at the abbey.

[25] G.E. Cokayne, "Kent," in *The Complete Peerage* (London, 1929), 131.

[26] John Beeler, *Warfare in England, 1066–1189* (Ithaca, 1966), 300–1, accepted the idea that William's forces in England were virtually identical to this earlier troop, including the number of soldiers. Besides being unable to prove the continuous career of the group (particularly during William's imprisonment in Flanders), Beeler also implies that Verbruggen agrees with his conclusion. Verbruggen does accept Galbert's reports on William in Flanders, but he makes no estimates of William's soldiers in England. J.F. Verbruggen, *The Art of Warfare in Western Europe during the Middle Ages*, trans. Col. Sumner Willard and Mrs R.W. Southern (Woodbridge, 1997), 129.

and 1149 places him in England with William of Ypres. Since he is described as *Fromoldus castellanus*, he may have obtained a reconciliation with Thierry during this same period when William also regained control of his Flemish possessions. The timing was especially fortuitous for Fromold since the Bailleul castellan had just died on the Second Crusade. If, as seems likely, other Flemings like Fromold were in England to escape political problems at home, then Stephen's stipendiary force was obviously composed of knights of some consequence.[27]

The question of just who is a mercenary gets further clouded when historians determine that a familial or vassalic link places a knight under an obligation which redeems him from outright mercenary status. Thus, Pharamus of Boulogne escapes the mercenary stigma on account both of his relationship to the queen and estates he held in Surrey.[28] Unfortunately, William's status with Stephen as a vassal or just an employee remains undetermined. He may have indeed arrived in England as a mercenary, but what effect would his acquisition of Kent have had on his relation to the king? In the case of Fromold (and by extension, many of the other Flemings), did a vassalic link tie him to William? There is even some evidence that William may have had an otherwise unknown brother, Regnier, with him in England. Even though the grant to which Regnier was a witness may be a forgery,[29] the monks of Oseney Abbey either remembered his actual presence or calculated that William of Ypres naturally tapped into a family network for his soldiery.

We have to turn to Matilda's forces in order to find some of the more perfidious characters of the Anarchy. Nor should we be surprised to find some of William of Ypres's relatives in the other camp. Robert fitz Hubert made his first appearance little more than a month after the earl of Gloucester and the empress landed at Arundel in the autumn of 1139. On the night of 7 October, fitz Hubert stole into the castle at Malmesbury and occupied it. Malmesbury had been in fitz Hubert's hands for a week when the king arrived; eight days later the pressure of the siege, along with negotiations on the part of William of Ypres, saw the castle surrendered back to the king.[30] Robert fitz Hubert's audacious capture of Malmesbury – even before he took service with either side in the civil war – caught the chroniclers' attention and has thus left us with more details than normal about a hired warrior. John of Worcester calls him *miles*, a knight, the son of a certain noble named Hubert. This assertion of noble origins is further

---

27 Warlop, 213, 476–77, n. 53. Warlop's evidence comes from the cartularies of Loo, Berques, and Bourbourg.
28 See Beeler's comments on Pharamus of Boulogne, whose presence in England he explained through his kinship with the queen and small landholdings in Surrey, 301.
29 *Regesta Regum Anglo-Normannorum*, III: 627.
30 *HN*, 36; John of Worcester, *The Chronicle of John of Worcester*, ed. J.R.H. Weaver (Oxford, 1908), 61. William of Malmesbury indicates that he held the castle for fifteen days while John of Worcester writes that the siege took only eight days.

strengthened by the fact that Robert was a blood-relation, *consanguineus*, of William of Ypres.[31]

Following his quick suppression at Malmesbury, Robert fitz Hubert soon hired himself out to the earl of Gloucester. The *Gesta Stephani* is explicit on this point, noting that Robert was the *stipendiarius* of the earl. This status, however, did not bring down condemnation; rather it was Robert's zealous interest in only his own aggrandizement, not in either side of the Anarchy. He stole away one night with his own retainers from the earl's army just months after the escapade at Malmesbury. Again relying on stealth, he infiltrated the impressive strong-hold at Devizes through use of unusually crafted scaling ladders made of leather.[32] The sources agree that with Devizes as his base, Robert meant to carve out his own principality between the two factions warring for the throne. He sent to Flanders for more knights (*pro militibus*) and began to terrorize the country-side. Somehow in the process of ravaging the district, he ran afoul of John the Marshal at Marlborough. John imprisoned fitz Hubert and then later bartered him away to the earl of Gloucester. What happened next is cloudy, but the end result was that the Angevin supporters hanged fitz Hubert before the walls of Devizes in an unsuccessful attempt to induce his followers to surrender. After these events the king approached the garrison with a large monetary offer and was able to regain the fortress without a siege.[33]

At this point, fitz Hubert's exploits provide a fleeting glimpse at some of the compatriots whom he brought into England. In his analysis of mercenaries at the end of the twelfth century, Georges Duby noted emphatically that knights were not among the ranks of mercenaries.[34] Such was not the case in England during this period. Robert fitz Hubert had a noble pedigree and was related to one of northwest Europe's most distinguished houses. The *Gesta Stephani* notes that the garrison he installed at Devizes was composed of relatives and fellow knights. More specifically, John of Worcester's account tells that before fitz Hubert went to the gallows, two of his nephews were hanged.[35]

---

31 *Ibid.*, 61: "Miles quidam nomine Robertus, cuiusdam nobilis viri Huberti filius . . . Willelm. d'Ipre, ut fertur consanguineus ipsius Rotberti."

32 Fitz Hubert's reliance on devious stratagems likewise drew down only convenient, but not specific, condemnation. Paragons of chivalric prowess such as William Marshal would happily trick their opponents and receive praise. Fitz Hubert's real crime was again his unmitigated greed.

33 For the different accounts of Robert fitz Hubert at Devizes, see *HN*, 43–44; *GS*, 104–8; and John of Worcester, 61–63.

34 Georges Duby, *The Legend of Bouvines*, trans. Catherine Tihanyi (Berkeley, 1990), 80: "In fact, mercenaries do not seem to be recruited from the nobility no matter how impoverished it might be: the sons of poor knights might be looking for pay, but they want to wage battle hon-orably." Duby's point captures the negative connotation of "mercenary" clearly but does not explain why a knight fighting for pay is not a mercenary.

35 *GS*, 108, calls them *cognati et commilitiones*. The information on fitz Hubert's nephews is in Florence of Worcester, *Chronicon ex Chronicis*, ed. Benjamin Thorpe, 2 vols. (London, 1849), II: 119–23. It comes from a Gloucester-based interpolation which Weaver, *John of Worcester*, 5–10, 61–3, did not think reflects John of Worcester's usual pro-Stephen

With so many warriors of noble background composing the salaried ranks of armies in England, it is no wonder that chroniclers never chose the word *routier* to describe them. The word existed already,[36] but contemporary writers were aware that men such as William of Ypres and even Robert fitz Hubert belonged in a different category. For them, such impressive warriors could only find fit company among the *milites* of the realm. Nor should this surprise us since that category had not yet been closed off by the rise of chivalric ideals. The heterogeneity of knightly ranks is particularly evident in England where the Domesday surveys have made it possible to make estimates of the landed wealth of much of the Anglo-Norman knighthood. Even before Sally Harvey's analysis of Domesday landholdings, D.C. Douglas had already described the knights in England as a "very miscellaneous class," composed of humble retainers who might serve alongside men holding such large estates that they were actually the social equals of their immediate lords. Harvey's study lent statistical weight to Douglas's assessment with her estimate that one and a half hides constituted the "normal landed basis of the eleventh-century knight." That amount kept the Anglo-Norman knight above the most wealthy peasants, but just barely. The income from one and a half hides "might enable [a knight] to sustain the equipment of his profession, though it would leave no surplus for status-seeking."[37] Thus the word *miles* defies explicit definition in Anglo-Norman England, let alone the rest of Europe. From "knight" to "foot-soldier," it was "used in Domesday Book to describe persons of every imaginable level of wealth, social status and military training."[38] William of Poitiers relates with descriptive adjectives how the Conqueror delivered orders first to his magnates, then to "middling nobles" – *milites mediae nobiles* – and lastly to the common knights – *milites gregarios*.[39] In the end, the variety of meanings leaves us to define *milites* best by what they were not: clerics and the bottom rung of society's noncombatants.

The situation had not changed by Stephen's reign, although increasingly the term *miles* was acquiring those attributes that indicated it referred to knights rather than just any soldier. This is the crux of the transitional period: *miles* is coming closer to designating the typical knight – one who often attended his lord, even in peacetime, who probably held a fief, and whose specialized equipment and skills attested to his social preeminence – but the term is still a good distance from that position. Observing this heterogenous group of warriors, the chroniclers, such as William of Poitiers, relied on adjectives to distinguish between the ranks. We should see the term *miles stipendiarius* in this same light.

---

sympathies. Since the *GS* contains similar information, I see no reason to question the validity of the nephews' presence.

[36] Du Cange, see under *rumpere*, for its evolution in the eleventh century.

[37] D.C. Douglas, *William the Conqueror* (Berkeley, 1964), 275; Sally Harvey, "The Knight and the Knight's Fee in England," *Past and Present* 49 (1970): 15, 20–21.

[38] C. Warren Hollister, *The Military Organization of Norman England* (Oxford, 1965), 115.

[39] Harvey, 28.

It did not set the stipendiary, or mercenary, apart from fief-holding knights; instead, it place the stipendiary within the group while explaining their particular relationship to the lord.

Even though money served as the medieval mercenary's basis of service, we must see that he understood his service in terms of lordship and vassalage. How else do we explain William of Ypres's dedication to Stephen's cause after the debacle at Lincoln? Once Stephen returned to a still contested but stronger kingship, he made William's feudal links to him all the more apparent. Moreover, even though William and other Flemings began in the 1140s to repair their relations with Count Thierry of Flanders, they continued to defend Stephen's interests instead of returning to their old patrimonies. If we see the vassalic elements in either William or Fromold's service, then we can understand why they might feel compelled to stay in England so long as their feudal lord on the continent did not require them. By contrast, the career of Robert fitz Hubert demonstrates the opposite effect. The fact that he fought for a salary did not initially exemplify his destructive appetites; rather it served as just another charge against him, coming after his treachery, depredations against church and populace, and overall bad behavior. If we can see this, then paid warriors no longer need to be a skeleton in the feudal closet. They became problematic indeed from the mid-twelfth century onwards as their numbers and types increased. Until that transition, however, mercenaries operated within feudal structures as acceptable types. They became problems when they did not keep faith with their employer-lords, no differently than did "purely" feudal soldiers.

ANGLO-NORMAN WOMEN AT WAR:
VALIANT SOLDIERS, PRUDENT STRATEGISTS
OR CHARISMATIC LEADERS?

Jean A. Truax

MODERN society has been conditioned by the writings of Machiavelli, Rousseau and Hegel to think of war as the supreme testing ground for both leadership and patriotism.[1] Thus, some modern feminists seek an expanded role for women in the military as a way of earning an equal position in society[2] and are eager to find historical precedents for such activity. Perhaps motivated by such concerns, Mary R. Beard wrote:

> Where . . . [medieval women] had power as rulers or in ruling families, they often instigated and proclaimed wars and even marshaled their troops as they went into battle. They incited men to ferocity at the fighting fronts. They accompanied men on marauding expeditions. They fought in the ranks. They took up arms to defend their homes.[3]

During the Anglo-Norman period, references to women at war are frequent enough to permit the historian to test both the truth of Beard's statements and the validity of the assumptions underlying them.

Obviously, women who acted as feudal overlords, whether in their own right or as the representatives of male relatives, controlled the resources of money and manpower necessary for waging war. Thus, in 1101, Adela of Blois, ruling on behalf of her husband who was absent on the First Crusade, dispatched a hundred knights to help Prince Louis of France in his campaign against Bouchard IV of Montmorency, who had refused to answer a summons to the

---

[1] Jean Bethke Elshtain, *Women and War* (New York, 1987), 70–75.

[2] Ibid., 231–33, 239. Wendy Chapkis and Mary Wings, "The Private Benjamin Syndrome," in *Loaded Questions: Women in the Military*, ed. Wendy Chapkis (Washington DC, 1982), 20. For the use of this tactic by suffragists during the First World War, see Lesley Merryfinch, "Militarization/ Civilianization," in *Loaded Questions*, 11.

[3] Mary R. Beard, *Women as Force in History: A Study in Traditions and Realities* (New York, 1987), 279. Also "As the empire of the East crumbled and feudal wars took the place of wars for imperial expansion, women belonging to aristocratic and royal families inspired wars, frequently initiated them, and sometimes used arms themselves." (286) A more recent study is by Megan McLaughlin, "The Woman Warrior: Gender, Warfare and Society in Medieval Europe," *Women's Studies* 17 (1990): 193–209. McLaughlin argues that women were more accepted as warriors in the early medieval period because military organization was essentially domestic in character.

royal court.[4] Eadmer recorded that when Anselm left Rome in 1103, he crossed the Alps with an escort of soldiers provided by Countess Matilda of Tuscany.[5] Even religious women occasionally resorted to armed force, as indicated by the letter of Archbishop Theobald of Canterbury to the abbess of Amesbury, accusing her of attempting to deprive Jordan, the treasurer of Salisbury, of the church of Froyle by "violence and armed force."[6]

Even women whose husbands were alive and on the scene seem to have had their own military forces. For example, Orderic Vitalis made it clear that the empress Matilda had companies of soldiers on the continent that belonged personally to her rather than to her husband, Geoffrey of Anjou. He noted that in 1139: "the countess's retainers captured Ralph of Esson, a powerful lord, in Lent and handed him over to their lady to be kept in fetters."[7] Matilda had her predecessors, for her grandmother Matilda I, the wife of William the Conqueror, sent her own troops to help a favored ally on at least two occasions. Robert of Torigny noted that she sent soldiers to help Ernulf of Hainault in his attempt to remain count of Flanders in 1071.[8] In the second instance, Matilda acted not only independently, but in direct opposition to her husband, sending troops and money to help her son, Robert Curthose, in his rebellion of 1077–78 against his father. William of Malmesbury wrote: "A slight disagreement arose between . . . [William and Matilda], because of their son . . ., whom his mother was said to have supplied with a military force out of her revenues."[9] Orderic Vitalis recorded that William ordered one of the queen's messengers to be arrested and blinded. The chronicler had the angry king exclaim:

> The wife of my bosom, whom I love as my own soul, whom I have set over my whole kingdom and entrusted with all authority and riches, . . . supports the enemies who plot against my life, enriches them with my money, zealously arms and succours and strengthens them to my grave peril.[10]

Interestingly, William of Malmesbury believed that Matilda had used her own

---

[4] Suger, *Vie de Louis VI Le Gros*, ed. and trans. Henry Waquet (Paris, 1964), 14–19; OV, 6:156–58.

[5] Eadmer, *Historia Novorum in Anglia*, 155; Anselm, *Epistolae*, in *Sancti Anselmi Cantuariensis archiepiscopi opera omnia*, ed F.S. Schmitt, 6 vols. (Stuttgart-Bad Canstatt, 1963–68), no. 325.

[6] John of Salisbury, *The Letters of John of Salisbury, Volume One, The Early Letters (1153–1161)*, ed. W.J. Millor, S.J. and H.E. Butler, rev. C.N.L. Brooke (Oxford, 1986), p. 188, no. 114: "violenter et manu armata." See also p. 189, no. 115, in which the archbishop refers to the abbess having "ejected him with violence and without any process of law" (*violenter et absque ordine iudiciario eiecistis*).

[7] OV, 6: 512–14: "Satellites enim comitissae in quadragesima Radulfum de Axone virum potentem comprehenderunt, dominaeque suae vinculis artandum tradiderunt." The incident took place in 1139.

[8] Robert of Torigny, interpolations in William of Jumièges, *Gesta Normannorum Ducum*, ed. Jean Marx (Paris, 1914), 286.

[9] William of Malmesbury, *Gesta Regum Anglorum* [*GR*] (London, 1964), 453; OV, 3:102–8.

[10] OV, 3:102.

money to finance Robert's rebellion, while Orderic accused her of having used her husband's money for the project. In any case, even though Matilda and the other women did not personally command the contingents of troops that they dispatched, the evidence is clear that they independently controlled the disposition of these military forces.

Furthermore, Anglo-Norman noblewomen controlled financial resources that could be spent on military projects. For example, Abbot Suger reported that the castle at Le Puiset had been built by Queen Constance, the wife of Robert II (996–1031).[11] In the late tenth century, Aubrée, the wife of Ralph of Ivry, hired the architect Lanfred to construct an impregnable fortress at Ivry. After construction was complete, she had Lanfred executed, so that he could not build a similar castle for anyone else. There is no doubt that Aubrée looked on the project as her very own, for she died at her husband's hands after attempting to expel him from her castle.[12]

Countess Ida of Boulogne[13] also seems to have expended both her time and her financial resources on a military expedition, the First Crusade. When her son, Godfrey of Lorraine, began to discuss the sale of the castle of Boulogne and its surrounding lands with Bishop Otbert of Liege, Ida traveled there to participate in the negotiations.[14] When she arrived, however, she found that Godfrey had dispossessed the monks of St. Hubert and deprived them of many revenues. Ida convinced her son to restore the monks' property and to give them the parish of Sensenruth. She herself donated to them a church at Baisy.[15] The combined need to raise money and to prepare spiritually for the hazardous undertaking touched off a flurry of donations by the countess and her son. Ida and Godfrey jointly donated land at Genappe to the abbey of Afflighem,[16] and Ida gave "goods and serfs" to the church of St.-Amour at Bilsen with the consent of her son.[17] In another transaction, Abbess Richeza of Ste.-Gertrude at Nivelles purchased the villages of Genappe and Baisy from Ida and Godfrey for "a very great price."[18] The life of the Countess written by a monk of St.-Vaast mentions a trip to England,[19] and Godfrey's modern biographer, John Andressohn,

---

11 Suger, 132.

12 OV, 4:114, 290; Robert of Torigny in *Gesta Normannorum Ducum*, 288.

13 Ida of Boulogne is of course not technically an Anglo-Norman woman, but she appears frequently in Anglo-Norman writing because of her friendship with Anselm. For Anselm's correspondence with Ida, see nos. 82, 114, 131, 167, 208, 235, 244, 247. At the beginning of the *Historia Novorum*, 29, Eadmer mentions that when Anselm was on his way to England in 1092 before becoming archbishop of Canterbury, he stopped at Boulogne to "confer with the Countess Ida."

14 Karl Hanquet, ed., *La Chronique de Saint-Hubert dite Cantatorium* (Brussels, 1906), 204.

15 Ibid., 204–6.

16 Alphonse Wauters, *Table Chronologique des Chartes et Diplomes Imprimes concernant L'Histoire de la Belgique* (Brussels, 1866), 1:598.

17 Ibid., 599.

18 Ibid., 602. A later confirmation by the Emperor Henry IV refers to the sale as having been made by Ida alone [609].

19 *Vita B. Idae, ASB*, 13 April, 143.

speculated that Ida also sold her property across the Channel to the Church as part of the fund-raising campaign.[20] A letter from Count Stephen of Blois to his wife Adela indicates that she provided financial support for the Crusade in the same way, for Stephen wrote that by March, 1098, he had doubled through his crusading activities the amount of riches that his wife had originally given him.[21] Thus these noblewomen were vitally interested in the military ventures of the male members of their families and generously expended both their time and their property in support of such causes.

It is clear from these examples that although women like Aubree and Ida did not participate directly in the fighting, they committed both their organizational skills and their property to military projects. Women also frequently became directly involved on at least one side of the most common type of medieval military encounter, the siege of a castle.[22] While some of these women seem to have been little more than passive victims of male violence,[23] other examples indicate that sometimes women played a commanding role in the defense of their castles. For example, the *Anglo-Saxon Chronicle* recorded that when Earl Ralph of Norfolk fled England after the earl's Rebellion in 1075, his wife held his castle for him until she herself was given a safe conduct out of the country.[24] Similarly, in 1095, when William Rufus captured Robert of Mowbray, earl of Northumbria, his wife and his steward held his castle until the king threatened to put out the captive's eyes.[25] Orderic Vitalis wrote that in 1123 Hugh de Montfort, in rebellion against Henry I, commanded his wife, his brothers and his retainers to hold the stronghold at Montfort-sur-Risle, while he himself went on to Brionne to warn Waleran of Meulan.[26] Robert of Torigny did not mention the activities of Hugh's wife during the siege, but did state that before the siege, Hugh acted on the advice of his wife and refused to give information about his stronghold to the king.[27] In these cases, although the chroniclers gave few details, they

---

[20] John Andressohn, *The Ancestry and Life of Godfrey of Bouillon* (Hallandale FL, 1972), 26.
[21] Heinrich Hagenmeyer, *Epistolae et Chartae ad Historiam Primi Belli Sacri Spectantes: Die Kreuzzugsbriefe aus Jahren 1088–1100* (Innsbruck, 1901), 149.
[22] Kelly DeVries, *Medieval Military Technology* (Lewiston NY, 1992), 125.
[23] In the *Gesta Stephani*, for example, we read that in 1141 King Stephen's forces besieged the countess of Chester in Lincoln Castle. K.R. Potter, *Gesta Stephani* (Oxford, 1976), 110. The same work tells the rather romantic story of Richard fitz Gilbert's wife, who was trapped in Cardigan Castle by the marauding Welsh until Miles of Gloucester "advanced boldly to the castle through the midst of the enemy, through the fastnesses of dark woods, over the high peaks of mountains, and bringing her safely back with her company returned triumphant and with glory" (18). Similarly, Baldwin de Redvers' wife and supporters were besieged at Exeter when he rebelled against King Stephen in 1136. As the garrison neared starvation, Baldwin's wife went to King Stephen ". . . barefooted, with her hair loose on her shoulders, and shedding floods of tears" (40). The king rejected her petition, however, and relented only when members of his own party begged him to allow the city to surrender (42).
[24] *ASC* 1075 AD; Florence of Worcester, *Chronicon ex Chronicis*, 2 vols. (London, 1964), 2:11; Simeon of Durham, *Historia Regum [HR]*, RS 75, 2:206.
[25] *ASC* 1095 AD; *HR*, 226.
[26] OV, 6:334.
[27] Robert of Torigny, *Chronicle*, 4:105.

obviously considered the wife one of the commanders of the castle defenders and held her responsible for the success or failure of the effort.

Another example provides a few more details about a woman's participation as a decision-maker and shows her negotiating the terms of surrender with the enemy. When the empress Matilda arrived in England in October, 1139, her stepmother Adeliza of Louvain received her at Arundel Castle, which she held as part of her dowry from the late King Henry. The former queen was acting on her own authority in this case, since as Marjorie Chibnall has pointed out, the lady's second husband, William de Albini, remained a firm supporter of King Stephen.[28] According to Florence of Worcester, when King Stephen besieged the castle, the former queen argued that she had not invited the king's enemy into England, but rather had merely granted hospitality to a family member. Mollified, the king granted the empress safe passage to Bristol.[29] This example makes it clear that the Anglo-Norman chroniclers believed women to be capable of directing the defense, not only of their husbands' property, but also of their own in case of armed attack.

Orderic Vitalis particularly seems to have delighted in stories of such wifely devotion and was lavish in his praise of women left to guard their husbands' property in the face of danger. For example, he wrote a stirring account of the activities of Robert Bordet's wife, Sibyl, while her husband was absent from Tarragona, visiting Rome and returning to Normandy to raise additional military forces. Orderic Vitalis wrote:

> She was as brave as she was beautiful. During her husband's absence she kept sleepless watch; every night she put on a hauberk like a soldier and, carrying a rod in her hand, mounted on to the battlements, patrolled the circuit of the walls, kept the guards on the alert, and encouraged everyone with good counsel to be on the alert for the enemy's stratagems. How greatly the young countess deserves praise for serving her husband with such loyalty and unfaltering love, and watching dutifully over God's people with such sleepless care![30]

Unfortunately, either Orderic Vitalis's information or his imagination failed at that point, for he neglected to record whether the Moors ever attacked. However, his fulsome praise for the young countess illustrated his faith in a wife's ability to successfully command a military force in defense of her husband's property.

Similarly, Orderic Vitalis also praised Robert Giroie's wife Radegunde for

---

[28] Marjorie Chibnall, *The Empress Matilda: Queen Consort, Queen Mother and Lady of the English* (Oxford, 1991), 80.

[29] Florence of Worcester, 2:117. On the other hand, William of Malmesbury censured the former queen for having "broken the faith she had repeatedly pledged by messages sent into Normandy." William of Malmesbury, *Historia Novella* [*HN*] in *Historia Regum Anglorum atque Historia Novella*, 2 vols. (London, 1964), 2:725.

[30] OV, 6:404. For an account of the activities of Robert Bordet and his successors in Spain, see Lawrence J. McCrank, "Norman Crusaders in the Catalan Reconquest: Robert Burdet and the Principality of Tarragona, 1129–55," *Journal of Medieval History* 7 (1981): 67–82.

her unsuccessful attempts to defend her husband's fortress at Saint-Ceneri against an attack by Robert of Belleme. The attack occurred in July, 1092, while Robert Giroie was away from home serving with the forces of the future Henry I in his wars against his brothers. A rumor reached the castle that Robert had been killed, which caused some of the defenders to abandon their efforts. Radegunde had to surrender, because in Orderic's words, "one woman could not uphold what she believed to be right against determined men."[31] The chronicler portrayed Radegunde as the commander of the castle and made her responsible for the decision to surrender. Reporting her death in the same year, Orderic Vitalis described Radegunde as "upright and honorable."[32]

Another of the chronicler's stories portrayed a woman resorting to physical violence in defense of her husband's castle. In 1119, when Eustace of Breteuil rebelled against Henry I, he fortified his castles against his father-in-law and "sent his wife Juliana . . . to Breteuil, and provided her with the knights necessary to defend the fortress."[33] However, the citizens were loyal to the king, and opened the gates of the town to him, forcing Juliana and her forces to take refuge in the castle. Seeing that no escape was possible, Juliana sought a meeting with her father. When Henry arrived, his treacherous daughter attempted to shoot him with a cross-bow.[34] Orderic had no words of praise for this display of wifely loyalty, and gleefully reported that when Juliana finally had to surrender, her father forced her to leap down from the walls of the castle into the frozen moat, where she "fell shamefully, with bare buttocks."[35] King Henry's unusual and somewhat brutal punishment of his rebellious daughter suggests that he considered her not an impotent and harmless woman, but rather a dangerous opponent to be humiliated. Robert of Torigny omitted this colorful story, but did relate that Eustace of Breteuil lost his property because "his wife Juliana, the bastard daughter of King Henry, arrogantly and foolishly expelled his [King Henry's] wardens from the castle of Breteuil, against the king's wishes and her own fealty."[36]

Thus, these writers not only believed that it was possible for a woman to command military forces, but seem to have taken it for granted that she would do so when necessary. The various accounts of the capture of Malmesbury Castle by Duke Henry of Normandy in 1153 illustrate the strength of this assumption. According to the *Gesta Stephani*, as the armies of Duke Henry and King Stephen faced each other across the rain-swollen Avon River, the king's castellan treacherously betrayed the castle to Duke Henry.[37] Conversely, Henry

---

31 OV, 4:292–94.
32 Ibid., 4:294.
33 Ibid., 6:212.
34 Ibid., 6:212–14.
35 Ibid., 6:214.
36 Robert of Torigny, in *Gesta Normannorum Ducum*, 290: "uxor eius, Juliana, filia regis Henrici notha, nimis arroganter et stulte, contra voluntatem et fidelitatem regis, custodes suos de munitione Britolii ejecit."
37 *GS*, 232.

of Huntingdon believed that the bad weather made it impossible for King Stephen to cross the river and relieve the castle.[38] These writers were, of course, Anglo-Normans living in England. By contrast, the Norman chronicler Robert of Torigny, living at a distance from the action and perhaps receiving less first-hand information than the others, stated that Countess Gundreda of Warwick had expelled the king's guards and handed the fortress over to Duke Henry.[39]

Similarly, Orderic Vitalis wrote a particularly emotional account of the surrender of the fortress of Devizes to King Stephen in 1139. The king arrested bishops Roger of Salisbury and Alexander of Lincoln after a brawl at court between their retainers and those of Count Alan of Brittany. Roger of Salisbury's other nephew, Bishop Nigel of Ely, fled to the fortress of Devizes, where he was soon besieged by the angry king. Stephen kept the imprisoned bishops on a starvation diet and also threatened to hang Roger le Poer, who was the bishop of Salisbury's son and the king's chancellor, from the castle gates unless Nigel capitulated. Henry of Huntingdon and the *Gesta Stephani* both stated that the three bishops agreed to surrender the fortress because of the king's threats and their own sufferings.[40] William of Malmesbury turned Roger of Salisbury's sufferings into a voluntary fast undertaken to "subdue the spirit of the bishop of Ely" so that he would agree to surrender the castle.[41] Orderic Vitalis, however, once again operating at a greater distance from the events than the English chroniclers, stated that Nigel of Ely remained obdurate in the face of his uncle's pleas. The Norman writer placed Matilda of Ramsbury, Roger le Poer's mother, in command of Devizes. When King Stephen threatened to hang her son, Matilda surrendered immediately, exclaiming, "I gave him birth, and it can never be right for me to cause his destruction; instead I should offer my life in exchange for his if necessary."[42] Like Robert of Torigny, Orderic Vitalis seems to have been ignorant of the exact circumstances of the surrender and therefore to have assumed that a woman would naturally be left in command of an absent husband's castle and that in case of an attack, she would make the decision to hold fast or to surrender the fortress.

The chroniclers seem to have particularly delighted in the comparatively rare cases of women who actually directed the movements of troops in the field and participated in offensive actions. William of Malmesbury praised Countess Matilda of Tuscany as "a woman, who, forgetful of her sex, and comparable to the ancient Amazons, used to lead forth her hardy troops to battle."[43] The author, however, offered no specifics, perhaps because of his great distance from the events, and so continued with an account of the circumstances surrounding the accession of Urban II to the papal throne. Orderic Vitalis gleefully

---

[38] Henry of Huntingdon, 286.
[39] Robert of Torigny, *Chronicle*, 172.
[40] *GS*, 78; Henry of Huntingdon, 265.
[41] *HN*, 718.
[42] OV, 6:532–34.
[43] William of Malmesbury, *Gesta Regum*, 467–68.

embroidered such tales, even though he also provided few concrete details about his subjects' activities. For example, when a quarrel between Helwise of Evreux and Isabel of Tosny led to warfare between their husbands, Orderic Vitalis pictured Isabel riding to war armed as a knight. He remarked:

> She showed no less courage among the knights in hauberks and sergeants-at-arms than did the maid Camilla, the pride of Italy, among the troops of Turnis. She deserved comparison with Lampeto and Marpesia, Hippolyta and Penthesilea and the other warlike Amazon Queens.[44]

Unfortunately, Orderic Vitalis offered no details about Isabel's exploits; his story continued with an account of the fighting between the two men.[45] Isabel appeared later in his tale only as part of the audience to which her son and some other knights told stories of visions that they had seen or of which they had heard reports.[46] Earlier in his work, the chronicler had stated that after her husband died, Isabel remained a widow and, feeling the need to reform her life, finally became a nun at Haute-Bruyère. In this passage, Orderic Vitalis seemed to disapprove of Isabel's former lifestyle, since he noted that she "repent[ed] . . . the mortal sin of luxury in which she had indulged in her youth."[47] His admiration for Isabel's military exploits, however, was unquestionable.

In the same way, the Anglo-Norman chroniclers also celebrated and sometimes enhanced the memories of women of the past who had commanded military forces. For example, Henry of Huntingdon noted that when King Ina of Wessex fought against the South Saxons, his wife Aethelburh stormed the castle at Taunton and razed it to the ground.[48] One of Henry's favorite heroines was Aethelflaeda, the Lady of the Mercians, who became the ruler of Mercia after the death of her husband and actively assisted her brother Edward the Elder in his campaigns against the Danes. The version of the *Anglo-Saxon Chronicle* known as the *Mercian Register* preserves only a bare account in the years 910–918 of the fortresses that she built, her capture of the towns of Derby and Leicester, and her death at Tamworth while besieging York.[49] Henry of Huntingdon embellished Aethelflaeda's story, writing that at Derby she "commanded a vigorous assault to be made on the fortress and a desperate conflict took place at the very entrance of the gate."[50] Henry wrote that if Aethelflaeda had not died suddenly, "she would have surpassed the most valiant of men."[51] In a short

---

[44] OV, 4:212–14.
[45] Ibid., 4:214–18.
[46] Ibid., 4:218.
[47] Ibid., 3:128.
[48] Henry of Huntingdon, 112. The term "castle" is an anachronism here. The *Anglo-Saxon Chronicle*, 722 AD merely refers to Queen Aethelburh having destroyed Taunton.
[49] *ASC*, 910–18 AD.
[50] Henry of Huntingdon, 158.
[51] Ibid.

poem in her honor, the chronicler specifically called attention to her military prowess and even compared her to Julius Caesar.[52]

Other Anglo-Norman chroniclers also paid tribute to Aethelflaeda. William of Malmesbury wrote:

> This most powerful woman assisted her brother greatly with her advice and was of equal service in building cities. You could not easily discern whether it was more due to fortune or her own exertions that a woman should be able to both protect her own men and to terrify foreigners.[53]

Florence of Worcester also preserved the memory of Aethelflaeda's military conquests and spoke of her in glowing terms.[54]

Geoffrey of Monmouth may actually have modeled the exploits of two of his heroines on the careers of the noblewomen of his own day.[55] For example, when Locrinus abandoned his wife, Gwendolen, for another woman, Gwendolen retreated to Cornwall, where she "assembled all the young men of that region and began to harass Locrinus with border forays."[56] After her forces killed Locrinus in battle, Gwendolen ruled the kingdom for fifteen years, until her son came of age, and then returned to Cornwall, which she ruled for the rest of her life.[57] In a second case, King Leir's daughter, Cordelia, ruled the kingdom after her father's death for five years, until her two nephews Marganus and Cunedagius rebelled against her. The two men "laid waste to a number of provinces and met the queen herself in battle."[58] In the end, they captured Cordelia and put her in prison, where she committed suicide.[59] Geoffrey also recorded that when Arthur left Britain for the continent to meet the forces of the emperor, "he handed over the task of defending Britain to his nephew, Mordred, and to his Queen, Guinevere."[60] Thus, just as they praised contemporary women as mili-

---

[52] Ibid.

[53] William of Malmesbury, *Gesta Regum*, 196.

[54] Florence of Worcester called her "a woman of incomparable prudence, and eminent for her just and virtuous life" and noted that she had ruled the Mercians with "firmness and equity" (1:128). Perhaps thinking of Aethelflaeda's role as a builder of cities, Henry of Huntingdon made the emperor Constantine's mother Helen responsible for building the city walls at London and Colchester (30).

[55] Without becoming involved in a discussion of whether Geoffrey was writing history, propaganda or fiction, it seems safe to say that his work reflected the conditions of the world in which he lived. J.S.P. Tatlock, *The Legendary History of Britain: Geoffrey of Monmouth's Historia Regum Britanniae and Its Early Vernacular Versions* (1950; New York, 1974), 284–320. For a discussion of the place of Geoffrey of Monmouth in English historical writing, see Henry F. Greek, "Geoffrey of Monmouth and his World: The *Historia Regum Britanniae* and the Traditions of Norman Propaganda Writing" (Master's thesis, University of Houston, 1991).

[56] Geoffrey of Monmouth, *Historia Regum Britanniae*, in Edmond Faral, *La Légende Arthurienne: Etudes et Documents* (Paris, 1929), p. 95, pt. 1, bk. 3.

[57] Ibid.

[58] Ibid., 105.

[59] Ibid.

[60] Ibid., 253.

tary commanders, these writers judged the women of the distant past by Anglo-Norman standards and assumed that they could also boast of the same accomplishments.

Given this acceptance and admiration for women as military commanders, the historian expects the civil war in which the empress Matilda contested the English throne to provide many examples of the prospective queen controlling the strategies of her military forces. Orderic related that after King Henry's death, Geoffrey of Anjou "immediately sent his wife Matilda into Normandy,"[61] where the castles of Argentan, Exemes and Domfront surrendered to her at once. Presumably, a body of soldiers accompanied the empress, but this is not stated. In any case, Geoffrey himself soon followed with his own army. Later, at the siege of Le Sap, Count Geoffrey suffered a wound from a javelin in his right foot. Matilda joined him later in the battle, "bringing many thousands of soldiers with her."[62]

In England, Matilda traveled with her military forces and had many adventures and narrow escapes. The anonymous author of the *Gesta Stephani* marveled:

> Never have I read of another woman so luckily rescued from so many mortal foes and from the threat of dangers so great; the truth being that she went from the castle of Arundel uninjured through the midst of her enemies and escaped without scathe from the midst of the Londoners when they were assailing her, and her only, in mighty wrath, then stole away alone, in wondrous fashion, from the rout of Winchester, when almost all her men were cut off; and then when she left besieged Oxford, came away, as has been said, safe and sound.[63]

Matilda, however, is not usually considered the primary commander of her English forces – that task is supposed to have been left to Robert of Gloucester. Chibnall has stated: "she remained as far as possible in the background during battles, both from total inexperience in military leadership and because her capture would have meant the end of her cause."[64] Yet, if the chroniclers are to be believed, at Winchester and Oxford, the empress seems to have franchized the primary commander of her forces. The *Gesta Stephani* stated that Matilda, with a large body of troops, arrived at Winchester first, began the siege, and then summoned her followers to come to assist her. The author included both King David of Scotland and Robert of Gloucester among those who answered her call.[65] Similarly, Henry of Huntingdon wrote: "after some time she, with her uncle the king of the Scots, and her brother Robert, collecting their forces, settled down and besieged the castle of the Bishop of Winchester."[66] In this case,

---

61 OV, 6:454: "Mathildam uxorem suam mox in Normanniam premisit."
62 Ibid., 6:472. Even the combined forces were not able to take the fortress.
63 *GS*, 144.
64 Chibnall, 97.
65 *GS*, 126–28.
66 Henry of Huntingdon, 275: "Post dies autem cum avunculo suo rege Scotorum, et fratre suo Roberto, viribus coactis veniens obsedit turrim Wintonensis episcopi."

Matilda was included with other commanders, but it is possible that by mention-ing her first, the author intended to indicate that she was in overall command of the effort. At Oxford, the *Gesta Stephani* stated that Matilda strengthened the garrison, dispatched troops of cavalry on raiding expeditions, and fortified castles to hold King Stephen's men in check and to protect her own adherents.[67] Thus, while the empress did not lead her troops in battle, it is clear that she made the strategic decisions that determined where and when they would fight.

In addition, the activities of King Stephen's wife, Matilda of Boulogne, as a military commander are also well documented. In 1138, while her husband attacked Hereford, the queen besieged Dover. According to Orderic, while the queen led the forces attacking the city on the land side, she sent word to her kinsmen in Boulogne to blockade the sea approaches to the city so that the enemy could not receive any supplies.[68] The *Gesta Stephani* related that after King Stephen's capture at Lincoln, Queen Matilda sent envoys to the empress Matilda to beg for her husband's release. Her pleas fell on deaf ears, however, so the queen

> expecting to obtain by arms what she could not by supplication, brought a magnificent body of troops across in front of London from the other side of the river and gave orders that they should rage most furiously around the city with plunder and arson, violence and the sword, in sight of the countess and her men.[69]

Later, when the empress besieged Winchester, most of the sources place Queen Matilda in command of the forces that rode to the relief of the city. According to the *Gesta Stephani*:

> The queen . . ., with a splendid body of troops and an invincible band of Lon-doners, who had assembled to the number of almost a thousand, magnificently equipped with helmets and coats of mail, besieged the inner ring of besiegers from outside with the greatest energy and spirit.[70]

Similarly, the *Anglo-Saxon Chronicle* stated: "when they [Robert of Gloucester and Matilda] were inside the city, then came the king's queen with all her forces and besieged them, so that there was great famine within the city."[71] According to Henry of Huntingdon, bishop Henry of Winchester "summoned to his relief the queen and William of Ypres and almost all the barons of England."[72] By contrast, Florence of Worcester's account focused on the activities of the

---

67 *GS*, 138.
68 OV, 6:520; Henry of Huntingdon, 261; Robert of Torigny, *Chronicle*, 135.
69 *GS*, 122.
70 Ibid., 128–30.
71 *ASC*, 1141 AD.
72 Henry of Huntingdon, 275: "Episcopus autem misit pro regina et Willelmo Yprensi, et pro universis fere proceribus Angliae." A similar statement occurs in William of Newburgh, *Historia Regum Anglicarum*, RS 82, 1:41.

empress Matilda and, while it acknowledged the queen's presence at Winchester, did not speak of her as the commander of the forces.[73]

It is significant that Henry of Huntingdon mentioned William of Ypres in company with Queen Matilda in discussing the siege of Winchester, for modern historians have often considered him the real commander of the royal forces after the king's capture at Lincoln. R.H.C. Davis wrote: "when Stephen was in captivity it was William who made himself responsible for the safety of the queen, William who organized a new army, and William who led it to victory at Winchester."[74]

On the other hand, Davis also admitted that the Norman nobles hated William because he was a foreigner.[75] Contemporary sources made friction between the Normans and the Flemings the cause of the collapse of Stephen's expedition to Normandy in 1137. Orderic wrote:

> [King Stephen] . . . greatly esteemed William of Ypres and the other Flemings and placed exceptional reliance on them. Because of this the magnates of Normandy were much incensed, craftily withdrew their support from the king, and, out of envy for the Flemings, hatched all kinds of plots against them.[76]

At Argentan, fighting broke out between the Normans and Flemings, and men were killed on both sides. Seeing his army melting away before his eyes, Stephen agreed to a truce with the Angevins.[77] Like most of the rest of Stephen's supporters, William of Ypres fled from the battlefield at Lincoln, leaving the king to fight almost alone until his capture. Henry of Huntingdon sought to excuse William's flight, stating: "as an experienced general, perceiving the impossibility of supporting the king, he deferred his aid for better time."[78] However, the anonymous author of the *Gesta Stephani* seems to have harbored some ill-feelings, for he wrote that at the battle of Lincoln "a great many, like the Count of Meulan and the famous William of Ypres fled shamefully before coming to close quarters."[79] Significantly, this is the only time that the *Gesta Stephani* mentions William of Ypres, which is perhaps an indication of the distaste felt for the mercenary captain by some of the king's supporters.

---

[73] Florence of Worcester, 2:135.

[74] Ralph H.C. Davis, *King Stephen, 1135–1154* (London, 1990), 66. William was of noble birth, the illegitimate son of Philip of Loo and therefore a grandson of Robert the Frisian. He was outstandingly loyal for a mercenary, perhaps because he had found refuge with Stephen after his unsuccessful attempt to become count of Flanders. Stephen rewarded him handsomely with lands. See also Davis's appendices dealing with land ownership, 125, 140.

[75] Davis, 25, 66; Chibnall, 73.

[76] OV, 6:484.

[77] Ibid., 6:484–86. Robert of Torigny stated that one of the Flemish soldiers stole a barrel of wine from the forces of Hugh of Gournay, and that this touched off "a fierce feud between the Normans and Flemings, which compelled the king to return without having accomplished anything." *Chronicle*, p. 132.

[78] Henry of Huntingdon, 274.

[79] *GS*, 112: "plurimus autem antequam manu consererent, ut comes Mellonensis et Willelmus ille de Ipra, proh pudor! fugitantibus."

Under these conditions, it is doubtful that even so talented a military leader as William of Ypres could have singlehandedly rallied the English barons to the imprisoned king's cause. Orderic himself wrote, "But Count Waleran, William of Warenne, and Simon [of Senlis] remained loyal to the queen, and vowed to fight manfully for the king and his heirs."[80] William may indeed have organized the rebuilding of the king's shattered forces and he may have commanded them in the field at Winchester, but the chronicle accounts clearly indicate that the queen was the focus of the baron's loyalty, that the armies in the field were seen as belonging to her, and that she was responsible for broad strategic decisions about where and when to employ those forces.

The remaining ambiguity surrounding Matilda's role highlights the paradox which confronts any historian considering the many cases in which Anglo-Norman women are alleged to have participated in military actions. It seems indisputably clear that Anglo-Norman women acting as feudal overlords controlled the money and manpower necessary for waging war and that they directed where and when those resources would be employed. Beyond this, however, the evidence is contradictory. References to women left in command of besieged castles are numerous, but there is a frustrating lack of detail about the exact role that these women played. Furthermore, descriptions of the same event sometimes differ, and often only one of the accounts mentions the presence of a woman in command. The few accounts of women leading offensive actions are also frustratingly ambiguous, and it seems doubtful that any of the women actually fought in battle and exchanged blows with the enemy.

In this regard, it is significant that we do not read of any women being injured or killed in battle, although we might count Aethelflaeda, the Lady of the Mercians, as a wartime casualty if we attribute her death at Tamworth to the diseases so prevalent in army camps in all periods of history. Similarly only in the *Historia Regum Brittaniae* do we read of a woman, Queen Cordelia, being captured on the battlefield. Only one woman, Juliana of Breteuil, is recorded to have wielded a weapon, and the incident in question was an attempted murder, not a pitched battle between opposing military forces. However, despite the fact that Anglo-Norman woman apparently did not fight in battle alongside their male contemporaries, there is no doubt that the chroniclers considered them capable of commanding the defense of besieged castles and directing the movements of armies in the field. In their minds, a woman did not need actual combat experience in order to be qualified to make strategic decisions.

Additional light can be shed on this question by examining the parallel case of another group of non-combatant commanders, male clerics who were forbidden by their religious vows to shed blood.[81] Florence of Worcester portrayed Wulfstan of Worcester (described as "a man of deep piety and dove-like

---

80 OV, 6:546.
81 I owe this insight to an unpublished paper by Randall Rogers, "Clerical Roles in Crusading Warfare," presented at the 2nd Annual International Conference of the Texas Medieval Association held September 11, 1992 at Southern Methodist University, Dallas, Texas. See

simplicity"[82]), as the leader of the city's defenders in 1088. The chronicler noted that when the defenders decided to cross the Severn River to meet the enemy, they first asked the bishop for his permission.[83] Similarly, Archbishop Thurstan of York rallied the men of Yorkshire and led them to victory against King David of Scotland at the battle of the Standard in 1138.[84] Richard of Hexham stated that although Thurstan himself was forced to stay behind because of his ill health, he sent the priests of his diocese to march with their people into battle.[85] St. Anselm participated even more directly in the command of the military forces that he was required as archbishop of Canterbury to supply to his feudal overlord, the king. Anselm sent knights to support William Rufus in his invasion of Wales in 1097, and the allegedly inferior quality of these forces was one of the sources of conflict between the king and the archbishop.[86] After their reconciliation, Anselm assumed military command of southeastern England while Rufus campaigned in the north.[87] In 1101, when Robert Curthose invaded England, the archbishop led the Canterbury knights to Pevensey and camped there in the field with them.[88] Anselm and other bishops routinely assumed command of the military forces that they were required to supply to their feudal overlord, even though they themselves were forbidden to shed blood in battle.

On a humbler level, Robert of Torigny noted that the castle of Arques, which surrendered to Geoffrey of Anjou in 1144, was held by a monk named William, who was killed by an arrow during the siege.[89] Similarly, when King Louis VI and Count Thibaut of Blois besieged Toury in 1111, Suger gave credit to a bald priest for rallying the troops and finding a way to breach the walls, thus accomplishing what the count himself had been unable to do.[90] Like the bishops, these lesser clerics also found themselves in positions of military command and proved themselves worthy of the charge. Thus, there is a striking parallel between the roles played by women and clerics in medieval warfare. Both groups rarely, if ever, actually fought in battle, for a variety of reasons such as advanced age, lack of physical strength, lack of training, religious vows and

also Walter Porges, "The Clergy, the Poor, and the Non-Combatants on the First Crusade," *Speculum* 21 (1946): 1–23.

[82] Florence of Worcester, 2:24.

[83] Ibid., 2:25.

[84] Ibid., 2:111; Robert of Torigny, *Chronicle*, 135; William of Newburgh, 34; Richard of Hexham, *Historia de Gestis Regis Stephani et de Bello Standardii (1135–1139)*, 3:160–62; Aelred of Rievaulx, *Relatio de Standardo*, 3:182. Henry of Huntingdon had the bishop of the Orkneys give a speech rallying the troops before the battle (262–63).

[85] Richard of Hexham, 161.

[86] Eadmer, 78.

[87] St. Anselm, nos. 191–92. For the importance of this incident, see Sally N. Vaughn, *Anselm of Bec and Robert of Meulan: The Innocence of the Dove and the Wisdom of the Serpent* (Berkeley, 1987), 191–92.

[88] Eadmer, 127.

[89] Robert of Torigny, *Chronicle*, 149.

[90] Suger, 138.

social prohibitions. However, it is clear that noblewomen, like clerics, acted as feudal overlords and therefore controlled military forces.

Perhaps seeking to justify leadership roles for twentieth-century women, modern historians have sometimes exaggerated the actual role played by medieval women in military combat. However, this analysis has shown that Anglo-Norman society did not link combat experience to leadership potential in the way that modern society does. The Anglo-Norman chroniclers clearly assumed not only that women were capable of making broad strategic decisions regarding the disposition of military forces, but also that their leadership in these matters would be accepted. A woman's presence with her troops was not only welcomed but provided them a powerful emotional rallying point. In Anglo-Norman society, unlike our own, non-combatants, whether women or clerics, were not barred from leadership positions that might include military command.

RURAL POPULATIONS AND THE EXPERIENCE OF WARFARE IN MEDIEVAL LOMBARDY: THE CASE OF PAVIA

Steven G. Lane

NICCOLÒ MACHIAVELLI, nourished on ancient examples and modern catastrophes, wrote in 1521 that a successful political entity, whether ruled by a republican or princely form of government, ought to base its strength on a "national" army; that is, one composed of "its own" troops. Reliance on the mercenary troops that had been in wide use by Italian cities and princes for the better part of two centuries, wrote Machiavelli, was no good. His distinction, in theory, was a simple one: some troops, perniciously, fought for money and made a career of it. The rest fought for love, and only out of necessity. It was with this latter sort of soldier that Machiavelli would have stocked his ideal militia.[1] Even though Machiavelli himself had helped in the organization of such militias in the Florentine countryside, in his writings, he seems studiously vague about the identity of these ideal, well-motivated soldiers. In writing of republics, he merely stated that one wanted an army of "citizens"; when treating of the prince, he only specified that such a figure wanted troops "of his own." In either case, Machiavelli failed to state with any precision from what sectors of society such soldiers should be drawn.

Machiavelli wrote near the end of the era of independent Italian city-states. By contrast, this paper will look at the beginning of that period, when the urban commune and its fighting force had recently appeared in Italy and when the "statehood" of these cities was still embryonic. Here, the question of political identification is even more slippery – these cities, after all, had barely sorted out their own political rhetoric at the time they began recruiting armies among the rural population.[2] This paper will closely examine this rural population.

---

[1] For Machiavelli's place in the late medieval "militia tradition" and his efforts at organizing a Florentine militia, see Charles C. Bayley, *War and Society in Renaissance Florence* (Toronto, 1961), 219–316. See also Quentin Skinner, *Machiavelli* (New York, 1981), 31–34, 74–77; Gennaro Sasso, *Niccolò Machiavelli*, 2 vols. (Bologna, 1993), 1:623–51.

[2] The earliest magistrates, known as "consuls," of the new Italian communes, were often associated with older power-holders during the decades surrounding the establishment of communal government, between 1080 and 1120. At Pavia, the earliest consuls, between 1112 and 1124, were largely drawn from a group with strong associations to Pavia's bishop. The consuls themselves, at Pavia and elsewhere, frequently met in the cathedral church of their

Northern Italy

The sense of identification which brought citizens into the ranks of cavalry and footmen seems clear; but how were rural dwellers (emphatically, non-citizens) to be brought into urban armies, and what role were they to play there? Machiavelli himself, centuries later, was opposed to outright conscription, urging instead an appropriate mixture of coercion and persuasion. We must consider here what mix of force and blandishment attended the early entry of rural inhabitants into the urban militias, with special reference to current research on the city of Pavia in the twelfth and thirteenth centuries. How important were these rural levies to the urban fighting force? What role did they play in war? Who fought, and how did they receive their training? What were the broader effects of warfare on rural populations?

The first century of communal history (roughly, the twelfth century) is sometimes thought to have been relatively pacific – true (it is said), there was a struggle with the emperor, but this war was the product of misplaced imperial ambition, which the cities successfully laid to rest. This century, however, was a

city, with separate communal "palaces" only beginning to appear in the latter half of the twelfth century. Out of a large literature, see Antonio Ivan Pini, *Città, comuni e corporazioni nel medioevo italiano* (Bologna, 1986), 70–76, for the "tentative" character of early communal government and the association of consuls and bishops. See also, if you will, S. Lane, "The Territorial Expansion of a Political Community: Pavia 1100–1300," University of Chicago dissertation, 1995, pp. 92–97.

time of intra-urban warfare every bit as intense as the struggles which would also later characterize the Renaissance. When the northern cities were not fighting jointly against Emperor Frederick I Barbarossa (1152–90), they were fighting locally against their neighbors, or regionally against opposing urban leagues.[3] The single overriding factor conditioning both these local wars and the increasing involvement of the rural population in warfare, was the creation of those urban territories, which so fascinated bishop Otto of Freising on his first trip to Italy.[4] In retrospect, we refer to these compact territories as "states" but, at the time, there was little precise language available to describe them. For a while, cities relied on older terms such as "county" and "diocese," before turning to a language evocative of sheer power: by the thirteenth century the favored term was "district," which meant simply the effective limit of a city's armed strength.[5] These districts often corresponded at their centers to older counties and dioceses, but at their fluid edges they were won by force. It was often these battles over territory which occasioned local war, in which tactics ranged from rapid raids and ambushes with a few dozen troops on each side, to the merciless destruction of entire cities, such as those twice visited by Milan on its much smaller neighbor Lodi.[6] This creation of urban "districts" had two significant consequences for the inhabitants of rural settlements. In the first place it entailed their more or less compulsory participation in the urban military. In the second place, it exposed their homes and lands to a continually increasing risk of destruction.

An important source of information on these questions is a set of depositions taken during a dispute between Pavia and its neighbor Piacenza, in 1184. The two cities had struggled for several decades to control the rural settlements lying between them. The 1184 dispute concerned five small settlements south of the Po, in the eastern region of the Oltrepò Pavese, in a border area between the two cities' zones of influence.[7] What these documents and others tell us about the

---

3 Out of the very extensive literature on the urban leagues of northern Italy, and their wars among themselves and with the emperor, see, for example, Gina Fasoli, "La Lega Lombarda: antecedenti, formazione, strutture," in *Probleme des 12. Jahrhunderts* (Stuttgart, 1968).

4 Otto of Freising, *The Deeds of Frederick Barbarossa*, ed. and trans. Charles C. Mierow (Toronto, 1994), pp. 125ff., bk. 2, chap. 13.

5 The terminology is well discussed in Aldo A. Settia, "Il distretto pavese nell'età comunale: la creazione de un territorio," in *Storia de Pavia*, vol. 3, pt. 1. I am grateful to Prof. Settia for the opportunity to consult a typescript of the essay.

6 See Ferdinand Güterbock, *Das Geschichtswerk des Otto Morena und seiner Fortsetzer über die Taten Friedrichs I. in der Lombardei*, MGH SRG ns, no. 7 (Berlin, 1930), 1–6, 34–36.

7 The settlements, four of which still exist, were Monticelli (Monticelli Pavese, now north of the Po), "plebs de Parpanese" or "Parpanese et plebs" (now Parpanese and Pievetta), Mondònico, S. Marzano, and "Ulmus" (somewhere between modern Parpanese and Castel S. Giovanni, possibly in the area of Cascina Olmellina). The depositions are preserved in the Archivio Storico Civico of Pavia, in the *Pergamene Comunali*, and are published by Luigi C. Bollea, *Documenti degli archivi di Pavia relativi alla storia de Voghera (929–1300)* (Pinerolo, 1909), nos. 45–58. Ettore Falconi and Roberta Falconi, eds., *Il Registrum Magnum del*

role of rural inhabitants in urban armies and the broader effects of local war on rural population must be discussed.

The 1184 depositions allow us to look back on fifty years of urban aggrandizement in the countryside. Initially, this pressure appears to have involved only the peaceful collection of taxes, but by the 1160s both Pavia and Piacenza had turned to armed coercion in order to install governors in these small Oltrepò villages. Despite some scholarly suggestions that the first century or so of urban dominance of the countryside was relatively peaceful, here at least the story was different.[8]

These local settlements often strongly resisted the direct imposition of urban government. Their resistance, however, is less clear when it comes to indirect exactions such as taxes and military levies. To return to Machiavelli, we might ask whether there was yet any sense of political identification in the countryside which could have induced rural inhabitants to fight under urban banners unsupported by the threat of physical force. By 1184, the answer seems to be a qualified "yes." At the very least, dwellers in these fringe settlements had come to accept the idea that there was a "land" or "district" of Pavia, and that they somehow "belonged" to it. On the other hand, this "belonging" was often understood in a limited or negative fashion. One of the litmus tests imposed in 1184 to determine which city should control a given settlement hinged upon deciding the direction in which the inhabitants fled when war threatened. A rural inhabitant's territory, then, was where he hid when he had to. By the 1180s, in the borderland, one also had to choose which city's currency would prevail in the local market. Further definition was added by occasional economic embargoes, such as those which forbade export of grain from a city's territory in times of shortage or famine. The urban territory was thus a fact well-established in the imagination of rural populations.

How did a rural levy work, and how important was it in swelling the ranks of urban armies? Such rural troops were not conscripts in the narrow sense. Those who gave depositions in 1184 complained of many things, but burdensome military service and large-scale conscription were not among them. The documents suggest that the levy was assessed like a tax, with each settlement assigned to contribute at common expense a fixed number of various kinds of troops. Such

comune de Piacenza (Milan, 1984), nos. 44, 60 and 62 pertain to the same case. The case is mentioned by Aldo A. Settia, Comuni in guerra: armi ad eserciti nell'Italia delle città (Bologna, 1993), p. 107, no. 67 in his discussion of the role of rustici in urban armies. For a fuller discussion see also Lane, Territorial Expansion, 173–211.

[8] Pini, 77–78, has recently claimed that armed subjection of the contado was virtually non-existent in the first century of the commune's existence. In the case of Pavia, the city had begun to impose taxes as early as thirty years after the first mention of consuls. Another ten years would see the first uses of force to assure the city's authority over rural communities. Nor are these examples peculiar to Pavia, since Pavian action was paralleled by similar behavior on the part of its neighbor Piacenza. I hope to analyze the evidence of these depositions much more fully in a large treatment of lordship and rural communities in the Pavian countryside.

levies may have been drawn from large areas of the countryside with each local settlement contributing its share according to its relative wealth, presumably as determined by the urban assessors. The numerous witnesses who recalled having "paid their share" suggest that these military obligations were routinely assessed in cash. If we adopt Maitland's definition of "unfreedom" as the degree of discretion an overlord exercised when imposing services or exacting payments from his dependents, then one would be hard-put to argue that the services imposed by the cities contributed greatly to the "unfreedom" of the rural population. Military service of some sort was part of a package of obligations negotiated between rural settlements and the cities of Pavia and Piacenza from about the 1140s. I say negotiated only because these and other obligations were characteristically expressed in formal oaths which were periodically renewed. In this sense they were not merely imposed from above, but publicly formalized.

The obligations themselves were not particularly heavy. A levy might be the result of the city's own plans for war, or, in the late twelfth century, the result of the demand of a superior such as the emperor. We know, for example, that Pavia imposed a levy on its own countryside in 1162 in order to furnish troops for the emperor's siege of Milan.[9] The call went out first for skilled warriors such as crossbowmen. Either shortly before or shortly after the capitulation of the city, Barbarossa called for manual laborers to aid in levelling Milan's walls. In each case, the burden on individual settlements was mild: in a typical case, Pieve di Parpanese sent two archers to the siege of Milan, and five laborers to its destruction.

Numbers such as these allow us to make some rough guesses as to the numerical contribution of the countryside to urban warfare. We have a tax return from 1181 covering two-thirds of the Pavian countryside; with the exception of one large settlement, the returns for Oltrepò are missing, but we do have sporadic earlier figures for Oltrepò settlements, including Parpanese, where troop numbers are also available.[10] Three assumptions are necessary in order to arrive at our estimate. The first is that Parpanese's assessment was higher in 1181 than the £15 it paid in 1154. (This assumption will yield a more conservative military contribution in the end.) The second assumption is that the two-thirds tax return of 1181, totally about £1700, really does show about two-thirds of the total tax rendered (there seems no reason to guess that the Oltrepò settlements were fantastically wealthier than other areas of the countryside). The last assumption is that there was a relationship between a town's tax assessment and the number of troops it was asked to provide to the levy. Here again, tax assessments seem the most likely basis on which military assessments were made. If the entire Pavian *contado* contributed around £2400 in 1181, and the value of Parpanese's contribution rose to £20 between 1154 and 1181, a rough calculation suggests the

---

9 This levy is widely mentioned by the witnesses of 1184.
10 For the document of 1181, which gives returns from a tax known as the *fodrum* (certainly derived from the imperial tax of the same name), see Bollea, doc. 40.

Pavian countryside might have yielded upwards of 600 laborers for the destruction of Milan. For specialized soldiers the numbers are smaller; Parpanese contributed only two archers to the siege of Milan, which suggests a total levy of perhaps 250. By comparison, if we may trust the figures of a chronicler from Lodi (who was probably an eyewitness), the communal army of Milan at the city's surrender in 1162 numbered 300 cavalry and 1000 footsoldiers.[11] These calculations are guesswork, but still suggest that a concerted effort to raise troops and money in the countryside must have considerably swelled the ranks of urban armies.

Where did these rural recruits fit into the urban army? The classic civic militia of an Italian city was divided into cavalry and foot, a social as well as a functional distinction.[12] Rural levies do not appear to have included mounted warriors, but they provided almost everything else. The tasks such men performed were often humble ones. Inhabitants of some of the disputed settlements were routinely called on by Piacenza in the 1140s and the 1150s for wars against Parma, where they acted as "cart-men," apparently meaning overseers of the army's baggage train (and providers of the necessary oxen).[13] Others worked on urban fortifications and earthworks. But the rural settlements sent skilled fighters as well. We most often hear of archers of various kinds. It is tempting to conclude that these settlements might have pooled their resources to train local militias, and that, consequently when they sent their own men, they sent a more proficient force than one totally comprised of untrained peasants, armed only with mattocks and scythes.

We know that the knights and footmen of the cities engaged in their own war-games, often quite furious, as a form of training. The depositions of 1184 hint tantalizingly at something similar in the countryside. "Some men of the *pieve*," said a witness, "have weapons in common with some men of Parpanese, and they have a standard-bearer, to whom they are bound by oath." Further, we hear of settlements meeting the military obligations by furnishing their own men, under local leaders. This in turn suggests the existence of a force akin to a local militia, perhaps responsible for defense and local security. The urban levy must have provoked a varied response in the countryside, with some places sending a few paid archers, others sending a small body of local troops which may have fought under its own banner.

None of this sounds very threatening for the local population. The documents convey no sense that service in urban armies was a life-risking proposition for rural troops. In fact, intra-urban warfare often placed a premium on capturing the enemy for ransom rather than killing him outright, and chronicle depictions of battles are as likely to end with tallies of prisoners and the prices they fetched, as they are to end with body counts. The wealthy urban cavalry were by far the most tempting target for ransom, and rural footmen must have been low

---

11 Güterbock, 153.
12 For this distinction, see Settia, 93–114.
13 For a broader discussion of the "cart-men", see Settia, 115–26.

on this scale of esteem. Rural witnesses occasionally remembered the names of urban nobles who had lost their lives to war, but none ever complained of having lost brothers or sons in battle. On the other hand, the constitution of urban territories could prove to be a threat to rural populations and appears to have contributed to a decline in local security which, in certain areas of the countryside, was precipitous.

A thoroughly ordinary document of lease issued by the archpriest of Olubra in 1233 finished with an ominous provision: the stipulated rent, he said, need not be paid "in the event there is war between Pavia and Piacenza or between the emperor and Piacenza, of such severity that the place of Olubra is not, and cannot be, inhabited."[14] Nor were such provisions, for a war so devastating as to leave large population centers of the *contado* uninhabited, new in the 1230s; a witness of 1184 recounted that, during an imperial expedition against Piacenza, buildings in S. Marzano were burned and the latter town was abandoned, such that "no one stayed in S. Marzano except the abbot and his household." Documents with provisions similar to this lease are numerous in the monastic and private archives of the period, clustering in areas of endemic friction between cities, for example in the northern areas of Pavian territory in the direction of Milan, or in the borderland with Piacenza. In such areas, in times of tension, it was common practice for those leasing property to make explicit provisions for the possibility of wars which might disrupt the use of that property, or lay it waste completely. As the countryside's contribution to the urban economy grew, so did the strategic value of scorched-earth tactics against the enemy's *contadini*.

We do not hear of these raids causing notable loss of life in the countryside. The witnesses were much more apt to dwell on material losses and sometimes spoke of the various armies simply as "brigands." Indeed, there was little in a rural settlement that could not be carried off. We hear of livestock being driven away, hoarded grain being dug up and removed, even of the wooden buildings themselves being disassembled by marauding Piacenzans, the wood being then taken away in ships. In the worst situations the local church, often a repository for the laity's most precious goods, would be robbed. Some, but not all of these goods, might later be recovered by the intercession of well-placed friends and overlords of one city or the other.

It is clear from such episodes that the ambiguous position of the border settlements left them open to destructive reprisals on the part of military leaders who plundered first and asked questions afterward, if ever. And, though public oaths governed the services owed by the rural population to the neighboring cities, these arrangements do not seem to have provided any explicit security against raiding and destruction. Another sort of agreement was necessary, referred to in the depositions as *fidantia*, a word meaning simply a promise of safe conduct.

---

14 Archivio Collegiata di Castel S. Giovanni, document of 4 April 1233. On this archive, see Giovanni Agnelli, "Archivio della collegiata di Castel S. Giovanni de Olubra," *Archivio Storico per le Provincie Parmensi* 1 (1892): 1–23.

The two most notable of these agreements were ones made by the men of S. Marzano with the bishop of Piacenza between 1164 and 1168 and by the men of Mondònico with Pavia and the emperor, probably in the wake of the expedition mentioned above. These safeconducts were not given freely; the bishop received an unspecified sum for the one which he granted; and the Pavians and the emperor were given a considerable amount of grain and money in theirs. The *pieve* also attempted to make an agreement with the emperor, the payment for which was a fixed sum of grain for every pair of oxen.

Older references to *fidantiae* mention periods when certain rural locations had been under the protection of both cities at once. When a Piacenzan aristo- crat first appeared in Parpanese around 1159, the denizens complained of the consuls he tried to force on them, saying that neither city had ever imposed consuls there at any time in the past, and that the people of Parpanese were accustomed to enjoying safeguard from both cities. Sometime between 1162 and 1164, the town of Mondònico appealed to the Pavians on the basis of an old safeconduct, to try to secure remission of a tax imposed by Piacenza.

The continuing efforts of these rural settlements to gain some measure of security for their goods and households was yet another measure of the danger to which their ambiguous border status exposed the inhabitants. Even the outlay of substantial sums of locally-collected money was not always enough to spare the rural populace. Henricus Ursi of S. Marzano claimed that in 1184 he had once returned from a few days' visit to a mill he owned to find that his village had been burned by imperial troops in his absence. But such experiences were surely not confined to the borderlands. As the dependence of rural population on the cities grew, so too did the dangers to which they were exposed. These dangers did not end with the erection of urban territories; before long, civil strife within the cities themselves spilled over into the countryside. By 1250, in the small communities of the mountainous Oltrepò, the most important obliga- tions of rural populations were to garrison the local fortifications and to stand guard over common lands.

A grand political experiment the Italian city-state may have been, but for the farmer and the rural landlord, it meant something quite different: an ever- increasing readiness for war.

Part IV

WAR AT SEA

THE FIRE-SHIP OF AL-SĀLIH AYYŪB
AND MUSLIM USE OF "GREEK FIRE"[1]

Douglas Haldane

On the 15th of Sha'ban A.H. 647 (23 November, 1249), during the battle of Mansura, Sultan al-Malik al-Sālih Najm al-Dīn Ayyūb died from complications arising from gangrene, bladder disfunction, and sores in the lungs. He was forty-two.[2] His remarkable wife, Shajur al-Durr, concealed his death for three months, preserving the morale of the Muslim army defending Egypt from Louis IX's first crusade, and allowing al-Sālih's son, Turan Shah, time to assume command. According to al-Maqrīzī (d. A.H. 845/A.D. 1441),[3] Shajur al-Durr secretly sent al-Sālih's body back to Cairo in a *harrāqa* or fire-ship.[4]

Maqrīzī's explicit use of the term *harrāqa*, rather than any one of many other Arab ship designations, raises questions about Muslim fire-ships. What about the *harrāqa*'s construction and operation made it suitable as a funerary vessel? And how did it compare to Byzantine fire-ships using what Byzantine authors called "sea-fire" or "prepared-fire" and non-Greek authors called "Greek Fire"?[5] The incendiary "Greek Fire" played a central role in the balance of power in the Arab-Byzantine arms race. Its history serves as a lens to examine the broader field of medieval Mediterranean naval history.

At this point a clarification of terminology is in order. The term "fire-ship" here means a ship equipped with a device to shoot the incendiary liquid "Greek Fire," rather than a ship sailed into an enemy fleet either on fire or as an incendiary bomb. Arab and European historians of the Crusades broadened the term

---

[1] This paper was originally presented at the 1993 Middle East Studies Association (MESA) conference. Thanks go to Sherman Jackson and Frederick van Doorninck Jr. for their encouragement and assistance, Paul E. Chevedden for providing a forum for the paper and his valuable criticism, Warren Schultz for acting as my second at MESA so that I could continue my research in Cairo, and Michael Bates for pointing out the need to qualify the difference between Muslim fire-ships and lighters.

[2] Taqi al-Dīn, "Ahmad ibn Ali al-Maqrīzī," *al-Khitat*, 2 vols. (Bulaq, 1854), 2:374; Felix Klein-Franke, "What was the Fatal Disease of al-Malik al-Salih Nagm al Dīn Ayyūb?" in *Studies in Islamic History and Civilization*, ed. Moshe Sharon (Leiden, 1986), 156; Jamal al-Din Yusuf ibn Taghrī Birdī Abū al-Muhāsin, *al-Nujūm al-Zāhira fi Mulūk Misr wa al-Qāhira*, 6 vols. (Cairo, 1956–1969), 6:328.

[3] Years of the Muslim calendar are listed first; *anno domini* is listed second.

[4] Al-Maqrīzī, 2:374.

[5] Alphonse Dain, "Appellatons grèques du feu grégois," in *Mélanges de philologie, de littérature et d'histoire anciennes offerts à A. Ernout* (Paris, 1940), 121ff.

"Greek Fire" to include any incendiary device. In this paper, the term "Greek Fire" means the original liquid incendiary, shot at enemy vessels from a flame-throwing tube mounted on a ship.

Use of incendiaries in Mediterranean warfare dates back to at least the classical Greek period.[6] What made "Greek Fire" unique, in its sensational debut during the Arab assault on Constantinople in 674, was that it could be directed as a stream of fire at an enemy. Callinicus, a Syrian refugee architect newly arrived in Constantinople, developed the weapon only the year before the assault.[7] Emperor Constantine Pogonatus fitted out some *dromon* galleys with cauldrons carrying the new incendiary while other *dromons* bore siphons for firing the mixture. The new incendiary burnt the Arab fleet "ship and man" and saved Constantinople.[8] "Greek Fire" once again saved the city in the final Arab assault of 717–718.

Understandably, the Byzantine state kept the mechanics and components of the formidable weapon a closely guarded secret. Callinicus's descendants alone prepared the mixture and only in Constantinople.[9] Emperor Leo VI, in his early tenth-century *Naumachia*, states: "Once the strategies are understood well, they are able to be counteracted or counterdevised by the enemy, but until use, keep each device secret."[10] The Arabs exploited failed Byzantine weapons; it was doubly important to keep an effective weapon out of their hands. Severe punishment, even divine wrath, was promised anyone leaking the secret to the enemy.[11] These threats however did not stop dissemination; and by the early ninth century the secret was out.

By at least 220/835, if not before, the Aghlabids of North Africa controlled fire-ships.[12] Euphemius, the renegade commander of the Byzantine fleet in Sicily, may have used the secret of "Greek Fire" as payment for the Arab army he needed to besiege Syracuse in A.D. 827.[13] The Spanish Ummayads had

6   John R. Partington, *A History of Greek Fire and Gunpowder* (Cambridge, 1960), 1.
7   Theophanes, *The Chronicle of Theophanes*, trans. Harry Turtledove (Philadelphia, 1982), 46–47; Theophanes, "Chronographia," ed. Johann Classen, 2 vols. (Bonn, 1889), 1:542, 5; S.D. Cheronis, "Chemical Warfare in the Middle Ages. Kallinikos' 'Prepared Fire,' " *Journal of Chemical Education* 14.8 (1937): 362.
8   Theophanes, 1:542, chaps. 6–9.
9   Georgius Cedrenus, *Synopsis Historion I*, in R.J. Forbes, *More Studies in Early Petroleum History* (Leiden, 1959), 80.
10 Leo VI, *Naumachia*, ed. Alphonse Dain (Paris, 1943), 31, 72. By A.D. 750, the Egyptian fleet had counteracted the effect of "Greek Fire" by smearing a combination of cotton and mineral substances on their hulls, Severus ibn Muqaffa, *History of the Patriarchs of the Egyptian Church*, ed. and trans. Yakub A. Masih and O.H.E. Burmeister, 4 vols. (Cairo, 1943); Wladyslaw B. Kubiak, "The Byzantine Attack on Damietta in 853 and the Egyptian Navy in the 9th Century," *Byzantion* 40 (1960): 47.
11 Constantine Porphyrogenitus, *De Administrando Imperio*, ed. Gregory Moravcsik, trans. R.J.H. Jenkins (Washington DC, 1967), 13.84.10–23–85, 1–21; Forbes, 82.
12 A.A. Vasiliev, *Byzance et les Arabes*, 2 vols. (Brussels, 1935), 2:375; Al-Marrakeshi ibn Idharī, *al Bayān al-Mūghrib fi ijtisar ajbar muluk al-Andalus wa al-Mūgrib*, 2 vols. (Leiden, 1948), 1:105–86.
13 Michel Canard, "Byzantium and the Muslim World to the Middle of the Eleventh

learned the secret by 229/844.[14] Perhaps the Byzantines conceded the secret to the Spanish Umayyads as part of the alliance discussions against the Aghlabids in 839–40.[15]

The Aghlabids valued their new weapon; at least two fire-ships accompanied the fleet of Abd Allah ibn al-Aghlab on his journey from North Africa to Palermo when he became the first Arab governor of Sicily. To the Arabs' great distress, the Byzantine navy captured and fled with an Aghalbid fire-ship off this island. According to ibn Idhari, the Arabs gave chase in another fire-ship until all hope of recovery was lost.[16] The persistence of the Arab pursuit is explained by the fact that they lost not only the flame-throwing gear, but also the incendiary mixture. Although the gear could be replaced on site, Gebel Zeit on the Red Sea was the closest source of the petroleum that probably formed the base of the distillate mixture.

Arab possession of "Greek Fire" probably evened the balance of power in the struggle for control of Sicily and southern Italy. The battle for Sicily was waged primarily on land; the victories at sea, without an accurate accounting, superficially appear to have gone as often to the Arabs as to the Byzantines. Moreover, the secret of "Greek Fire" was part of the Aghalbid legacy that the Fatimids inherited with the establishment of their dynasty in North Africa during the early ninth century. The Fatimid fleet was outfitted with "Greek Fire" in preparation for the dynasty's expansion into the eastern Mediterranean.[17]

The Fatimids made extensive use of fire-ships, particularly in guarding spice merchants engaged in the India trade. The Fatimid vizier al-ʿAfdal bolstered the fleet at the port of Aydhāb with five *harrāqas* in 512/1118 after a mercantile dispute with the governor of Mecca.[18] Despite the destruction of the Fatimid fleet at Fustāt in 1169, fire-ship technology and the fire-ships themselves survived in outlying ports for Ayyubid exploitation. By the end of the Fatimid period, "Greek Fire" technology was widely known; its use remained extremely specialized, however, and required trained professionals.

In an attempt to solve some of the mystery surrounding "Greek Fire," J. Haldon and M. Byrne reconstructed a form of Byzantine flame-throwing apparatus based on evidence from two sources: a late ninth-century Latin

Century," in *The Cambridge Medieval History*, ed. John M. Hussey, 8 vols. (Cambridge, 1966), 4 pt. 1:728.

14 Ekkehard Eickhoff, *Seekrieg und Seepolitik zwischen Islam und Abendland* (1954; Berlin, 1966), 197.

15 Canard, 730. "Greek Fire" technology soon spread throughout the Arab Mediterranean world; fire-ships also appear in Egypt in the mid-ninth century A.D., Ibn Muqaffa, 2.1:62; (Arabic) 43.

16 Ibn Idharî, *al-Bayân*, 1:106.

17 Michel Canard, "L'impérialisme des Fatimides et leur propagande," *Annales del'Institut d'Etudes Orient*, 6:188.

18 Al-Maqrīzī, *'Atāz al-Khunafā biʿAkhbār al 'Umma al-Fâtimīn al-Khulafa*, ed. J. al-Din Shayyal, H. Muhammad, M-H.M. Ahmad, 3 vols. (Cairo, 1967–73), 3:57.

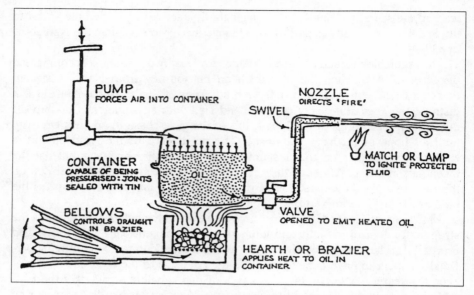

PUMP
FORCES AIR INTO CONTAINER

NOZZLE
DIRECTS 'FIRE'

SWIVEL

CONTAINER
CAPABLE OF BEING
PRESSURISED: JOINTS
SEALED WITH TIN

OIL

MATCH OR LAMP
TO IGNITE PROJECTED
FLUID

BELLOWS
CONTROLS DRAUGHT
IN BRAZIER

VALVE
OPENED TO EMIT HEATED OIL

HEARTH OR BRAZIER
APPLIES HEAT TO OIL IN
CONTAINER

Haldon and Byrne's reconstruction of the Byzantine "Greek Fire"
flame-thrower (p. 95). Reprinted by permission

manuscript containing Leo VI's *Naumachia* and Anna Comnena's twelfth-century *Alexiad*.[19]

Haldon and Byrne suggest that a cauldron was filled with an incendiary liquid and sealed. Then, it was placed on a pre-heating hearth in the ship's bow. Connected to the cauldron was the siphon, or pump, for putting its contents under pressure. Operation of the siphon forced the mixture through a hose to a tube that ejected the liquid.

The *siphonator*, a trained "pump man," or more appropriately, "fire-man," operated the device and ignited the liquid at the tube's mouth when firing.[20] A good *siphonator* could shoot his fire in any direction he wished, "often downwards or laterally", as the terrified Pisans learned in 1100 when they met the fleet of Alexis I off Rhodes.[21] Alternatively, flame-throwers could be mounted along the ship's sides. Flame-throwers in this position enabled the fire-man to rake enemy vessels as his own ship passed through their ranks rather than wait until his ship lay upwind of the enemy.[22]

---

[19] Forbes, 83; Leo VI, *Naumachia*, 20; Anna Comnena, *The Alexiad*, trans. E.A.S. Dawes (New York, 1967), 293; Annae Comnenae, *Alexias*, ed. A. Reifferscheid (Leipzig, 1884), 1:134, lines 21–22; John Haldon and Michael Byrne, "A Possible Solution to the Problem of Greek Fire," *Byzantinische Zeitschrift* 70 (1977): 91–100.

[20] Ibid., 96.

[21] Anna Comnena, 293; Annae Comnenae, 1:134, lines 21–22.

[22] Emmerich Pászthory, "Über das 'Griechische Feuer'," *Antike Welt* 17 (1986): 32.

The closest Arab equivalent to Byzantine *siphonators* were the "naphtha throwers" (*naffātūn*). Al-Tabari (d. 310/923), records that three *naffātūn* were assigned to each forty-five-man crew of a *bāraja*, another form of fire-ship.[23] *Naffātūn* were also used to quell the Zanj, or Zanzibaran, slave revolt in the Basra salt flats during the first half of the ninth century. Covered with talc to protect them from the adhesive naphtha, these men "sprayed fire" on the Zanj and their houses.[24] Ibn al-Athīr (d. 630/1233) does not say how they accomplished this, but, in this case, the *naffātūn* appear to be on land using a hand-held device.

These devices may have been similar to hand siphons mentioned by Leo VI as "recently developed by our state" and used soon afterwards against the Arabs at Dvin in 325/927. These hand-held tubes could spray the enemy with adhesive incendiary liquid. Much later, the Mamluk sultan Qalawūn's troops used them against one of the last Crusader strongholds at al-Marqab in 684/1285.[25] As Ibn ʿAbd al-Zāhir (d. 692/1293) relates, among the iron weapons at al-Marqab were "flame-throwing tubes . . . such as exist only in the royal magazines and arsenals."[26] These tubes may have been a Byzantine concession to Qalawūn for renewal of the treaty against the Crusaders.[27]

Although the Byzantines failed to stop the proliferation of "Greek Fire," they succeeded in guarding the secret of the incendiary's composition to this day. No Byzantine text details the components of the incendiary. By contrast, Muslim authors were not as reticent.

During the late twelfth century Murda ibn Ali al-Tarsusi wrote a manual for Saladīn describing a variety of incendiary weapons, many called "Greek Fire" by the Crusaders.[28] One recipe called for a distillate of tar, resin, sandarac, powdered sulphur, clarified dolphin fat, and goat kidney fat. The mixture was then sprinkled with sulphur, poured into a clay vessel wrapped in wool, placed on a mangonel, lit, and thrown.[29]

Joinville's history of Louis IX's first crusade describes the effect:

> This is what the Greek fire was like: it came straight at you, as big as a vinegar barrel, with a tail of fire behind it as long as a long spear. It made such a noise as it came that it seemed like thunder from heaven; it looked like a dragon

---

[23] Abū Jaʿfar Muhammad ibn Jarīr al-Tabari, *Tārīkh al-Umam wa al-Mulūk*, ed. De Goeje Foundation, 16 vols. (Leiden, 1879–1892), 3:1582.
[24] ʿIzz al-Dīn Abū al-Hasan ibn Muhammad Ibn al-Athīr, *al-Kāmil fi al-Tārīkh*, 7 vols. (Beirut, 1965), 7:383.
[25] Leo VI, 30, 65; Vasiliev, 2:150.
[26] Leo VI, 30, 65; Muhī al-Dīn Ibn ʿAbd al-Zāhir, *Tashrīf al-Iyān wa al-ʿAusūr fi Sīrat al-Malik al-Mansūr*, ed. Murād Kāmil (Cairo, 1921), 78; Francesco Gabrieli, *Arab Historians of the Crusades*, trans. E.J. Costello (New York, 1969), 335.
[27] Michel Canard, "Le Traité de 1281 Michel Paleologue et le Sultan Qalaʿun, Qalqashandi Subh al aʾsha XIV," *Byzantion* 10 (1935): 670.
[28] Claude Cahen, "Un Traité d'amurerie composé pour Saladin," *Bulletin d'Etudes Orientales* 12 (1948): 103–63.
[29] Cahen, 123.

flying through the air. It gave so intense a light that in camp you could see as clearly as by daylight in the great mass of flame which illuminated everything. Three times that night they bombarded us with Greek fire, and four times they fired it from the revolving crossbow.[30]

Al-Tarsusi's preparations do not call for firing the mixture from a tube as would produce the ball of flame that Joinville initially describes, instead he calls for the use of a mangonel, perhaps Joinville's "revolving crossbow." Al-Tarsusi provided another incendiary formula used against ships. The oil was heated to the verge of combustion, and poured on to the water. When the water carrying the incendiary surrounded the enemy ships it was ignited. The Muslim navy probably did not have the wood resources to afford using a ship as a floating bomb, but rather resorted to formulas like al-Tarsusi's and to *harrāqas* like those deployed by the Mamluk amirs that al-Qalqashandī (d. 821/1418) says contained "a cannon that throws oil on what is in front of [it]."[31]

Some of the earliest references to *harrāqas* in the ninth century speak of their use on the Tigris as transports, lighters, and ships of war against the Zanj.[32] Not all of these were active fire-ships; the term *harrāqa* probably had a broader meaning designating the class of ship that was most often fitted with flame-throwing gear if needed. In later references, *harrāqas* also appear to be smaller boats. For example, engineers building a dam to protect Fustāt from flooding in 749/1348 surveyed the project from a *harrāqa*.[33] Al-Maqrīzī reports that, in the mid-thirteenth century, the Mamluk sultan Baibars rebuilt the Egyptian fleet with forty galleys, equipped with castles to throw fire, and many *harrāqas*.[34] Perhaps the latter, being smaller, were more easily produced. Al-Maqrīzī also recounts that during the siege of Damietta in 618/1221, the Muslims used a "big fire ship", suggesting most others were smaller.[35]

During Louis IX's first crusade, Muslims carried ships on camel back to Bahr al-Mahalla, a backwater of the Nile in the Frankish rear. Later, the Franks captured seven Muslim fire-ships on the same body of water, but not before "the Muslims escaped with their gear."[36] Such *harrāqas* may have been simple craft, small enough to load onto camel-back, at least in pieces, and the flame throwing gear was not permanently mounted, but movable within the vessel or from it entirely.

The *harrāqa* was probably a smaller version of the Byzantine *cheland*, a small galley. In preparation for his 945/6 campaign against Crete, Nicephoras Phocas fitted *chelands* with "Greek Fire" rather than the larger *dromons*, because the former's small size and maneuverability made it a more effective

---

30 John of Joinville, *The Life of St. Louis*, trans. Reni Hague (London, 1955), 75.
31 al Qalqashandi, *Subh al-'Asha fi Sina'at al-Insha'*, 4 vols. (Beirut, 1987), 4:49.
32 Ibn al-Athīr, 7:139.
33 Al-Maqrīzī, *al-Khitat*, 2:167.
34 Ibid., 2:194–95.
35 Ibid., 1:218.
36 Ibn Wasil, *Mufarraj al-Kurub*, in Gabrieli, 292–93.

fire-ship.[37] Al-Tabarī's forty-five-man *bārja* dating to 251/866, was less than half the size of Leo VI's smaller *dromons* built fifty years later.[38]

We can now see that Shajar al-Durr's choice of a *harrāqa* to return the body of al-Sālih Ayyub is telling. As a small ship, the *harrāqa* minimized the number of people involved and maintained the secret of al-Sālih's death. If cornered by Frankish forces, it could defend itself with one or two men armed with "Greek Fire." Being fast, the *harrāqa* was more likely to elude Frankish patrols. Because *harrāqas* were numerous and a common sight in many contexts, one alone would not cause suspicion.

Arab and Byzantine sources complement each other on the subject of "Greek Fire". Where Byzantine texts readily supply us with details concerning the flame-thrower's mechanism, they maintain the secret of the incendiary composition. Muslim sources, on the other hand, readily supply us with information about a variety of naptha-based compounds (some of which may have been used with flame-throwers), but fail to describe the delivery system. Medieval texts suggest indirectly that the Muslims used "Greek Fire" from at least as early as the ninth century. Its proliferation among the Aghlabids in North Africa made it available to the Fatimids before their expansion into the eastern Mediterranean. However, the only direct evidence for flame-throwing tubes on board ship comes in the late-fifteenth century.

Any discussion of the proliferation of "Greek Fire" among the Muslims must be qualified by the fact that the qualities of "Greek Fire" limited its areas of deployment. On land, the Muslims favored broader use of bomb-type incendiaries like those devised by al-Tarsusi. Anyone with a lit match and a strong arm or catapult could use them, as they did not require any special skill. In siege warfare, mobility was at a premium and "Greek Fire" flame-throwers were not easily moved. Accuracy, on the other hand, was not a great concern because large stores of bombs were available and any incendiary that fell short or long was bound to create some collateral damage. A miss with a bomb at sea was as good as no bomb at all.

"Greek Fire" was well suited for use at sea since it could deliver devastating blows where pin-point accuracy was not called for, and the incendiary and gear required a minimum of storage space on already crowded galleys. But "Greek Fire" was essentially a highly combustible material under heat and pressure and subject to explosion. Fire-men, the Byzantine *siphonators* and Muslim *naffātūn*, had extremely specialized and hazardous assignments and were probably few in number. Since it took a crew of between one and three people to operate a "Greek Fire" flame-thrower, the deployment of fire-men through a fleet was much easier to accomplish than throughout the ranks of an army holding a city under siege.

---

[37] George Finlay, *A History of Greece*, 7 vols. (Oxford, 1887), 2:316.

[38] Ibn al-Athīr, 3:1582; Leo VI, 20, 8–9. Fatimid fire-ships of the mid-tenth century also ranged to Leo's smaller hundred-man size, Asʿad ibn al-Khātir Ibn al-Mamāti, *Kitāb Qawānīn al-Dawāwīn*, ed. A. Attiyah (Cairo, 1943), 340.

The Muslim *harrāqa* was probably the equivalent of the Byzantine fire-ship, and Muslims used "Greek Fire" from early on. But, until more solid evidence comes to light, either in the literature or as the product of a nautical excavation, we can go no further than this.

THE BATTLE OF MALTA, 1283:
PRELUDE TO A DISASTER

Lawrence V. Mott

ON 8 June 1283, a naval battle took place in the Grand Harbor of Malta which would have profound repercussions on the ability of the Angevins to wage war for the rest of the conflict known as the War of the Sicilian Vespers. Not only would the battle bring to prominence for the first time Admiral Roger de Lauria, who would go on to become one of the great admirals of the period, but it would also lay the groundwork for the failure of the French crusade against Aragon two years later. The battle of Malta is one of the rare cases in the war where an Aragonese fleet met a fleet composed entirely of Provençal ships and crews. The only other instance occurred at the battle of Las Rosas, but, as will be shown, the quality and type of French units deployed at that battle were to a large extent dictated by the results of the earlier battle at Malta. For the above reasons, the battle of Malta offers an opportunity to evaluate both the ships and tactics of two homogeneous fleets without the ambiguities that attend the interpretation of a battle in which one of the fleets, composed of units from various city-states, is plagued by the problems of unity of command, differing tactics within the fleet, and less than enthusiastic participation on the part of one or more of the units. Moreover, the results of the battle of Malta suggest that, contrary to the conventional wisdom, the ships and tactics used by the fleets in the western Mediterranean were virtually identical, the Catalans and Aragonese employed subtle, but effective, differences in ship design and tactics to become the pre-eminent naval power in the western basin. This paper will analyze the differences in the tactics and ships utilized by both sides in the battle of Malta, and outline the effects the Angevin defeat there would have on the failed crusade of Philip III.

The battle of Malta was not the first naval engagement between the Aragonese fleet and the forces of Charles of Anjou, but the result of an engagement which had occurred nine months before. Following the Sicilian revolt against Angevin rule in April 1282, Pedro III of Aragon (1276–1285) laid claim to Sicily based on his wife's connection to the Hohenstaufen family. He invaded Sicily in June and by late September of 1282, Charles had been forced to abandon the siege of Messina and cross the straits to Reggio on the coast of Calabria. The actual size of the fleet Charles took with him to Reggio is hard to determine based on the chronicles. Neocastro and Desclot are in virtual agreement, with the former putting the number of vessels at fifty-two galleys, while

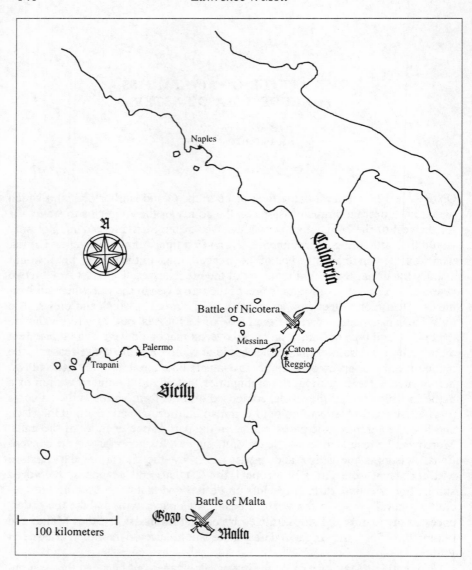

Figure 1. Map of southern Italy, Sicily and Malta

the latter simply states there were a total of seventy vessels, including auxiliaries.[1] Muntaner gives an apparently inflated figure of a total of 120 galleys plus assorted transports.[2] Based on the chronicles, it appears that the Angevin fleet was composed of twenty-two to twenty-four galleys with an accompanying flotilla of thirty to forty *tarides*, armed *lenys*, and barges.

In response to Charles's retreat to Reggio, Pedro III had a fleet assembled in Messina in order to intercept the Angevin fleet as it attempted to pass north through the straits (Figure 1). Nominal command of the fleet at this time had been given to the natural son of King Pedro, Jaime Perez, but for this operation Pedro de Queralt and Ramon de Cortada were placed in command. Muntaner states that the king wished his son to remain in order to oversee the fleet at Messina, but the appointment of Queralt and Cortada may have signaled a growing lack of faith in the leadership abilities of Perez. In any case the two vice-admirals were placed in command of sixteen galleys.[3]

At first glance, the Angevin fleet would seem to have held the advantage, but it was a fleet made up of a conglomerate of units from Genoa, Pisa, Provence, and the Principality of Naples. What is more, at that point it was a fleet that had very little enthusiasm for a fight. Part of this lack of enthusiasm came from the fact that the Genoese and Pisan were essentially mercenaries who had no particular stake in the outcome. Moreover, while the fleet had been at Sicily, the Genoese had been openly fraternizing with the Sicilians who had revolted against Charles.[4] However, the main reason for the reticence by the various units to engage the enemy had been created by Charles of Anjou himself. Because of the relative lack of seaworthiness of galleys, it was customary throughout the Mediterranean for fleets to be dispersed and laid up during the winter months in order to repair and refit the ships. After the Angevin fleet had retired to Reggio, following the common practice, Charles had disbanded the fleet so that the various units could return to their homeports.[5] While this practice was common enough, the locale where Charles decided to disband the fleet was poorly chosen. The result of this decision was a fleet with no unity of command, composed of various units, and simply striving to return home, that would have to pass within sight of the enemy fleet at Messina. In summary, the

[1] B. Neocastro, *Historia Sicula*, in *Rerum Italicarum Scriptores* [*RIS*], ed. L.A. Muratori (1921), vol. 13, pt. 3: chap. 53; B. Desclot, *Llibre del Rei en Pere*, in *Les Quatre Grans Cròniques*, ed. Ferran Soldevila (Barcelona, 1983), chap. 98.
[2] R. Muntaner, *Cronica*, in *Les Quatre Grans Cròniques*, chap. 66.
[3] In a letter to Count Guido of Montefeltro, Pedro III describes the battle and notes that the Aragonese fleet consisted of sixteen galleys. As a comparison, both Desclot and Speciale state that the Aragonese fleet was composed of fourteen galleys and Neocastro says there were fifteen galleys, while Muntaner places the number at twenty-two. *De rebus Regni Siciliae (9 settembre 1282–26 agosto 1283) documenti inediti estrati dall' Archivio della Corona d'Aragona* (Palermo, 1882), doc. CXV, p. 109; Desclot, chap. 98. Muntaner, chap. 67; Neocastro, chap. 53. N. Specialis 1727, *Rerum Sicularum* in *RIS*, 10: bk. I, chap. 18.
[4] Stephen Runciman, *The Sicilian Vespers* (Cambridge, 1992), 224, 233.
[5] Desclot, chap. 97; Muntaner, chap. 67; Neocastro, chap. 53.

Aragonese faced a leaderless fleet composed in part of mercenaries who would see no financial gain from a fight, and of individual units which had been disbanded. King Pedro appears to have recognized this when he reportedly described the Angevin fleet as "a people who are fleeing and who have lost all heart, and . . . are of many nations and are never of one mind."[6] Regardless of whether he said this or not, it was a shrewd observation and it undoubtedly was the main reason he felt his smaller fleet could have success against a much larger force.

The Angevin fleet had attempted to go north through the strait on October 11, but had been chased back into port by the Aragonese galleys. Desclot and Neocastro state that they were then held in port by unfavorable winds until October 14 when they again made an attempt to pass through the strait.[7] Again the Aragonese fleet came out in pursuit and this time caught the Angevin fleet at Nicotera. The result of the battle that followed was dictated as much by the composition of the Angevin fleet as by any particular battle plan on the part of the Catalans and Aragonese. The chronicles are in virtual agreement that none of the groups within the Angevin fleet trusted each other for support in the battle, and at the advance of the enemy they simply scattered and tried to escape without putting up any kind of resistance. The brunt of the attack was borne by the Pisans and the galleys of the Principality, which had attempted to flee back to Nicotera. By the end of the day, twenty-one Pisan and Angevin galleys had been captured along with an assorted group of *tarides* and barges.[8]

This battle was an unmitigated disaster for Charles. Not only had his fleet been soundly defeated and a large number of warships and transports been captured by the enemy, the majority of galleys captured had been those of the Principality, which left his territories in Calabria virtually defenseless. Pedro took advantage of the situation and proceeded to launch a number of raids into Calabria. One of these raids was lead by Jaime Perez in January 1283 against the arsenal at Catona just outside of Reggio, which was being held at that time by a force under the command of the count of Alençon, who was the nephew of the king of France and the brother of Charles of Anjou. Perez ferried a contingent of *almogavers* in four groups from Messina to Catona under the cover of darkness and apparently caught the garrison by complete surprise. According to Speciale, Muntaner and Desclot, the raid was a great success in which the garrison was wiped out.[9] Included among the dead was the count of Alençon, who had been apparently butchered in his bedchamber along with his household guard despite having surrendered.

---

6 Muntaner, chap. 67.
7 Desclot, chap. 98; Neocastro, chap. 53.
8 Pedro III in his letter to Count Guido states twenty-one Angevin galleys were captured. For comparison, Desclot and Neocastro state twenty-two galleys were captured along with assorted transports. Muntaner states that a total of forty-five galleys, armed lenys and barges were captured. *De rebus Regni Siciliae*: doc. CXV, p. 109; Desclot, chap. 98; Neocastro, chap. 53; Muntaner, chap. 67.
9 Desclot, chap. 102; Muntaner, chap. 70; Speciale, bk. 1, chap. 19.

There is general agreement that it was the conduct of this raid that led to the removal of Jaime Perez as admiral of the fleet, and the appointment of Roger de Lauria as his replacement. Most of the chronicles are mute concerning the reason for the removal of Perez as commander. It has been speculated that Perez's inability to control the *almogavers* and the subsequent death of the count of Alençon were the contributing factors for his being removed from command, but this alone seems to a rather weak excuse of his removal.[10] The *almogavers* were traditionally hard to control, and this was not the first nor the last time that they would run amuck. The death of the count certainly deprived the king of a very valuable hostage, but there may have been other reasons for the removal of Perez. Zurita, citing a chronicle by an anonymous author, states that Perez had undertaken the raid without royal permission and that he nearly lost his head because of the casualties he had sustained.[11] On the other hand, both Muntaner and Desclot state that King Pedro was present at Messina and that the raid was authorized by him after being approached by the *almogavers*.[12] Considering the men and ships involved in the undertaking, it seems highly unlikely that a sortie of this size could been organized without the king's knowledge.

However, concerning the loss of men, Desclot recounts how a company of *almogavers* was left behind during the withdrawal and goes into lengthy detail as to King Pedro's attempts to rescue them. Desclot states that there were only thirty men left behind, but this figure may only represent one group of several stranded by Perez. What this suggests is that the raid was not as singular a success as purported, and that reinforcements sent from Reggio may have forced Perez into a disorganized retreat that left a number of troops stranded. As will be discussed later, the *almogavers* were considered elite troops who were highly prized. If Perez did bungle the withdrawal and left a number of troops at Catona, it would have been a serious mistake and certainly grounds for his dismissal as admiral. As we have seen, King Pedro already seemed to have had misgivings about Perez's ability to lead the fleet, and a bungled raid capped off with the death of the count of Alençon may simply have deepened his doubts about his natural son to the point where he lost all confidence in him. Jaime Perez held the office of admiral until April 1283 when he was finally replaced by Roger de Lauria.

On 12 April 1283 at Messina, Roger de Lauria was appointed as the Admiral of the Crown, Catalunya, Valencia and Sicily.[13] Roger was not Catalan nor Aragonese, but had actually been born in the town of Scala in Calabria in 1250. His life followed that of a typical son of a feudal lord, and he was sent to the court of

---

[10] J. Pryor, "The Naval Battles of Roger of Lauria," *Journal of Medieaval History* 9 (1983): 183.

[11] J. Zurita, *Anales de la Corona de Aragon* (Zaragoza: Institucion "Fernando el Católico," 1977), chap. 24. This charge is repeated by Antonio de Herrera y Tordesillas, *Commenterios de los hechos de españoles, frances y veneciones en Italia* (Madrid, 1624), 7.

[12] Desclot, chap. 102; Muntaner, chap. 70.

[13] ACA, Cancillería real, R 54, f. 227r; G. La Mantia, *Codice diplomatico dei re aragonesi di Sicilia (1282–1353)* (Palermo, 1990), I: doc. 222.

King Manfred to be educated. However, his education was cut short when
Charles of Anjou invaded Italy, and his father died along with Manfred at the
battle of Benavento in 1266. His mother fled with him and his boyhood friend,
Conrad de Lancia, to the court of Aragon. Both young men found favor at the
court of Jaime I, and by 1270 Roger received lands from the king for services
rendered. The lands he was granted were in a relative hot spot for the Crown.
Not only did he have to contend with the continual border squabbles that arose
with Castile, but in 1276 he had to put down a general insurrection by the
mudejar population. His actions apparently pleased the king for we have a letter
sent to Roger thanking him for his service in the war and granting him 5,700
royal *solidos*.[14] When Jaime I died that same year, his son Pedro III ascended to
the throne and proceeded to name Roger as the bailiff of Concentaina and Alcoy.
Finally, on October 12, 1278 he was named governor of Valencia.[15] He is mentioned in command of a trading ship at Tlemcen in that same year, but other than
that his activities seem to have been limited to Valencia.[16] The next major
position he appears to have been given was that of governor of Reggio on
14 February 1283, a day after Charles had vacated it at the approach of Pedro
III's forces.[17]

The appointment of Roger de Lauria has been somewhat of a puzzlement. He
certainly had been involved in hard fighting during the insurrection, and his
position as governor had made him responsible for not only defense of the territory but also maintaining the naval forces of the city. Yet, as Pryor has pointed
out, he was surrounded by a number of men who had more experience with
regard to naval matters.[18] His friend Conrad de Lancia had held the title from
1278 until 1280 when it had passed to Jaime Perez. Pedro de Queralt, who had
been in command of the fleet that routed the Angevins at Nicotera, was certainly available, along with two competent vice-admirals, Ramón Marquet and
Berenguer Mallol. Pedro III's decision to choose Roger ahead of these other
candidates was probably based on several factors. The admiral of the fleet had
to be not only a tactician and strategist, but also a good administrator. The maintaining of a fleet required the commander to arrange for provisions, pay, equipment and maintenance. The other candidates undoubtedly had the skills
necessary, but Roger had been governor of one of Aragon's newest and most
important provinces and, as such, was responsible for both its land and sea
defenses. Roger was a trusted friend of the crown, and the king needed a commander he could trust to maintain the fleet after he had returned to Aragon.

Finally, the choice was probably influenced as much by the political situation

---

[14] R. Fullana Mira, "La Casa de Lauria en el Reino de Valencia," in *III Congrés de historia
de la Corona de Aragó, dedicat al periode compres entre la mort de Jaume I i la proclamció
del rey Don Ferrán d'Antequerra*, 2 vols. (Valencia, 1923), 1:82.
[15] Ibid., 1:83.
[16] Ibid., 86.
[17] Neocastro, chap. 59.
[18] Pryor, 183.

as the strategic one. After moving into Calabria in February 1283, Pedro had set about winning the hearts and minds of the inhabitants, and achieved some success. As part of this policy, he had appointed locally popular individuals to important posts, including Alaimo di Lentini as grand judge and Juan de Procida as chancellor of Sicily.[19] Pedro was actively trying to recruit men from Calabria, and what better choice for command of the fleet in the region than a native son. Roger had proven himself in Valencia and the king would have little to worry about concerning his loyalty since Roger had an undisguised hatred for the Angevins, and Charles of Anjou in particular. When the appointment of Roger to admiral is seen from both a political and military standpoint, the choice of Pedro III becomes much more understandable. If there were any misgivings about his ability as a naval commander, Roger would soon dispel them.

The fleet that Roger de Lauria inherited from Jaime Perez was without doubt the best in the western Mediterranean. This was due in large part to the crews which were composed primarily of Catalans and Sicilians. According to Muntaner, Pedro III had specified the composition of the crews before he departed:

> "Admiral, arm twenty-five galleys at once, and arm them in this way: that in each one there is one Catalan Master's Mate and a Latin one, and three Catalan pilots and three Latin, and likewise the same of *proers*, and the rowers should be all Latins, and the crossbowmen should be all Catalans. And in this way, that from now on, all fleets will be fitted in this way, and that for no reason will you change it."[20]

As can be seen from the passage, the Aragonese ships contained mixed crews. However, unlike the Angevin fleet, these crews were highly motivated; the Sicilians because they were fighting to oust the Angevins from their home, and the Catalans because they were fighting for their king and to acquire an important holding for Aragon and Catalonia. The distrust of one's allies, which was so rife in the Angevin fleet, was simply lacking. Adding to the apparent high morale of the fleet had to have been the belief of the crews that they were lead by highly competent and aggressive commanders.

Not only was the Aragonese fleet manned by highly motivated men, but also by units which were ideally suited for galley warfare. In the above passage, Pedro III specified that all of the crossbowmen should be Catalan, in part because the Catalan archers were the best in Christendom, the Genoese not withstanding. Most of what we know of them comes from Muntaner who described them thus:

> The Catalans are the best, in that they know how to make a crossbow, and each knows how to adjust his crossbow, and knows how to make a bolt, and a nut for the cord, and to string it, and to fasten it, and all that pertains to a crossbow; and the Catalans do not understand how anyone could be a crossbowman if he did not know, from beginning to end, all that pertains to the crossbow.

---

[19] Runciman, 238–40.
[20] Muntaner, chap. 76.

And so they carry all their tools in a box, as if they had a crossbow workshop, and no other people do this. The Catalans learn this while drinking their mother's milk, and the other people of the world do not do this; that is why the Catalans are the supreme crossbowmen of the world. And because of this, the admirals and captains of the Catalan fleets should give all attention that this singular ability, which is not in other nations, they do not loose and that they practice it.[21]

Muntaner does not give the actual number of crossbowmen carried on an Aragonese galley, but we can get a reasonable estimate from the *Ordinacións* of Pedro IV, dated 1354. The *Ordinacións* state that a *galéa grosa* was to carry forty *ballesters*, while a *galéa sotil* was to only have thirty. Each archer was to have a leather curass, two crossbows, and two claws, one of with two hooks. The two crossbows that they carried may well have been different.[22] In a charter party written in 1292, the contract states that the crossbowmen on the ship were to have two bows, one was to have stirrup and the other was to be a "two-foot crossbow," that is a bow requiring the archer to sit and use both feet to cock it.[23] The requirement that the archers have two types of crossbow can be traced back to regulations promulgated by Jaime I in 1258. The *Ordinacións* of 1354 also stipulate that has two hundred bolts, one hundred *de prova* and one hundred *de matzém*. Capmany translated the two types of bolts as "tested" and "government issue." Muntaner states that the crossbowmen had two types of bolts, *vires* and *tretes*, but whether these two types represent those in the *Ordinacións* or a particular style of bolt is unknown.[24]

The *ballesters* in the Aragonese fleet were supported by some of the best light infantry in the Mediterranean. The *almogavers* were fighters from the areas bordering the Muslim territories and as such were accustomed to raiding and fighting under a variety of conditions. The best description of them comes from Desclot:

And the people who have the name *almogavers* are a people who only live by arms, and are not of cities or villages, but only live in the mountains and the forests. And they make war with the Saracens every day and enter into the territory of the Saracens for a day or two, pillaging and seizing, and taking many Saracens prisoners and much of their goods. And these men live by their booty, and they suffer great hardships which other men could not suffer, that they are well even after two days without eating, if necessary, or they eat the herbs of the countryside which only for them are not harmful. And the *adelils* are the leaders who guide them, who know the lands and the trails. And they wear no more than a very short leather tunic or a shift, whether summer or winter, and on the legs close-fitting leather leggings, and on the feet good leather sandals. And they carry a good knife, and a good leather belt, and a

---

21 Ibid., chap. 130.
22 A. Capmany, *Ordenanzas de las armades navales de la Corona de Aragon* (Madrid, 1787), 19, 25.
23 ACA, Pergaminos de Jaime II, no. 120.
24 Ibid., chap. 130; Capmany, 25.

scabbard on the belt, and each carries a good lance, and two darts, and a leather pack on the back in which there is bread for two or three days. And they are a very strong people and swift in fleeing or pursuing, and they are Catalans and Aragonese and Saracens.[25]

At first glance the *almogavers* were hardly an inspiring sight, as Muntaner notes. When the *almogavers* sent to relieve Messina arrived, the people were dismayed by their ragged appearance, and despaired that they would be of any help.[26] But the *almogavers* were highly proficient warriors and, despite their light armor, they were not intimidated by heavily armed knights. As Charles tried to retreat from Messina across the straits to Reggio in September 1282, a group of *almogavers* attacked his army and managed to get in among the troops trying to embark. In the resulting battle, they managed to burn a number of ships and to slaughter at least five hundred French knights.[27] In another instance when confronted by mounted knights, they broke their lances in half and then ran in among the horses, gutting them, and then pouncing on the fallen knights.[28] Unencumbered by restrictive armor, the *almogavers* used quickness and mobility for protection. Their agility and background made them perfect marines for the Aragonese navy, since they could keep their feet better on a pitching slippery deck than a heavily armored knight, and they already had the experience necessary for the type of slashing raids practiced in galley warfare. These troops were highly prized by the Aragonese and Catalan commanders, and if Jaime Perez did loose or strand a number of these men during his raid at Catona, it is little wonder Pedro III replaced him as admiral.

The rowers were armed as well and expected to participate in the battle. Based on the *Ordinacións* of 1354, we know that the rowers were actually divided into groups. In the first row of benches in the bow sat the *cruillers* and *aliers*, both of whom wore a leather cuirass and carried a shield. The *aliers* sat on the outboard end of the benches and were there to protect the sides of the bow. The *cruillers* sat inboard and handled the ground tackle and supported the men on the forecastle. Because of their position and duties, the *aliers* were the highest paid group of rowers. In the stern in the last row of seats were the *spatlers* who served a similar function to the *aliers* and carried the same armor.[29] According to the *Ordinacións*, the *remers simples* were only expected to carry a sword, but an inventory from 1359 suggests that they sometimes worn an iron cap, a collar and a cuirass, and carried a shield. In battle, the rowers would stay at the oars until the galley had grappled with the enemy and then leave the benches to join the fight.[30]

[25] Desclot, chap. 78.
[26] Muntaner, chap. 64.
[27] Ibid., chap. 65.
[28] Ibid., chap. 134.
[29] Capmany, 25–6.
[30] Laures F. Foerster, "The Warships of the Kings of Aragon and their Fighting Tactics During the 13th and 14th Centuries," *International Journal of Nautical Archaeology* 16.1 (1987): 24.

The fleet of which Roger de Lauria took command was highly motivated, manned by what could be described as professionals, and was battle-tested. The fleet did not have to be reorganized or assembled, and no training of the crews was needed. Yet, he may not have had a complete complement of men. While Muntaner states the fleet was well-manned and rested, Desclot declares that there was a shortage of experienced men and good weapons since most of the Catalan and Aragonese soldiers had returned with Pedro III to Catalonia.[31] There may be some truth in the statement. Pedro III had returned to Catalonia in April 1283 and most likely took a number of ships and men with him. Philip III of France had moved into Navarre and Pedro most likely took a number of galleys with him to counter any raids against the Catalan coast. Muntaner states that he left with only four Catalan galleys, but if that was the case one has to wonder why Roger had only twenty galleys to pursue the French when after the battle of Nicotera he should have had the twenty-two Aragonese galleys, plus the twenty-one enemy galleys which were captured.[32]

Charles of Anjou faced an entirely different set of problems. The botched evacuation from Messina and the subsequent battle of Nicotera had been a blow to Charles. Not only had he lost most of the galleys from the Principality, but he had also discovered that his erstwhile allies could not be counted on in a close fight. However, the lessons of the battle had not been lost on him and he set about assembling a fleet composed entirely of his French subjects. Realizing that only by controlling the waters around Apulia, Calabria and Sicily did he have a chance of recovering his territories, Charles wrote to the seneschal of Provençe from Reggio in November 1282 and ordered him to assemble a fleet composed entirely of men and ships from southern France.[33] In this letter, he orders twenty well-armed galleys and two thousand crossbowmen and spearmen to be assembled at Marseille. Based on the correspondence, it appears that the Angevin fleet was manned in a manner similar to that of Roger de Lauria's in that there appears to have been an equal mix of archers and spearmen in the fleet, with about one hundred men for each galley.

It has been generally assumed that the *ballisters* of Provence were substantially inferior because of the generally poor performance of the Angevin naval forces in the War of the Sicilian Vespers, and because of their lack of any reputation. Though the Provençal archers did not have the notoriety of the Catalans or the Genoese, that does not necessarily imply incompetence on their part. Many of the crossbowmen came from the Narbonne region as well as from Marseille, areas which shared a cultural background similar to that of the Catalans, and it would seem to be a mistake to assume a total lack of proficiency on their part simply because they happened to be part of a losing effort. Likewise the *lancearius* were probably similar to the *almogavers* in their function, though they probably wore the standard iron cap and leather cuirass. Again, though

---

31 Desclot, chap. 110.
32 Muntaner, chap. 76.
33 A. Bouard, *Actes et Lettres de Charles I Roi de Sicile* (Paris, 1926), doc. 1222, p. 365.

these men lacked the reputation of their counterparts, that does not mean they were either incompetent or untrained. Marseille was a large and important Mediterranean port, and therefore had the same constant need for crossbowmen and spearmen to man their galleys and merchantmen as did other Mediterranean port cities. The men recruited for the fleet were probably for the most part experienced personnel and not raw recruits. Charles could also recruit the men from the Provençal galleys which escaped the battle of Nicotera. In other words, the fleet that Charles assembled was manned by competent, experienced personnel, and not raw recruits of questionable ability as has been implied by some. They may not have had the proficiency level of the Aragonese crews, but that does not mean they were substantially inferior. However, in recruiting for the new fleet Charles apparently stripped Marseille of every experienced man, and pressed into service those who did not join willingly. This decision would have profound repercussions for Marseille and the French fleet in general.

Charles chose two men from Marseille to command the fleet, Barthomeu Bonvin and Guillaume de Cornut, the latter of whom is said to have sworn an oath to bring back Roger de Lauria dead or alive.[34] While there is no information as to their naval experience, the two admirals probably had gained a substantial background having been members of important merchant families in Marseille, and having served in the city government and the Angevin administration.[35] From Charles's correspondence, we know that Johanne Yvaldo had been in command of the Provençal galleys in August 1282, but the poor performance of the galleys at Nicotera apparently led to his removal as there are no further references to him in the correspondence or the chronicles. The first mention of either admiral comes from a document for the victualing of the fleet at Marseille, dated 17 April 1283, in which Bonvin is identified as the fleet admiral.[36]

Sometime in late April or early May the Provençal fleet weighed anchor and set sail for Naples. The orders received at Naples from the prince of Salerno, Charles's son, were for the fleet to go to Malta to relieve the garrison at the Castrum Maris, now known as San Angelo, located at the end of a point in the Grand Harbor. The French garrison had been restricted to the castle from the outset of the war due to a general insurrection which was later bolstered by an Aragonese contingent under Manfred de Lancia. Malta lay in a strategic position, and both sides were anxious to control it. As a result, the composition of the fleet was apparently changed. Charles, in ordering provisions for when the fleet arrived at Roseti, stated that the port should be ready to provide victuals for eighteen galleys, a *panfil*, and eight armed boats, which confirms the statement by Desclot that a number of auxiliaries were attached to the fleet at Naples.[37] The reason for the difference between the eighteen galleys stated in

---

34 Desclot, chap. 110; Muntaner, chap. 81.
35 G. LeSage, *Marseille Angevine* (Paris, 1950), 117, 120.
36 Bouard, doc. 1125, p. 368.
37 Ibid., doc. 1126, p. 368.

the document and the twenty galleys mentioned in the earlier documents and the chronicles is unknown.

The course the fleet set for Malta probably took it around the western end of Sicily in an attempt to avoid the Aragonese fleet at Messina. Muntaner states that the Angevin fleet went through the straits, but, as Pryor has points out, this would have required it to row against the current in the strait while passing within sight of the enemy.[38] Most likely in order to avoid any entanglements with the Aragonese, the fleet left Naples and sailed past the island of Ustica on its way around the western tip of Sicily, as both Desclot and Neocastro state.[39] How Roger received news of their sailing is unclear since none of the chronicles appear to agree. Muntaner states that while out raiding the Apulian coast Roger captured three light galleys sent by Bonvin to watch the Boca del Faro for the Aragonese fleet and that it was from the crews he learned of Bonvin's sailing.[40] Desclot states the news was spread by fishing boats which had seen the Provençal galleys, while according to Neocastro, on hearing rumors of the sailing of the enemy fleet Roger sent a *sagetia* to reconnoiter Naples to confirm the sailing of the Angevin fleet.[41] The truth of the matter may well be a combination of both accounts. The decision of Bonvin and Cornut to send galleys to watch the enemy fleet would have been a prudent move, and the use of light galleys to scout and report on enemy movements was a common tactic. Likewise, it would have been very difficult for the Angevins to skirt the island of Sicily without being noticed by merchant ships or fishing vessels. In either case, Roger de Lauria probably had news of the Provençals within two to four days of their sailing.

The chronicles also disagree as to the course he took from Messina to intercept the Angevin fleet. According to Muntaner and Speciale, after receiving news of the enemy he took the shortest route to Malta by passing south through the Straits of Messina.[42] However, Desclot and Neocastro state that the Aragonese fleet left Messina and then turned west in pursuit, eventually following them around Sicily and to Malta.[43] It is impossible to tell which version is the most likely. If Roger de Lauria did have accurate intelligence that the Provençal fleet was headed for Malta, he would have most likely set a course directly for Malta instead of engaging in a long and fruitless pursuit around Sicily. However, if he only knew that the Provençals had sailed but did not know their intentions, then it would have been prudent for him to follow after them to prevent a possible attack on a Sicilian port.

The Provençal fleet probably arrived at the Grand Harbor sometime on June 4. Manfred de Lancia, on receiving word from Queen Constance in Messina that

---

38 Pryor, 184.
39 Desclot, chap. 101; Neocastro, chap. 76.
40 Muntaner, chap. 83.
41 Desclot, chap. 111; Neocastro, chap. 76.
42 Muntaner, chap. 82; Speciale, bk. I, chap. 26.
43 Desclot, chap. 111; Neocastro, chap. 76.

the French were coming, lifted his siege of the Castrum Maris and retreated to the old city of Città Notabile with his troops and siege engines. The Provençals apparently made the six mile trek to the city to attack Manfred and the Maltese nobles there, but were soon pushed back to the castle at the harbor. The chronicles are not clear, but it appears that by the time Roger de Lauria arrived at Gozo in the evening of June 7 the Provençals had been forced back into the Castrum Maris and Il Borgo which was the small village next to it. After Roger landed at Gozo, he sent word to Manfred and inquired about the enemy fleet. After receiving news from Manfred and local fishermen that the fleet had been at Gozo and had then left for Malta, he moved his fleet that very same night to Malta and the entrance of the Grand Harbor. Bonvin and Cornut had set out two *lenys* as pickets at the harbor entrance, but instead of actively patrolling, they had tied up on either side of the harbor entrance. According to Muntaner, an armed boat, guarded by two lenys, was able to slip into the harbor using muffled oars and discover the disposition of the French galleys. It is quite probable that he also received intelligence from *almogavers* on shore.[44]

Just before sunrise, Roger moved his fleet to the harbor entrance and deployed it for battle (Figure 2). In arranging his ships, he used the common tactic of deploying the galleys in a line abreast and then passing heavy cables between them so that enemy ships could not pass between the galleys. The Genoese apparently developed this tactic sometime in the twelfth century, and by the thirteenth century it had been adopted by most Mediterranean fleets. That the tactic arose with the Genoese and was actively practiced by the Catalans is not surprising. Both peoples relied heavily on missile weapons, the crossbow in particular, to decided the issue in naval combat. The general tactic, as we will see, was to close with the enemy and shower him with projectiles until his crews were so depleted that they could be overwhelmed by a boarding party. Without cabling the galleys together, a battle would quickly devolve into a disorganized melee with the likelihood that the low sides of the galleys would be exposed to attack and immediate boarding. If the attacking crews were composed of heavily armored troops, the result could be disastrous for a lightly armored defender.

However, the cabling of the galleys together was not necessarily a defensive posture. In a number of battles, including that of Malta, the ships were placed in an open formation so that their oars were clear and they could actually row forward as a unit. In such a formation, the light galleys and armed lenys were not lashed together but placed as a mobile reserve behind the cabled galleys. This formation was often modified if large vessels were in the fleet. In such a case the heavy transports, the *uxers* and *tarides*, were cabled together in the center, while the galleys were placed on the wings, and the lighter vessels at the rear. When used as a defensive posture, the galleys were rafted together in a line

---

[44] Muntaner, chap. 83; Neocastro, chap. 76; Speciale (chap. 26) states that Roger received the news from Manfred Lancia, while Desclot (chap. 112) states that local people provided the information on their arrival at Malta.

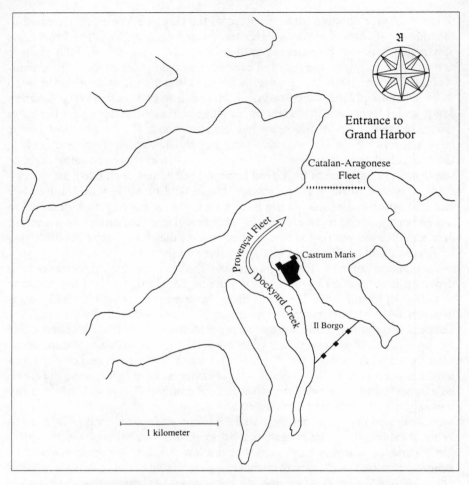

Figure 2. Map of the Grand Harbor showing the disposition of the fleets
on 8 June 1283

abreast so closely that oars actually overlapped and were lashed together. While
the chronicles are silent about disposition of troops on galleys in this formation,
it is quite likely that gang planks were placed between the ships so that men
could be easily transferred from one ship to another as the situation demanded.
In all of these cases, the main objective was to prevent the battle from turning
into a general boarding brawl in which individual ships could be cutout and
overwhelmed.

Before the battle, Roger had his ships cabled in an open formation and then
proceeded to do something which Muntaner considered quite mad. Instead of
falling on the Provençals in their sleep, he woke his adversaries and announced
he was prepared for battle. Muntaner states that he did this by sounding his

trumpets and nakers, while Desclot asserts he sent an armed boat in to Dockyard Creek to challenge the Provençal fleet to battle.[45] Muntaner's statement that Roger did this so that he could not be accused of having won the battle by attacking men in their sleep sounds chivalric, but, as Pryor has pointed out, Roger's decision to do this was probably more of a tactical ploy.[46] While Roger may have had the initiative, the prospects of attacking a fleet beached underneath an enemy castle must have given him pause. A fleet of galleys beached stern-first gave a defender a number of advantages, and it was highly unlikely he could have moved the fleet very far into the harbor without being spotted from the Castrum Maris. Unlike the attacker, the defender could easily transfer and mass troops to any location in the fleet, and the rowers could be armed and used as troops since there would be no need for them at the oars. If beached under or near a friendly castle, the fleet could expect reinforcements and even artillery fire. The difficulties associated with a seaborne assault on a beached fleet were widely recognized. Speciale, when writing of the battle of Cape Orlando in 1299, noted how a fleet drawn-up in this manner was virtually unassailable.[47] Another example comes from the Castilian attack on a beached Catalan fleet in 1359. The king of Castile with thirty-three galleys and over forty ships caught eleven galleys of the Catalan fleet beached at Barcelona. Despite the numerical superiority of the Castilians, the Catalans were able to defend themselves by a turning the ships' boats on their sides and using them as mantlets between the galleys. They also brought up catapults from the city and reinforced the galleys with local troops. Despite persistent attacks over two days, the Castilian fleet was eventually forced to withdraw with nothing more to show for their endeavors than several damaged ships.[48]

Roger de Lauria was undoubtedly aware of the hazards of attacking a beached fleet. He would have also had to contend with Dockyard Creek and the Castrum Maris. In order to attack the Provençals, he would have had to arrange the fleet in a column, due to the constricted waters of the channel, which is less than 250 meters wide at the entrance. Besides having to parade the fleet underneath the castle, which most likely had some form of artillery, an attack on the beached fleet would have meant committing his fleet piecemeal to a battle in very confined water. By awakening the enemy, Roger was attempting to draw them out in order to neutralize a potential disadvantage and to avoid having to commit his fleet piecemeal. However, he gave up the advantage of surprise and apparently allowed the Angevins to array themselves for the battle.

While it is apparent why Roger would want to lure the Provençals out of Dockyard Creek, the reason Bonvin and Cornut came out has not been addressed. As discussed earlier, both men were probably knowledgeable concerning galley tactics and were surrounded by experienced commanders. The

---

[45] Muntaner, chap. 83; Desclot, chap. 113.
[46] Pryor, 185.
[47] Speciale, bk. IV, chap. 13.
[48] Pedro IV of Aragon, *Cronica* in *Les Quatre Grans Cròniques*, chap. 6: 24–6.

chronicles portray the decision as having been made primarily on bravado and later authors have assumed it was based on a desire to close with the enemy. These explanations are simplistic and assume a certain level of incompetency on the part of the French commanders. When one looks at the overall tactical situation, there appear a number of good reasons why Bonvin and Cornut did not wish to be caught in Dockyard Creek. The main incentive for the French fleet to come out was that their landward side was not secure. A beached fleet did have a tactical advantage, but only if it did not face a potential threat from the land. As mentioned earlier, despite the presence of the fleet, the French garrison and the relief had been forced to stay within the castle for protection. The Provençal admirals faced the prospect of an assault from the land as well as the sea. Events had shown that the Angevins could barely cope with the forces of Manfred de Lancia, and the prospect of having to potentially face an assault from the land forces as well as the Aragonese fleet must have been daunting. Even if Roger and Manfred did not attack immediately, the Provençal fleet could not afford to be bottled up. While the Grand Harbor is an excellent anchorage, the harbor itself is surrounded by high ground, particularly the spit of land the Angevins were trapped on. If Bonvin and Cornut dallied in Dockyard Creek, they could have been easily blockaded. They could not send men from the fleet to deal with Lancia without exposing the undermanned galleys to a foray from Roger's fleet. Yet, if they waited, their fleet would be exposed to continual harassment from the land. Manfred had trebuchets with him, and the narrow nature of the inlet would have exposed the fleet to artillery fire from across the inlet and from the besiegers in front of the castle. The close proximity of the fleet to the enemy would have also invited raids from across the inlet and, as has been shown above, a group of *almogaver* raiders could create a great deal of mischief with a beached fleet using relatively few men. Finally, the Angevin admirals had virtually no way to provision the fleet. The fleet had been sent to bring provisions to the garrison which was being starved out, and the village and the castle simply lacked the wherewithal to feed the crews of twenty galleys for any length of time.

There may have been one other reason for the French decision to come out. According to Desclot, the Angevins sent out an armed boat to reconnoiter the enemy fleet. After coming within bowshot, it returned to the admirals with the inaccurate report that only eleven Catalan galleys were present.[49] If this account is true, then Bonvin and Cornut may have been lured out by a faulty scouting report. In either case, whether to prevent being blockaded and destroyed piecemeal or because they felt they had numerical superiority, it is apparent that Bonvin and Cornut had good reasons to come out into the central harbor for an open fight, and their decision to do so was probably correct based on the information available to them. In summary, both combatants had very good reasons for deciding to have the battle in the open space of the Grand Harbor.

---

[49] Desclot, chap. 113.

The resulting situation was not a major tactical advantage for Roger. Both fleets were evenly matched with respect to the number of men and galleys, and by awakening the Provençals Roger had lost the initiative. Where he did gain an advantage was probably in the resulting confusion in the Provençal fleet as the crews awoke and rushed to the galleys in darkness. The Aragonese fleet had time to prepare for battle, while the Provençal preparations were most likely haphazard due to the urgency of the situation. After one hundred knights from the castle had joined the galleys, the Provençals came out of Dockyard Creek and arranged themselves for battle. Both sides waited for daybreak and then rowed towards each other, coming together in the center of the harbor. As the fleets came together the Provençals opened the battle with a hail of arrows, javelins, stones and lime.

A preliminary bombardment with projectiles against an opposing fleet before engaging in close-quarter combat was a common tactic and for that reason galleys carried a variety of projectiles such as those listed in the *Siete Partidas* written in the third quarter of the thirteenth century:

> And for shooting [the galleys] should have crossbows with a stirrup, crossbows of two feet, and crossbows with a winch, and darts, and stones, and arrows as much as can be taken, and jars with lime for blinding the enemy, and others with soap in order to make them fall, and besides all this, pitch for fire in order to burn the ships, and of all these armaments they should have a great abundance so that they will not lack them.[50]

The first two types of crossbows in this list have been previously discussed, but that last is of interest since it appears to have been the main type of artillery used on board galleys. The *ballista de torno* was a large crossbow mounted on a stand and cocked with a winch, which shot all of the above mentioned items. We find mention of them in Muntaner when he is giving advice to the king concerning his planned attack on Sardinia. Muntaner advises loading on board each galley three of these crossbows. However, it is hard to discern if these were intended for the ships or for siege warfare since in the next line he mentions *trabucs* and *manganels* which are clearly siege weapons, and the overall emphasis of the passage appears to be towards land operations.[51] The other mention of them on ships comes from a 1419 inventory of the galley *Canes*. Besides two *bombards* listed, there are two *ballistas de tornos*.[52] Except for these two cases, the use of artillery by the Catalans and Aragonese is singularly lacking in the chronicles and the ship inventories. The inventory of the Catalan fleet of 1354 makes no mention of any form of artillery, even though it details every other major piece of equipment on the ships including the boarding planks used to load horses on the *uxers*.[53] Likewise, there is no mention in the *Ordinacións* or the inventories of soap, lime, stones or pitch for causing fires. The Catalans

---

[50] Alfonso X, *Las Siete Partidas* (Madrid, 1807), pt. 2, tit. 24, law 9.
[51] Muntaner, chap. 272.
[52] Capmany, appendix 5.

probably had some form of shipboard artillery, but it is obvious they did not rely on it to any significant degree.

The above is not to argue that others did not use these weapons. The use of lime mentioned by Desclot was common throughout the Mediterranean, and it even appears in *Tirant lo Blanc* where the Turks are described throwing lime to order to blind. Likewise, soap must have been a relatively effective device since its use was also common. With regards to this weapon, the *almogavers* had a distinct advantage. Unencumbered by heavy armor and a shield, they would have been able to operate relatively freely in such a slippery environment, which may well be one reason such lightly armed soldiers were used by the Aragonese.

Probably the weapon overemphasized the most by historians is the use of fire. While the *Siete Partidas* mentions the use of pitch to burn enemy ships, the chronicles covering the War of the Sicilian Vespers are virtually devoid of references to the use of fire, much less Homeric descriptions of burning ships which one would expect to find if fire was a common or effective naval weapon. The only chronicler who refers to its use at the battle of Malta and the later battle of Naples is Malaspina, who tends to insert short comments on the use of fire in rather formulaic phrases describing the ferocity of the battles.[54] There are numerous references to the use of fire in sieges, both by the naval forces and the besieged, but reports of its use by thirteenth- and fourteenth-century naval units against one another are harder to come by. The contract for the Angevin Red Galley includes glass bottles filled with sulphurous fire and tubes for shooting fire, but any reference to their use is singularly lacking.[55] We are left with the apparent contradiction of having specific references in laws and contracts to a weapon for which there is little evidence that it was ever used on a widespread basis.

The answer may be that naval commanders had several reasons for not utilizing fire as a weapon except under specific circumstances. While firepots and other incendiary devices could play havoc on an enemy ship, once the desired conflagration had been achieved, there was no way to control it. Considering that the battles were fought at close quarters in ships which were roped together, there would have been the strong likelihood of the fire spreading indiscriminately to other galleys, including the ship which used the weapon in the first place. Moreover, there was the problem of handling the inflammable material on board a ship involved in combat. An accident in preparing or launching the projectile could have resulted in major damage to the ship and crew, while also seriously reducing the galley's combat effectiveness. Finally, the object of naval warfare of the period was not to destroy the enemy vessels, but to capture

---

53 ACA, Cancillería real, R. 1541.
54 Sabae Malaspina, *Rerum Sicularum Historia 1250–1285*, in *Cronisti e Scrittori Sincroni Napoletani*, ed. Giuseppe del Re (Darmstadt, 1975), bk. 10, chaps. 8, 15.
55 J. Pryor, "The Galleys of Charles I of Anjou King of Sicily," *Studies in Medieval and Renaissance History* 14 (1993): 79. J. Partington, *A History of Greek Fire and Gunpowder* (Cambridge, 1960), 27.

them. The construction of galleys was a costly affair and the capture of enemy vessels not only spared the government a considerable expense but could also provide a ruler with an instant flotilla, as in the case of the galleys captured at Nicotera. By using fire, a combatant was effectively destroying one of the main prizes which naval commanders strove to capture through battle. While fire could provide a momentary tactical advantage in a battle, the fact that it could be equally dangerous to both sides coupled with the desire to capture enemy vessels probably limited the use of fire as a general naval weapon and restricted it to specific situations.

At this initial stage in the battle, the normal response for the Catalans to the Provençal missile attack would have been to return fire with their javelins and stones. However, instead of engaging in an artillery duel, Roger de Lauria ordered "the men of the galley he was on that they say from one to the other, that they not loose any weapons except the crossbows and should hide themselves well and suffer the attacks."[56] The Catalans endured the bombardment until around midday when the Provençals apparently ran out of ammunition and began to throw the mortars and pestles they used to grind up the lime they had been throwing. At this point, Roger ordered the fleet to close with the Provençals and to use their javelins and projectiles which they had held back. The resulting onslaught of javelins, stones and arrows was devastating, and the Provençal knights and crews were thrown into confusion. With the enemy decimated and disorganized, the Catalans closed with the Provençal galleys and boarded them. The battle lasted until dusk, when Admiral Bonvin broke free and fled out to sea, leaving the other galleys to be captured. The number of galleys which escaped varies among the sources, with Muntaner stating only one galley escaped while Malaspina contends up to fifteen reached open water. The account of Desclot is probably the closest in which he states that seven Provençal galleys broke free. Even these seven galleys were so damaged and the crews so depleted that two had to be abandoned and sunk.

Considering that the crews of the two fleets had a similar composition of crossbowmen and spearmen, one would have expected the casualties to have been heavy on both sides since neither fleet had an obvious tactical advantage. However, in fact, while the Catalan fleet took few casualties, the Provençal crews were decimated. The Catalan losses were light as indicated by the account of Roger de Lauria after the battle in which he notes that 288 men had to be recruited to replace men lost in combat. This is almost exactly the same as the figure of three hundred dead given by Muntaner, which would suggest a casualty rate of less than ten percent.[57] While the losses for Catalans were relatively light, those for the Provençals were devastating, not only for the fleet but for the province as well. With respect to the Angevin fleet, Muntaner claims that 3,500 Angevins were slain and that, "between the wounded and other which had

56 Desclot, chap. 113.
57 La Mantia, doc. 222, p. 546; Muntaner, chap. 83; Pryor, "Naval Battles": 189.

hidden below, there were only five hundred left alive, and of those many died afterwards because of their mortal wounds." Desclot states that 860 men and nobles were captured. More important is his comment on the effect of the battle on the population of Marseille: "And that they [the people of Marseille] had such pain is not a marvel, for there was no one which had not lost a son, a father, a brother, a husband or kinsman." Given that the evidence indicates Angevin losses were between 3,500 and 4,000, Desclot's assertion is not an exaggeration. Baratier has estimated that the population for Marseille and its surrounding environs was approximately 20,000 at the end of the thirteenth century.[58] If this estimate is correct, the defeat at Malta was nothing short of catastrophic for the population. Not only had the community lost nearly twenty percent of its population, it had been a very selective loss, in that the twenty percent loss was restricted to only the able-bodied male population. The demographic effect on the community of Marseille must have been staggering. Not only had the battle cost the lives of Admiral Cornut and his kinsmen, it had effectively stripped Marseille and the Provençal province of its best naval personnel. The extent of the loss and its crippling effects would not become apparent for two years.

As noted above, while the Angevin fleet was at a disadvantage in being trapped within the harbor, it was not at a tactical disadvantage when the battle began. It has been generally assumed that the superiority of the *almogavers* and Catalan bowmen accounted for the lopsided casualties. Yet this assumes that the Provençal archers and spearmen were essentially incompetent. Considering the *almogavers* wore no armor and the crossbowmen only leather cuirasses, the question is not why the experienced Catalans could inflict heavy losses on their opponent, but why the Provençal crews appear to have been so ineffective against the Catalans. The municipal statues of Marseille dated to 1253 clearly show that the Provençal authorities placed a great deal of importance on the crossbow as a maritime weapon, which suggests that the Provençal crews were most likely proficient in its use, if not equal to the Catalans.[59] While the high morale, weapon proficiency and combat experience of the Catalan crews, in conjunction with the high level of casualties routed crews tended to take in medieval naval battles, probably accounts in part for the disparity in casualties between the two fleets, it would appear that there must be another reason for the low Aragonese losses.

A possible explanation lies in the previous quoted passage from Desclot in which Roger de Lauria commands his men to hide behind the bulwarks of the galleys. It has been generally assumed that Mediterranean galleys of the period were constructed essentially the same. However, the passage suggests that the forecastles and sterncastles of the Catalan galleys may have been built up so that the crossbowmen and *almogavers* were not only higher than their opponents, but had the benefit of high bulwarks to hide behind. If the Provençal galleys had the

---

[58] Desclot, chap. 113. E. Baratier, *La Démographie Provençal du XIII au XVI Siècle* (Paris, 1961), 66, note 1.
[59] R. Pernoud, *Les Statuts Municipaux de Marseille* (Paris, 1949), 56–8.

same construction as the Catalan galleys, the lopsided casualties beg the question as to why the Provençal crews did not simply follow the Catalan example by hiding behind the bulwarks of their ships until the missile barrage had passed. In his descriptions of various battles, Muntaner frequently refers to the effectiveness of the crossbowmen *en taula*, as at the battle of Malta:

> Of the crossbowmen it is not necessary to speak, because they were *en taula*, and they are so dexterous that they could not shoot a single time without killing or wounding those they attacked; thus the combatants *en taula* have the advantage.[60]

The word *taula* today refers to a table, but its use by Muntaner is in reference to a raised fighting platform on the ships.[61] While he frequently uses the term in reference to Catalan galleys, there is not a single occurrence of the term being used to describe an Angevin warship.

Other sources also suggest that the Catalans constructed their galleys with raised and protected forecastles and sterncastles. An inventory of the Catalan fleet taken in 1354 shows that the oared transports called *uxers* had planked castles placed forward and aft.[62] Interestingly, these castles appear only on the *uxers* and not the galleys. This difference maybe be due to the castles being structures added to the *uxers* as part of arming them for combat, whereas the raised forecastles and poops were integral parts of the galleys. In any case, the inventory consistently notes if the *uxers* not only have these castles, but if the castles have the necessary planking which is referred to as *entaulament*. It is clear from these references that the term *en taula* not only indicates a raised platform, but that this area was protected by raised bulwarks of some kind.

Another hint comes from the description of the pursuit of the Angevin fleet by the Catalans prior to the battle of Nicotera, in which Malaspina describes the Catalans as pursuing the enemy with galleys "having high poops and forecastles equally elevated."[63] This description of galleys with raised forecastles and poops matches exactly the thirteenth-century depictions of heavy war galleys in the Palacio de Moncada in Barcelona.[64] Not only do the ship depictions on the painted ceiling *tablitas* match this description, but virtually all the other depictions of galleys from this period show warships with low or nonexistent forecastles and certainly not the raised platforms and bulwarks implied in the texts. Often the only protection shown is a low rail. Depictions of Catalan ships also include galleys with no apparent protection for the combatants, but these may

---

[60] Muntaner, chap. 83: "E dels ballesters non cal dir, que eren ballesters en taula, que en tal guisa eren atresats, que no tiraven treta que no matassen, o no gastassen lom que ferien; que en les batalles en taula fan los joch."

[61] Laures, 24.

[62] ACA, Cancillería real, R. 1526.

[63] Malaspina, bk. 9, chap. 19.

[64] L.V. Mott, "Ships of the 13th-century Catalan Navy," *International Journal of Nautical Archaeology* 19.2 (1990): 105–6.

simply be of light galleys which were usually held in reserve and not of the *galea grossa* put in the front of the fleet.

The advantages of having raised bulwarks to protect the spearmen and archers is obvious, but this begs the question as to why the Angevin ships did not adopt them after their defeats at Malta and then at Naples in June of 1284. In part, the answer may be that the raised fighting castles added considerable weight and windage to the galleys, both of which would have reduced the overall speed of the ship. The chronicles suggest that Catalan warships were not particularly fast, and it may be that Angevin shipwrights considered the advantages of better crew protection not worth the sacrifice in speed. That this was the fundamental choice facing shipwrights is suggested by galley construction in the late fifteenth century. Genoese, Venetian, and Neapolitan galleys at the start of the sixteenth century did not carry a raised fighting platform, but were known for their speed under oars. The Spanish galleys, while considered slow, had forward fighting platforms, called *arrumbadas*, and had the reputation of being heavily constructed.[65] They also had the reputation of being good sailors as compared to their Italian counterparts, which suggests they had a deeper draught and wider beam. Though sheer speculation, it is possible that the characteristics of fifteenth-century galleys of different nationalities were simply the reflection of design attributes held over from the thirteenth century when Iberian shipwrights opted for heavily constructed galleys while their Provençal and Italian counterparts designed their galleys for speed. From the passage of Desclot and the tactics used by the Catalan admirals at the battle of Las Rosas, it is clear that the Catalans understood this distinction, while their Angevin counterparts did not.

The two years following the battle of Malta brought a number of changes to the Angevin fleet and to Marseille. In June of 1284, Charles of Salerno gave battle to the Aragonese fleet under Roger de Lauria off Naples against the advice of his father Charles of Anjou. The result was that the Neapolitan fleet was routed and at least ten galleys were captured along with Charles of Salerno himself. While this was a brilliant victory which enhanced Roger de Lauria's reputation, the battle did little to change the strategic balance. Prior to the battle, Charles of Anjou probably was able to muster up to 130 galleys and eighty *tarides*, so that the loss of ten to thirteen galleys at the battle of Naples amounted to only a fraction of the force at his disposal.[66] However, the galleys that were lost were all Provençal, as the Neapolitan galleys had fled at the beginning of the battle, so that, once again, the Aragonese had captured valuable ships and men which the French could ill afford to lose. Not only did the Angevins lose experienced personnel, they also lost two experienced leaders in Henri de Nice and the Sicilian admiral Riccardo de Riso.

These losses did not deter Charles of Anjou or Philip III from preparing a

65 J. Guilmartin, *Gunpowder and Galleys* (London, 1980), 204–10, 299.
66 Pryor, "Naval Battles": 198.

naval force to support the crusade called by Pope Martin IV against Pedro III and the Crown of Aragon for their attempts to control Sicily in opposition to papal wishes. Philip III had already agreed to undertake the crusade in February 1284 after some extended haggling with the papacy concerning the nature of the grant of Aragon to Philip's son and the amount of money the Church would donate to the crusade. After agreeing to the crusade against Aragon, Philip III had moved swiftly and by May 1285 had marshaled an army of 8,000.[67] Philip was aware that Pedro III was mired in political problems at home and that he could not rely on the support of the Aragonese nobility to help defend Catalonia. Philip's plan was to move south into Catalonia and capture first Gerona and then Barcelona before Pedro could muster any effective resistance or call for help from Sicily. However, because of the terrain, the French were forced to supply the army by sea, and they proceeded to establish string of bases from Marseille to Las Rosas on the Catalan coast. Las Rosas was located only twenty miles from Gerona and so became the lynch pin of French campaign. The importance of maintaining control of the sea was not lost on Philip III and approximately one quarter of the money raised for the crusade went to support the fleet.[68] As Pryor has pointed out, the chronicles are hopelessly confused about the size of the fleet, but it appears that Philip was able to collect approximately 210 ships, of which at least one hundred were galleys.[69]

On paper, the Angevin fleet appears to have been highly formidable and the loss of ships during the last two years would seem to have had little effect on the overall strategic picture. In part, this appearance of strength stemmed from an aggressive construction program started by Charles of Anjou and continued by Philip III after Charles's death in January 1285. Marseille had revolted against Angevin rule in 1251, and Charles had moved swiftly to end the rebellion and instituted reforms known as the *chapitres de paix* of 1257. The *chapitres de paix* of 1257 had guaranteed Marseille commune some independence, but it had also given Charles of Anjou near total control over the administration and finance.[70] On gaining control of Marseille, Charles had instituted a variety of naval policies designed to turn the port into a major naval base, including a program of building shipyards and the necessary infrastructure required to support a large fleet. The fact that Marseille, and the entire southern French littoral, could continue to produce large numbers of ships despite the continual losses inflicted on the Angevin fleet demonstrates that, at least in producing the hardware for war, the Angevin administration was relatively effective, even if this program undermined the merchant marine of the region.

In assessing the relative strengths of the Aragonese and French fleets at the

[67] J. Strayer, *Medieval Statecraft and the Perspectives of History* (Princeton, 1971), 116.
[68] Ibid., 114; Pryor, "Naval Battles": 195.
[69] H. Bresc, *Marseille dans la guerre des Vêspres siciliennes*, in *Marseille et Ses Rois de Naples* (Marseille, 1988), 47; Pryor, "Naval Battles": 196.
[70] E. Baratier, *Histoire de Marseille* (Toulouse, 1973), 92–3.

end of 1284, most authors have focused on the relative disparity in the number of ships each could muster. However, these assessments have overlooked the quality of the crews with which the French were manning their fleet. In assessing the affect of the war on Marseille, Bresc has concluded that the early battles had bled the region of its experienced admirals, marines, rowers, captains and seamen to the point that Marseille would not recover its maritime standing following the war.[71] As we have seen, the losses of men at the battle of Nicotera and Malta had decimated the Provençal maritime community, and the fleet that Philip III raised for the crusade was built and manned at Marseille, Aigues-Mortes, and Narbonne. The French had paid for the support of the Genoese and Pisans, but they had no great interest in the crusade, and their help would prove no more effective in this campaign than it had in the past. The upshot of the situation was that the French fleet was manned by inexperienced marines and sailors who had little or no combat experience. The French fleet may have appeared to be overwhelming, but it was a hollow force with inexperienced captains and green crews. Moreover, it was led by Guillaume de Lodève who had little naval experience and would prove as incapable of dealing with the Catalans as his predecessor Henri de Nice.[72] Philip III's fleet, despite its size, was manned and led by personnel who were ill-equipped to combat a highly motivated and well led Catalan naval force which was employing the same tactics which had already proved so devastating against seasoned Provençal fleets.

In surveying the naval aspect of the crusade against Aragon, the battle of Las Formigueras, in which Roger de Lauria defeated a French fleet and then went on to burn the supply ships in the harbor of Las Rosas, was probably the pivotal event in the campaign. This battle marked a turning point in the crusade and ultimately forced the French to retreat from Catalonia due to a lack of supplies. However, the disastrous effect the combination of inexperienced commanders and crews could have on the French fleet's performance had already become apparent earlier at the battle of Las Rosas in which a small squadron of Catalan galleys had defeated a French force over twice its size. As with the battle of Malta, this was one of the few engagements in which Catalan galleys faced a fleet composed entirely of French crews, and so provides for a comparison between the performance of the earlier Provençal fleet at Malta and the fleet assembled by Philip III. Of the various chronicles covering the crusade, only those of Desclot and Muntaner provide any details of this encounter. While there is little information as to the conduct of the battle beyond these two chronicles, the various accounts are in virtual agreement in that they state that the Catalan fleet consisted of between eleven and fifteen galleys while the French squadron contained twenty four to thirty.[73]

Unfortunately, while the chronicles of Desclot and Muntaner give us the most

---

[71] Bresc, 48.

[72] Baratier, 91.

[73] Desclot, chap. 158; Muntaner, chap. 130; Neocastro, chap. 97; *Gesta Comitum Barcinonensium*, ed. J. Barrau Dihigo and J. Massó Torrents (Barcelona, 1925), chap. 28, no. 39. The two

detailed accounts of the battle, the two chronicles are irreconcilable as to the tactics which were employed by the Catalans. Muntaner and Desclot agree that the two admirals, Ramón Marquet and Berenguer Mallol, decided to attack Las Rosas after receiving word that a fleet of fifty galleys had left the port, leaving only twenty-four galleys behind to guard it. Both chronicles agree that the Catalans scouted the port and that the French admiral Guillem de Lodève came out to confront them after they were spotted. The two chronicles also agree that the French deployed in a line abreast, and Muntaner further asserts that they were cabled together in a manner similar to that used in the battle of Malta. However, the two accounts are in absolute disagreement as to the tactics used by the Catalans. Desclot states that the Catalan squadron ran headlong into the center of the French line, and after breaking through it began to defeat the separated French galleys in detail. Muntaner contends that the Catalans took up a defensive posture and awaited the French attack. Only after the French galleys had been decimated by missile fire did the Catalans break formation and counterattack.

Of the two accounts, the one given by Muntaner is more detailed and appears to be the more accurate for a variety of reasons. Desclot asserts the Catalan admirals were prodded into action by accusations of cowardice from the nobility and the general populace. The two Catalan admirals were seasoned veterans and, as mentioned above, had participated in the battle of Nicotera. Considering their record of successes and their seniority, it would seem than any assertions of cowardice would have rung hollow and it is unlikely that these would have pushed both of them into a precipitous action. Moreover, Pedro III had been careful to husband his forces, and even Desclot recounts how he admonished both admirals to conserve their force as it might be required later to defend Barcelona. In this same vein, attacking the center of the French line in an open formation, as Desclot asserts, would have given the French the advantage and gone against the current naval doctrine of the time. The common tactic of the period was to deploy a fleet in a line abreast so that there was a strong center flanked by a wing on each side. The fleets would attempt to overreach the wings of the opposing fleet and thus encircle it. If a fleet was considerably smaller than the opponent and could not, or would not, retreat, it would raft the galleys together so that the enemy was confronted with a large floating fortress. While this gave the enemy the initiative, it allowed the defenders to transfer men from one ship to the next to beat back any assault, thus leaving the rowers free to fight. Attacking the center of the French line in open formation, even if the galleys were cabled together, would have violated doctrine of the time and given absolutely no advantage to the Catalans.

For the above reasons, I am inclined to believe Muntaner who had participated in several of the naval campaigns and had firsthand experience concerning naval tactics. Muntaner states that the French line consisted of fifteen galleys

most detailed accounts of the battle of Las Rosas, Desclot and Muntaner, state that the Catalans had eleven galleys compared to the twenty-four of the French.

cabled together in an open formation so they could still row forward. Behind this line were the remaining galleys which were used to prevent the escape of any of the Catalan ships. As we have seen, this was a typical disposition for an attacking fleet, and even Muntaner comments that the French galleys "were wisely placed." In response, the Catalans lashed their galleys together and the oars to one another so that the Catalan squadron was rafted together as a single unit and then awaited attack. The situation would certainly seem to have given the French the tactical advantage, but the results of the battle show that the Catalans were both better armed and prepared than their counterparts. Muntaner's description of the battle after the two fleets had come together drives home the point:

> And in the bows as in the sterns one might have seen lances and darts thrown by Catalan hands which passed through wherever they might overtake, and likewise the crossbowmen shot so that no arrow missed. There stood those of the galleys of Don Guillem de Lodève with sword or bordon in hand, without knowing what to do, and if someone had taken a dart or a lance, so little did they know of it, that they were as likely to throw it by the point as by the shaft.[74]

As at the battle of Malta, the Catalans waited until the French crews were decimated by missile fire and then boarded the enemy ships. The Catalan crews lacked a complement of *almogavers*, and yet this seems to have made little difference in the outcome. Desclot and Muntaner disagree as to how many ships were captured, with the former stating only seven were actually seized, while the latter contending that all of the French galleys were captured. While the two authors disagree as to the number of captured galleys, they are in virtual agreement as to the losses incurred by both sides. Desclot states that the French fleet lost over half of its personnel, while the Catalan fleet had lost only thirty-nine men and had four hundred wounded. Muntaner sets the French losses at four thousand and those of the Catalans as one hundred killed. Despite being outnumbered two-to-one, it is clear that the Catalans butchered the enemy fleet even though the French had the apparent tactical advantage and the initiative.

While the accounts undoubtedly contain a certain amount of hyperbole, the above shows how badly the loss of manpower had affected the French ships. While Muntaner gives no details as to the composition of the French fleet, Desclot tells us that it contained men from Marseille and the Narbonne region, the same areas which had been previously stripped of men to outfit the Angevin fleet. Muntaner claims that the French crews were made up of French knights, with no lancers or bowmen. This seems highly unlikely and Desclot mentions that the French had some bowmen with them. However, even Desclot's versions of the battle lack the usual description of a preliminary missile assault by the French, and the actual description does not contain any mention of the missile weapons the author described at the battles of Malta or Naples. Moreover,

---

[74] Muntaner, chap. 130.

despite their overwhelming superiority, the French seemed incapable of boarding any of the Catalan galleys even though the fleets had apparently come together without the preliminary missile barrage. The passage from Muntaner shows that the French fleet had been manned with knights and foot-soldiers who had neither the weapons nor the training to cope with the Catalans. Whether this was a conscious decision on the part of the French leadership or simply the result of the lack of manpower from previous losses is unknown. However, it is unlikely an experienced commander would have been as eager to give battle knowing how poorly his fleet was manned.

The battle of Las Rosas also demonstrates that the construction of the Catalan ships must have been sufficiently different in order to prevent the French from boarding and overwhelming the Catalan galleys using their superiority in heavily-armored knights. If the opposing galleys had possessed a similar construction, it seems likely that the mailed knights would have been able to force their way on to the Catalan galleys, which were defended only by lightly-armored crossbowmen and crewmen. Yet the description given by Muntaner and the lopsided losses given by both authors suggest that the Catalan bowmen were in a position to rain down a hail of arrows, lances and darts on their opponents with virtual impunity. Again, the evidence is circumstantial, but it suggests that there was a fundamental difference in the construction of the Catalan galleys. The fact that even when the French ships had grappled with the Catalan vessels, the French men-at-arms were incapable of boarding suggests that Catalan sides were sufficiently above those of the French to prevent effective boarding even when the French had the initiative and seemingly superior manpower.

The battle of Las Rosas clearly demonstrated the weakness of the French naval forces and set the stage days later for one of Roger de Lauria's most important victories. With his lines of supply and communication cut by the Catalan fleet, Philip III was forced to retreat toward France, despite having finally conquered Gerona. In the course of the retreat, Philip III fell ill and died, while his forces, scrambling back toward the frontier, were bled dry by constant attacks from Pedro III's forces. Despite the money expended by Philip III on the naval aspect of the crusade, the French do not seem to have been able to overcome the naval losses at the battles of Nicotera and Malta. Moreover, it appears from the method by which the French fleet was outfitted that the commanders and advisors of Philip III never seemed to have grasped the necessities of Mediterranean warfare. They rather manned their fleet with heavily-armed marines who proved completely inadequate. In this sense, the French fleet, despite its size, seems to have devolved. At the battle of Malta, the Provençal fleet was fitted much like that of the Aragonese. Yet by the time of the Aragon crusade the French fleet appears to have lost most of its spearmen and bowmen. Whether this decision was an impromptu or deliberate one is impossible to tell, but the disastrous defeats suffered by the French during the Aragon crusade testify not only about the strength of Catalan naval power but of French weakness in this regard.

None of the above argues that the results of the battle of Malta predetermined the success of the crusade against Aragon. A number of decisions on either side could have easily changed the outcome. Yet the severe losses inflicted at Nicotera, Malta, and Naples undoubtedly weakened the French fleet to the point that when it had to engage in operations independent of its erstwhile allies, it was incapable of matching the Catalans in quality of crews or leadership. Once Philip III made the decision to supply his forces by sea and once the Catalans began to apply pressure against the French lines of communication along the coast, the entire crusade was doomed to failure. In retrospect, the failure of the French naval forces during the crusade was laid at the battle of Malta which proved to be one of the most important engagements of the War of the Sicilian Vespers, though none of the participants realized it at the time. Not only had it brought to the forefront one of the greatest naval strategists and tacticians of the time, it had inflicted losses on the French fleet from which it would never recover.

BIBLIOGRAPHY

Primary Sources

Ibn al-ʿAdīm. ʿUmar b. Ahmad. *Zubdat al-halab min taʾrīkh Halab.* Edited by Sāmī al-Dahhān. Damascus, 1954.

d'Aguilers, Raymond. *Historia Francorum Qui Ceperunt Iherusalem.* Translated by John Hugh Hill and Laurita L. Hill. Philadelphia, 1968.

Anglo-Saxon Chronicle. Translated by George N. Garmonsway. London, 1990.

Annales Gandenses. Edited and translated by H. Johnstone. London, 1951.

Anonymi auctoris chronicon A.D. 1234 pertinens. Edited by J.B. Chabot. Paris, 1916.

Ibn al-Athîr. "Izz al-Dîn Abû al-Hasan ibn Muhammad." *al-Kāmil fi al-Tārīkh.* Beirut, 1965.

Bede. *Historia ecclesiastica gentis Anglorum.* Edited and translated by Bertram Colgrave and R.A.B. Mynors. Oxford, 1969.

Bollea, Luigi C. *Documenti degli archivi di Pavia relativi alla storia de Voghera (929–1300).* Pinerolo, 1909.

Bouard, Alain de. *Actes et Lettres de Charles I Roi de Sicile.* Paris, 1926.

al-Bundārī. Al-Fath ibn ʿAli. *Zubdat al-nusrah wa-nukhbat al-ʿusrah.* Edited by M.T. Houtsma. Leiden, 1889.

Capmany y de Montpalau, Antonio. *Ordenanzas de las armades navales de la Corona de Aragon.* Madrid, 1787.

The Carmen de Hastingae Proelio of Bishop Guy of Amiens. Edited by C. Morton and H. Muntz. Oxford, 1972.

A Choice of Anglo-Saxon Verse. Edited and translated by R. Hamer. London, 1970.

Christian Society and the Crusades, 1198–1229. Edited and translated by Edward Peters. Philadelphia, 1971.

Chronica Adefonsi Imperatoris. Edited by Emma Falque, Juan Gil, and Antonio Maya. Turnholt, 1990.

The Chronicle of Battle Abbey. Edited and Translated by Eleanor Searle. Oxford, 1980.

The Chronicle of Florence of Worcester. Translated by Thomas Forester. London, 1854.

Comnena, Anna. *The Alexiad.* Translated by E.A.S. Dawes. New York, 1967.

Constantine Porphyrogenitus. *De Administrando Imperio.* Edited by Gregory Moravcsik. Translated by R.J.H. Jenkins. Washington DC, 1967.

Crónica de la población de Avila. Edited by Amparo Hernández Segura. Valencia, 1966.

Crónica latina de los reyes de Castilla. Edited by Maria Desamparados Cabanés Pecourt. Valencia, 1964.

The Earliest Life of Gregory the Great by an Anonymous Monk of Whitby. Edited and translated by Bertram Colgrave. Lawrence KS, 1968.

Eddius Stephanus. *The Life of Bishop Wilfrid.* Edited and translated by Bertram Colgrave. 1927. Reprint, Cambridge, 1985.

English Historical Documents, c.500–1042. Edited and translated by Dorothy Whitelock. 3 vols. to date. London, 1953–.

Eulogium historiarum sive temporis. Edited by F.S. Hayden. 3 vols. London, 1863.

Eusebius, *Life of Constantine.* Translated by E.C. Richardson. 2 vols. New York, 1890.

De expurgatione Lyxbonensi. Edited and translated by Cook W. David. New York, 1936.

Faral, Edmond. *La Legende Arthurienne: Etudes et Documents.* Paris, 1929.

Felix, *The Life of St Guthlac.* Edited and translated by Bertram Colgrave. 1956. Reprint, Cambridge, 1985.

Feyerabend, Sigmund. *Reyszbuch desz heyligen Lands.* Franckfort im Mayn, 1584.

Abū al-Fidā'. *al-Mukhtasar fī ta'rīkh al-bashar.* 4 vols. Cairo, 1907–8.

Florence of Worcester. *Chronicon ex Chronicis.* 2 vols. London, 1964.

Fredegar. *The Fourth Book of Fredegar and Continuations.* Edited and translated by J.M. Wallace-Hadrill. London, 1960.

Fulcher of Chartres. *A History of the Expedition to Jerusalem, 1095–1127.* Translated by F.R. Ryan. Edited by H.S. Fink. New York, 1973.

Galbert of Bruges. *The Murder of Charles the Good.* Translated by James Bruce Ross. New York, 1960.

Gervase of Canterbury. *Historical Works.* Edited by William Stubbs. 2 vols. London, 1879.

Gesta Comitum Barcinonensium. Edited by J. Barrau Dihigo and J. Massó Torrents. Barcelona, 1925.

Gesta Stephani. Translated by K.R. Potter. Edited by R.H.C. Davis. Oxford, 1976.

Gregory of Tours. *The History of the Franks.* Translated by Lewis Thorpe. London, 1974.

Güterbock, Ferdinand. *Das Geschichtswerk des Otto Morena und seiner Fortsetzer über die taten Friedrichs I. in der Lombardei, MGH SRG* ns, no. 7. Berlin, 1930.

Hanquet, Karl ed. *La Chronique de Saint-Hubert dite Cantatorium.* Brussels, 1906.

Historical Poems of the XIVth and XVth Centuries. Edited by Robin H. Robbins. New York, 1959.

"Al-Hulal al Mawsiyya": Cronica arabe de las dinastias Almoravide, Almohade y Benimerin. Edited and translated by Ambrosio Huici Miranda. Tetuan, 1951.

Jiménez de Rada, Rodrigo. *Historia de rebus hispanie sive historia gothica.* Edited by Juan Fernández Valverde. Turnholt, 1987.

John of Joinville. *The Life of St. Louis.* Translated by Reni Hague. London, 1955.

John of Salisbury. *The Letters of John of Salisbury.* Edited by W.J. Millor and H.E. Butler. London, 1955.

John of Worcester. *The Chronicle of John of Worcester.* Edited by J.R.H. Weaver. Oxford, 1908.

al-Kātib al-Isfahānī. 'Imād al-Dīn Muhammad b. Muhammad. *al-Barq al-Shāmī.* Edited by Fālih Husayn. Amman, 1987.

————. *Kitāb al-fayh al-qussī fī al-fath al-Qudsī.* Edited by C. Landberg. Leiden, 1888.

————. *Sanā al-barq al-Shāmī, 562/1166–583/1187.* Abridged by al-Fath b. ʿAlī al-Bundārī. Edited by Fathiyah al-Nabarāwī. Cairo, 1979.

Kronyk van Vlaenderen van 580 tot 1467. Edited by P. Blommaert and C.P. Serrière, 2 vols. Ghent, 1839.

Leo VI. *Naumachia.* Edited by A. Dain. Paris, 1943.

Machiavelli, Niccolò. *The Prince.* Translated by George Hull. New York, 1981.

Ibn al-Mamāti, Asʿad ibn al-Khātir. *Kitāb Qawānīn al-Dawāwīn.* Edited by A. Attiyah. Cairo, 1943.

Map, Walter. *De Nugis Curialum.* Translated by Frederick Tupper and Bladen Ogle. London, 1924.

Al-Maqrīzī, Taqi al-Dīn. ʿAhmad ibn Ali. *ʿAtāz al-Khunafā biʿAkhbār al ʿUmma al-Fātimīn al-Khulafa.* Edited by J. al-Din Shayyal, H. Muhammad, M-H.M. Ahmad. 3 vols. Cairo, 1967–73.

————. *Kitāb al-sulūk li-maʿrifat duwal al-mulūk.* 4 vols. Cairo, 1934–73.

Mezières, Philippe de. *Le songe du vieil.* Edited by G.W. Coopland. 2 vols. Cambridge, 1969.

Abū al-Muhāsin, Jamal al-Din Yusuf ibn Taghrī Birdī. *al-Nujūm al-Zāhira fi Mulūk Misr wa al-Qāhira.* Cairo, 1956–69.

Ibn Muqaffa, Severus. *History of the Patriarchs of the Egyptian Church.* Edited and Translated by Y.A. Masih and O.H.E. Burmeister, 4 vols. Cairo, 1943.

————. *al-Khitat.* Bulaq, 1854.

b. Munqidh. Usāmah. *Kitāb al-iʿtibār.* Edited by Qāsim al-Sāmarrā'ī. Riyadh, 1987.

al-Muqaffaʿ, Sawîrus b. *History of the Patriarchs of the Egyptian Church.* Edited and Translated by Y. ʿAbd al-Masīh and O.H.E. Burmeister, 4 vols. Cairo, 1943–74.

Nangis, Guillaume de. *Chronicon et continuationes.* Edited by H. Geraud. Paris, 1843.

Nicetas Choniates. *Nicetae Chroniatae Historia.* Edited by J. van Dieten. Berlin, 1975.

Nikephoros Basilakes. *Nikephori Basilacae Orationes et epistolae.* Edited by A. Garzya. Leipzig, 1984.

Ordericus Vitalis. *Historia ecclesiastica.* Edited and translated by Marjorie Chibnall. 6 vols. Oxford, 1978.

Otto of Freising. *The Deeds of Frederick Barbarossa.* Edited and translated by Charles C. Mierow. Toronto, 1994.

Malaspina, Sabae. *Rerum Sicularum Historia 1250–1285.* In *Cronisti e Scrittori Sincroni Napoletani.* Edited by Giuseppe del Re. Darmstadt, 1975.

Pere III of Catalonia. *Chronicle.* Translated by Mary Hillgarth. Edited by Jocelyn M. Hillgarth. 2 vols. Toronto, 1980.

Neocastro, Bartolomeo di. *Historia Sicula.* Edited by Giuseppe Paladino. Bologna, 1921–22.

Niger, Ralph. *De re militari et triplici via peregrinationis Ierosolitane (1187/88)*. Edited by L. Schmugge. Berlin, 1977.

Pernoud, Regine. *Les Statuts Municipaux de Marseille*. Paris, 1949.

Political Poems and Songs. Edited by Thomas Wright. 2 vols. London, 1861.

Les quatre grans cròniques: Jaime I, Bernat Desclot, Ramon Muntaner, Pere III. Edited by Ferran Soldevila. Barcelona, 1961.

Regesta Regum Anglo-Normannorum: 1066–1154. Edited by H.A. Cronne and R.H.C. Davis. 3 vols. Oxford, 1968.

Il Registrum Magnum del comune de Piacenza. Edited by Ettore Falconi and Roberta Falconi. Milan, 1984.

Die Sachsengeschichte des Widukind von Korvei. Edited by H.-E. Lohmann and P. Hirsch. Hannover, 1935.

Sancti Anselmi Cantuariensis archiepiscopi opera omnia. Edited by F.S. Schmitt. 6 vols. Stuttgart/Bad Canstatt, 1963–68.

Severus, Sulpicius, *et al*. *The Western Fathers*. Edited by F.E. Hoare. New York, 1954.

Ibn Shaddād, Bahā' al-Dīn Yūsuf b. Rāfiʿ. *al-Aʿlāq al-khatīrah fī dhikr umarā' al-Shām wa-al-Jazīrah: [Ta'rīkh madīnat Halab]*. Edited by Dominique Sourdel. Damascus, 1953.

――――. *al-Nawādir al-sultānīyah, sīrat Salāh al-Dīn*. Edited by Jamāl al-Dīn al-Shayyāl. Cairo, 1962.

Abū Shāmah, ʿAbd al-Rahmān b. Ismāʿīl. *Kitāb al-rawdatayn fī akhbār al-dawlatayn*. Edited by M.H.M. Ahmad and M.M. Ziyādah. Vol. 1. Pt. 2. Cairo, 1962.

Society at War: The Experience of England and France during the Hundred Years War. Edited and translated by C.T. Allmand. Edinburgh, 1972. New edition, Woodbridge 1998.

Speciale, Niccolò. *Istorie Siciliane, Libro I*. Palermo, 1982.

Suger. *Vie de Louis VI le Gros*. Translated by Henri Wacquet. Paris, 1929.

Al-Tabari, Abû Jaʿfar Muhammad ibn Jarîr. *Tārīkh al-Umam wa al-Mulūk*. Edited by De Goeje Foundation, 16 vols. Leiden, 1879–92.

Ibn Tāhir. ʿAbd Allāh, *Makhtebhānūth Zabhnē*. Edited by Paul Bedjan. Paris, 1890.

Theophanes. *The Chronicle of Theophanes*. Translated by Harry Turtledove. Philadelphia, 1982.

――――. *Chronographia*. Edited by J. Classen. Corpus Scriptorum Byzantinae. Bonn, 1889.

Three Lives of English Saints. Edited by A.G. Rigg. Toronto, 1972.

Ibn Urunbughā al-Zaradkāsh. *al-Anīq fī al-manājanīq*. Edited by Nabīl Muhammad ʿAbd al-ʿAzīz Ahmad Nabīl Muhammad ʿAbd al-ʿAzīz Ahmad. Cairo, 1981.

van Berchem, Max and Edmond Fatio. *Voyage en Syrie*. 2 vols. Cairo, 1913–15.

Vegetius Renatus, Flavius. *Epitoma Rei Militaris*. Edited by C. Lang. Stuttgart, 1967.

Villani, Giovanni. *Chroniche Fiorentine*. Edited and translated by P. Wicksteed. London, 1906.

Vita Edwardi secundi. Edited and translated by N. Denholm-Young. London, 1957.

Ibn Wāsil, Muhammad b. Slim. *Mufarrij al-kurūb fī akhbār banī Ayyūb*. Edited by J. Shayyāl, S. ʿAshūr, and H. Rabīʿ. 5 vols. to date. Cairo, 1953–.

Willard, Rudolph. *The Blickling Homilies*. Edited by Bertram Colgrave *et al.* Copenhagen, 1960.

William of Jumieges. *Gesta Normannorum Ducum*. Edited by Jean Marx. Paris, 1914.

William of Malmesbury. *Gesta Regum Anglorum*. Edited by W. Stubbs. London, 1887–9.

———. *Historia Novella*. Edited by K.R. Potter. London, 1955.

William of Poitiers. *Histoire de Guillaume le Conquerant*. Edited by R. Foreville. Paris, 1952.

William of Tyre. *Chronique*. Edited by R.B.C. Huygens. Turnhout, 1986.

———. *A History of Deeds Done Beyond the Sea*. Translated by E.A. Babcock and A.C. Krey. 2 vols. New York, 1941.

Wyclif, John. "On the Seven Deadly Sins." In *Select English Works of John Wyclif.* Edited by Thomas Arnold. 3 vols. Oxford, 1871.

al-Yūnīnī, *Dhayl mir'āt al-zamān*. In *Die Jahre 1287–1291 in der Chronik al-Yūnīnīs*. Edited by Antranig Melkonian. Freiburg, 1975.

Ibn ʿAbd al-Zāhir, Muhī al-Dīn. *Tashrīf al-Iyān wa al-ʿAusūr fī Sīrat al-Malik al-Mansūr*. Edited by Murād Kāmil. Cairo, 1921.

Secondary Sources

Agnelli, Giovanni. "Archivio della cellegiata di Castel S. Giovanni de Olubra." *Archivio Storico per le Provincie Parmensi* (1892): 1–23.

Andressohn, John. *The Ancestry and Life of Godfrey of Bouillon*. Hallandale FL, 1972.

Avigad, Nahman. *Discovering Jerusalem*. Nashville TN, 1980.

———. "News and Notes: Jerusalem, the Jewish Quarter of the Old City, 1977." *Israel Exploration Journal* 28 (1978): 200–1.

Bachrach, Bernard S. "Angevin Campaign Forces in the Reign of Fulk Nerra, Count of the Angevins (987–1040)." *Francia* 16 (1989): 67–84.

———. "Animals and Warfare in Early Medieval Europe." In *Uomo de fronte al mondo animale nell'alto medio evo*, 2 vols. 1:707–64. Spoleto, 1985.

———. "Anthropology and Early Medieval History: Some Problems." *Cithara* 34 (1994): 3–10.

———. *Armies and Politics in the Early Medieval West*. Aldershot, 1993.

———. "Charles Martel, Shock Combat, the Stirrup and Feudalism." *Studies in Medieval and Renaissance History* 7 (1970): 47–75.

———. "Grand Strategy in the Germanic Kingdoms: Recruitment of the Rank and File." In *L'Armée romaine et les barbares du IIIe au VIIe siècle*. Edited by Françoise Vallet and Michel Kazanski. 55–63. Paris, 1993.

———. "The Hun Army at the Battle of Chalons (451): An Essay in Military Demography." In *Ethnogenese und Überrlieferung: Angewandte Methoden der*

Frühmittelalterforschung. Edited by Karl Brunner and Brigitte Merta. 59–67. Vienne–Munich, 1994.

———. "On the Origins of William the Conqueror's Horse Transports." *Technology and Culture* 26 (1985): 505–31.

———. "Some Observations on the Military Administration of the Norman Conquest." In *Anglo-Norman Studies VIII.* Edited by R. Allen Brown. 1–25. Woodbridge, 1986.

———, with Rutherford Aris. "Military Technology and Garrison Organization: Some Observations on Anglo-Saxon Military Thinking in Light of the Burghal Hidage." *Technology and Culture* 31 (1990): 1–17.

Baratier, Edouard. *La démographie provençal du XIIIe au XVIe siècle avec chiffres de comparasion pour le XVIIIe siècle.* Paris, 1961.

———. *Histoire de Marseille.* Toulouse, 1973.

Barber, Richard. *The Pastons: The Letters of a Family in the War of the Roses.* Woodbridge, 1986.

Barlow, Frank. *The Feudal Kingdom of England 1042–1216.* London, 1972.

Barraclough, Geoffrey. *The Origins of Modern Germany.* Oxford, 1947.

Bartlett, Robert. "Technique Militaire et Pouvoir Politique, 900–1300." *Annales* 41 (1986): 1135–59.

Battista, A. and B. Bagatti. *La fortezza saracena del Monte Tabor: AH. 609–15/AD. 1212–18.* Jerusalem, 1976.

Bauer, Albert and Reinhold Rau. *Quellen zur Geschichte der Sächsischen aiserzeit.* Darmstadt, 1971.

Bayley, Charles C. *War and Society in Renaissance Florence.* Toronto, 1961.

Beard, Mary R. *Women as Force in History: A Study in Traditions and Realities.* New York, 1987.

Beeler, John. *Warfare in England, 1066–1189.* Ithaca, 1966.

Beumann, H. *Widukind von Korvei.* Weimar, 1950.

Birt, Michael P. "Samurai in Passage: Transformation of the Sixteenth Century Kanto." *Journal of Japanese Studies* 11 (1985): 369–400.

Bloch, Marc. *Feudal Society.* Translated by L.A. Manyon. 2 vols. Chicago, 1961.

Boettcher, Thomas D. *Vietnam: the Valor and the Sorrow.* New York, 1985.

Bonner, Gerald, *et al.*, eds. *St Cuthbert, His Cult and His Community to AD 1200.* Woodbridge, 1989.

Bresc, Henri. *Marseille et Ses Rois de Naples.* Marseille, 1988.

Broshi, Magen. "Along Jerusalem's Walls." *Biblical Archeologist* 40 (1977): 11–17.

Brown, Delmer M. "The Impact of Firearms on Japanese Warfare, 1543–98." *Far Eastern Quarterly* 7 (1947): 236–53.

Brown, Elizabeth A.R. "The Tyranny of a Construct: Feudalism and Historians of Medieval Europe." *AHR* 79 (1974): 1063–88.

Brown, Peter. *The Cult of the Saints: Its Rise and Function in Latin Christianity.* Chicago, 1981.

———. *Society and the Holy in Late Antiquity.* Berkeley, 1982.

Brown, R. Allen. *The Normans and the Norman Conquest.* London, 1969.

———. *Origins of English Feudalism.* New York, 1973.

Brunner, Heinrich. "Der Reiterdienst und die Anfönge des Lehenwesens." *Zeitschrift der Savigny Stiftung für Rechtsgeschichte, Germanistische Abtheilung* 8 (1887): 1–38.

Brunt, P.A. *Italian Manpower, 225 B.C.–A.D. 14.* Oxford, 1971.

Burns, Robert I., S.J. "The Significance of the Frontier in the Middle Ages." In *Medieval Frontier Societies.* Edited by Robert Bartlett and Angus MacKay. 307–30. Oxford, 1989.

Cahen, Claude. "Un Traité d'amurerie composé pour Saladin." *Bulletin d'Études Orientales* 12 (1948): 103–63.

Campbell, James. "Some Twelfth-Century Views of the Anglo-Saxon Past." In *Essays in Anglo-Saxon History.* 209–28. London, 1986.

Chapkis, Wendy, ed. *Loaded Questions: Women in the Military.* Washington DC, 1982.

Charters, David A., Marc Miliner and J. Brent Wilson, eds. *Military History and the Military Profession.* Westport CT, 1992.

Chibnall, Marjorie. *Anglo-Norman England 1066–1166.* Oxford, 1986.

———. *The Empress Matilda.* Oxford, 1991.

Cho-yun, Hsu. *Ancient China in Transition. An Analysis of Social Mobility 722–222 BC.* Stanford, 1965.

Constable, Giles. "The Second Crusade as Seen by Contemporaries." *Traditio* 9 (1953): 213–79.

Contamine, Philippe. *War in the Middle Ages.* Translated by Michael Jones. Oxford, 1984.

Craster, Edmund. "The Patrimony of St Cuthbert." *EHR* 69 (1954): 177–99.

Creswell, Koppel A.C. *The Muslim Architecture of Egypt.* Oxford, 1952.

Dannenbaur, Heinrich. *Grundlagen der mittelalterlichen Welt: Skizzen und Studien.* Stuttgart, 1958.

Davis, Ralph H.C. *A History of Medieval Europe.* 1957. Reprint, London, 1988.

———. *King Stephen.* New York, 1967.

Delbrück, Hans. *Geschichte der Kriegskunst im Rahmen der politischen Geschichte,* 6 vols. Berlin, 1900–1936.

———. *Numbers in History.* London, 1913.

Deschamps, Paul. *Les châteaux des croisés en Terre Sainte.* 3 vols. Paris, 1934–73.

———. *Terre Sainte Romane.* Paris, 1964.

DeVries, K. *Medieval Military Technology.* Lewiston NY, 1992.

Dopsch, Alfons. *Die Wirtschaftsentwicklung der Karolingerzeit vornehmlich in Deutschland.* 2 vols. 1911–1913. Reprint, Weimar, 1962.

———. *Wirtschaftliche und Soziale Grundlage der Europäischen Kulturentwicklyng aus der Zeit von Caesar bis auf Karl den Grossen.* Vienna, 1924.

———. *The Economic and Social foundations of European Civilization.* Translated by Erna Patzalt by M.G. Beard and N. Marshall. London, 1937.

Douglas, D.C. *William the Conqueror.* Berkeley, 1964.

Duby, Georges. *The Legend of Bouvines.* Translated by Catherine Tihanyi. Berkeley, 1990.

————. *Rural Economy and Country Life in the Medieval West.* Translated by Cynthia Postan. London, 1968.

————. *The Three Orders: Feudal Society Imagined.* Translated by Arthur Goldhammer. Chicago, 1980.

Dupuy, Richard E. and Trevor N. Dupuy. *The Encyclopedia of Military History from 3500 BC to the Present.* New York, 1986.

Durliat, Jean. *Les finances publiques de Dioclétien aux Carolingiens (284–889).* Preface by K.F. Werner. Sigmaringen, 1990.

Duus, Peter. *Feudalism in Japan.* 3rd edn. New York, 1993.

Eickhoff, Ekkehard. *Seekrieg und Seepolitik zwischen Islam und Abendland.* Berlin, 1966.

Elshtain, Jean Bethke. *Women and War.* New York, 1987.

Engels, Donald W. *Alexander the Great and the Logistics of the Macedonian Army.* Berkeley, 1978.

Erdmann, Carl. "Die Burgenordnung Heinrichs I." *Deutsches Archiv für Geschichte des Mittelalters,* n.s. 6 (1943): 59–101.

————. *The Origin of the Idea of Crusade.* Translated by Marshall W. Baldwin and Walter Goffart. Princeton, 1977.

Faral, Edmond, *La legende arthurienne: études et documents.* 3 vols.

Farmer, David Hugh. *The Oxford Dictionary of Saints.* Oxford, 1987.

Fichtenau, Heinrich. *Living in the Tenth Century: Mentalities and Social Orders.* Translated by Patrick G. Geary. Chicago, 1991.

Finlay, George. *History of Greece.* 2 vols. Oxford, 1887.

Forbes, R.J. *More Studies in Early Petroleum History.* Leiden, 1959.

Foss, Clive. *Kütahya.* Vol. 1 of *Survey of Medieval Castles of Anatolia.* 2 vols. Oxford, 1985.

Fox, Robin Lane. *Alexander the Great.* New York, 1974.

Friday, Karl. *Hired Swords. The Rise of Private Warrior Power in Early Japan.* Stanford, 1992.

Fukuyama, Francis. *The End of History and the Last Man.* New York, 1992.

Fuller, J.F.C. *A Military History of the Western World.* 3 vols. New York, 1954–56.

Gabrieli, Francesco. *Arab Historians of the Crusades.* Translated by E.J. Costello. New York, 1969.

Gabriel, Albert. *Voyages archéologiques dans la Turquie orientale.* 2 vols. Paris, 1940.

Ganshof, F.L. *Frankish Institutions under Charlemagne.* Edited and translated by Bryce and Mary Lyon. Providence RI, 1968.

Gebhardt, Bruno. *Handbuch der deutschen Geschichte.* Stuttgart, 1954.

Giesebrecht, W. *Geschichte der deutschen Kaiserzeit.* Leipzig, 1881.

Gillingham, John and John C. Holt, eds. *War and Government in the Middle Ages: Essays in Honour of J.G. Prestwich.* Woodbridge, 1984.

Goffart, Walter. *Barbarians and Romans, A.D. 418–584: The Techniques of Accommodation.* Princeton, 1980.

González, Julio. *El reino de Castilla en la época de Alfonso VIII.* 3 vols. Madrid, 1960.

Goñi Gaztambide, José. *Historia de la bula de la cruzada en España.* Vitoria, 1958.

Guilmartin, John. *Gunpowder and Galleys.* Cambridge, 1980.

Hagenmeyer, Heinrich. *Epistulae et Chartae ad Historiam Primi Belli Sacri Spectantes: Die Kreuzzugsbriefe aus Jahren 1088–1100.* Innsbruck, 1901.

Haldon, John F. and Michael Byrne. "A Possible Solution to the Problem of Greek Fire." *Byzantinische Zeitschrift* 70 (1977): 91–100.

Hall, Bert and Kelly DeVries. "Essay Review – The 'Military Revolution' ". *Technology and Culture* 31 (1990): 500–7.

Hall, John W. *Government and Local Power in Japan 500 to 1700.* Princeton, 1966.

———. *Japan from Prehistory to Modern Times.* New York, 1970.

'Abd al-Haqq, Salim 'Abil. "Masrah Busrā wa-qal'athuhā." *Annales archéologiques arabes Syriennes* 14 (1964): 5–22.

Hillgarth, Jocelyn N. *The Problem of a Catalan Medieval Empire. EHR.* supp. 8 London, 1975.

Hinz, Walther. *Islamische Masse und Gewichte: Umgerechnet ins metrische System.* Leiden, 1970.

Hoffmann, Dietrich. *Das spätrömische Bewegungsheer und die Notitia Dignitatum.* Düsseldorf, 1969–70.

Hollister, C. Warren. *The Military Organization of Norman England.* Oxford, 1965.

Holt, P.M. *The Age of the Crusades: The Near East from the Eleventh Century to 1517.* London, 1986.

Holtzmann, R. *Geschichte der Sächsische Kaiserzeit: 900–1024.* Munich, 1943.

Huici Miranda, Ambrosio. *Las grandes batallas de la reconquista durante las invasiones africanas (Almoravides, Almohades y Benimerines).* Madrid, 1956.

Jacoby, David. "Crusader Acre in the Thirteenth Century: Urban Layout and Topography." *Studi Medievali,* 3rd ser., 20, fasc. 1 (1979): 1–45.

Jahnkuhn, Herbert. " 'Heinrichsburgen' und Königspfalzen." In *Deutsche Königspfalzen,* 2 vols. 2:61–69. Göttingen, 1965.

James, Edward. *The Franks.* Oxford, 1988.

———. *The Origins of France: From Clovis to the Capetians, 500–1000.* Edited by Maurice Keen. London, 1982.

Jäschke, Kurt-Ulrich. *Burgenbau und Landesverteidigung um 900. überlegungen zu Beispielen aus Deutschland.* 18–33. Sigmaringen, 1975.

Ibn al-Jawzī, Shams al-Dīn Yūsuf Sibt. *Mir'āt al-zamān fī ta'rīkh al-a'yān.* 1951–52. Reprint. Edited by J.R. Jewett. Chicago, 1907.

Johns, C.N. "Excavations at Pilgrims' Castle, 'Atlit (1932); The Ancient Tell and the Outer Defences of the Castle." *Quarterly of the Department of Antiquities in Palestine,* 3, no. 4 (1933): 145–64.

———. "Medieval 'Ajlūn." *Quarterly of the Department of Antiquities in Palestine* 1 (1932): 21–33.

Jones, Archer. *The Art of War in the Western World.* Oxford, 1987.

Jones, Michael E. "The Historicity of the Alleluja Victory." *Albion* 18 (1986): 363–73.

Karnow, Stanley. *Vietnam, A History.* New York, 1985.

Keegan, John. *The Face of Battle.* London, 1976.

Kennedy, Paul. "The Fall and Rise of Military History." *The Yale Journal of World Affairs* 1, no. 2 (1989): 12–19.

Keutgen, Frederich. *Untersuchungen über der Ursprung der deutschen Stadtverfassung*. Berlin, 1895.

Keynes, Simon and Michael Lapidge. *Alfred the Great: Asser's "Life of King Alfred" and Other Contemporary Sources*. London, 1983.

Klein-Franke, Felix. "What Was the Fatal Disease of al-Malik al-Salih Nagm al Dīn Ayyūb?" In *Studies in Islamic History and Civilization*. Edited by M. Sharon. Leiden, 1986.

Koehne, Karl. "Burgen, Burgmannen, and Städte. Ein Beitrag zur Frage der Bedeutung der ländlichen Grundrenten für die mittelalterliche Stadtentwicklung." *Historische Zeitschrift* 133 (1926): 1–19.

Köpke, Rudolph A. *Widukind von Korvei: Ein Beitraf zur Kritik der Geschictschreiber des zehnten Jahrhunderts*. Berlin, 1867.

Koistinen, Paul A. *The Military-Industrial Complex: A Historical Perspective*. New York, 1980.

Kurtz, Benjamin P. "From St. Antony to St. Guthlac: A Study in Biography." *University of California Publications in Modern Philology* 12 (1926): 103–46.

Lawrence, Arnold W. *Greek Aims in Fortification*. Oxford, 1979.

LeSage, Georges. *Marseille Angevine: Recherches sur son evolution administrative, economique et urbain de la victoire de Charles d'Anjou a l'arrivée de Jeanne 1er (1264–1348)*. Paris, 1950.

Leyser, Karl. "Henry I and the Beginnings of the Saxon Empire." *EHR* 83 (1968): 1–32.

Lewis, Archibald. *Knights and Samurai: Feudalism in Northern France and Japan*. London, 1974.

Liddell, Henry George and Robert Scott. *A Greek-English Lexicon*. Oxford, 1968.

Liddell Hart, B.H. *Strategy*. 1954. Reprint, New York, 1967.

Lintzel, Martin. *Ausgewöhlten Schriften*. 2 vols. Berlin, 1936.

Lloyd, Seton and D. Storm Rice. *Alanya ('Alā'iyya)*. London, 1958.

Lot, Ferdinand. *L'Art militaire et les armeés au Moyen Âge et dans la Proche-Orient*. 2 vols. Paris, 1946.

Lynn, John, ed. *Tools of War: Instruments, Ideas, and Institutions of Warfare, 1445–1871*. Urbana IL, 1990.

Lyon, Bryce D. *The Origins of the Middle Ages: Pirenne's Challenge to Gibbon*. New York, 1972.

Marsden, Erik W. *Greek and Roman Artillery: Historical Development*. Oxford, 1969.

Marshall, Christopher. *Warfare in the Latin East, 1192–1291*. Cambridge, 1992.

Mass, Jeffrey P. *Warrior Government in Early Medieval Japan. A Study of the Kamakura Bakufu, Shugo, and Jito*. New Haven CT, 1974.

Matthew, Donald J.A. *The Norman Conquest*. London, 1966.

McCrank, Lawrence J. "Norman Crusaders in the Catalan Reconquest: Robert Burdet and the Principality of Tarragona, 1129–55." *Journal of Medieval History* 7 (1981): 67–82.

McLaughlin, Megan. "The Woman Warrior: Gender, Warfare and Society in Medieval Europe." *Women's Studies* 17 (1990): 193–209.

Millis, Walter. *Military History*, Washington, 1969.

Mommsen, Theodor. "Das römischen Militärwesen seit Diocletian." *Hermes* 24 (1889): 195–279.

Morillo, Stephen. "Hastings: An Unusual Battle." *The Haskins Society Journal* 2 (1990): 95–104.

———. *Warfare under the Anglo-Norman Kings, 1066–1135.* Woodbridge, 1994.

Müller-Wiener, Wolfgang. *Castles of the Crusades.* London, 1966.

al-Munajjid, Salāh al-Dīn. *Dimashq al-qadīmah: aswāruhī, abrājuhā, abwābuhā.* Damascus, 1945.

Murphy, Thomas Patrick, ed. *The Holy War.* Columbus OH, 1976.

Murray, Alexander. *Reason and Society in the Middle Ages.* 1978. Reprint, Oxford, 1985.

Oberman, H.A. and T.A. Weisheipl. "The *Sermo epinicus* Ascribed to Thomas Bradwardine." *Archives d'histoire doctrinale et litteraire du moyen âge* 35 (1958): 295–327.

O'Callaghan, Joseph F. *The Spanish Military Order of Calatrava and its Affiliates.* London, 1975.

Oman, Charles. *History of the Art of War in the Middle Ages.* 2 vols. 1924. Reprint, New York, 1964.

Parker, Geoffrey. *The Military Revolution. Military Innovation and the Rise of the West, 1500–1800.* Cambridge, 1988.

Partington, James. *A History of Greek Fire and Gunpowder.* Cambridge, 1960.

Porges, Walter. "The Clergy, The Poor, and the Non-Combatants on the First Crusade." *Speculum* 21 (1946): 1–23.

Powers, James F. *A Society Organized for War: The Iberian Municipal Militias in the Central Middle Ages, 1000–1284.* Berkeley, 1988.

Powicke, Maurice. *Military Obligation in Medieval England.* Oxford, 1962.

Pringle, Denys. *The Defence of Byzantine Africa from Justinian to the Arab Conquest.* 2 vols. Oxford, 1981.

Reilly, Bernard F. *The Kingdom of León-Castilla under King Alfonso VI, 1065–1109.* Princeton, 1988.

Reuter, Timothy. *Germany in the Early Middle Ages, 800–1056.* London, 1991.

Ridyard, Susan J. *The Royal Saints of Anglo-Saxon England: A Study of West Saxon and East Anglian Cults.* Cambridge, 1988.

Riley-Smith, Jonathan. *The First Crusade and the Idea of Crusading.* London, 1986.

Rogers, Randall. *Latin Siege Warfare in the Twelfth Century.* Oxford, 1992.

Rosen-Ayalon, M., ed. *Studies in Memory of Gaston Wiet.* Jerusalem, 1977.

Round, John Horace. *Geoffrey de Mandeville.* London, 1892.

Runciman, Steven. *The Sicilian Vespers.* 1958. Reprint, Cambridge, 1992.

Russell, Frederick H. *The Just War in the Middle Ages.* Cambridge, 1975.

Sander, Erich. "Die Heeresorganisation Heinrichs I." *Historisches Jahrbuch* (1939): 1–26

Sasso, Gennaro. *Niccolò Machiavelli.* 2 vols. Bologna, 1993.

Schäfer, Dietrich. "Die *agrarii milites* des Widukind." *Sitzungsberichte des königlichen preussischen Akademie der Wissenschaften* 27 (1905): 569–77.

Schmitt, Johannes. *Untersuchungen zu den Liberi Homines der Karolingerzeit, Europäische Hochschulschriften Reihe III: Geschichte und ihre Hifswissenschaften Bd. 83.* Frankfurt/M, 1977.

Schlesinger, Walther. *Mitteldeutsche Beiträge zur Verfassungsgeschichte des Mittelalters.* Göttingen, 1961.

Schuchhardt, Carl. *Die Burg im Wandel der Weltgeschichte.* Frankfurt-am-Main, 1931.

Settia, Aldo A. *Comuni in guerra: armi ad eserciti nell'Italia delle città.* Bologna, 1993.

Shahādah, Kāmil. "Qal'at Shayzar." *Annales archéologiques arabes Syriennes* 31 (1981): 107–28.

Sharon, Moshe, ed. *Studies in Islamic History and Civilization in Honour of Professor David Ayalon.* Jerusalem-Leiden, 1986.

Shneidman, J. Lee. *The Rise of the Aragonese-Catalan Empire, 1200–1350.* 2 vols. New York, 1970.

Skinner, Quentin. *Machiavelli.* New York, 1981.

Smail, R.C. *Crusading Warfare 1097–1193.* 1967. Reprint, Cambridge, 1995.

Smith, Ralph B. *An International History of the Vietnam War.* New York, 1983.

Staab, Franz. "A Reconsideration of the Ancestry of Modern Political Liberty: The Problem of the so-called 'King's Freemen' (*Königsfreie*)." *Viator* 11 (1980): 51–69.

Stenton, Frank M. *Anglo-Saxon England.* Oxford, 1971.

Strayer, Joseph R. *Medieval Statecraft and the Perspectives of History.* Princeton, 1971.

———. *On the Medieval Origins of the Modern State.* Princeton, 1970.

Strickland, Matthew, ed. *Anglo-Norman Warfare.* Woodbridge, 1992.

Swanton, Michael. *Anglo-Saxon Prose.* London, 1975.

Tatlock, J.S.P. *The Legendary History of Britain: Geoffrey of Monmouth's Historia Regum Britanniae and Its Early Vernacular Versions.* 1950. Reprint, New York, 1974.

Thompson, James W. *Feudal Germany.* New York, 1928.

Tyerman, Christopher. *England and the Crusades, 1095–1588.* Chicago, 1988.

van Creveld, Martin. *Technology and War from 2000 BC to the Present.* New York, 1989.

van Velthem, Lodewijk. *Spiegel historiaal of rymspiegel.* Edited by Isaac Long. 4 vols. Amsterdam, 1727.

Vann, Theresa M., ed. *Women of Power: 1. Queens, Regents and Potentates.* Woodbridge, 1993.

von Ranke, Leopold. *Weltgeschichte.* 6 vols. Berlin, 1885.

Vasiliev, A.A. *Byzance et les Arabes.* 2 vols. Brussels, 1935.

Vaughn, Sally N. *Anselm of Bec and Robert of Meulan: The Innocence of the Dove and the Wisdom of the Serpent.* Berkeley, 1987.

Verbruggen, J.F. *The Art of Warfare in Western Europe during the Middle Ages, from the Eighth Century to 1340.* Translated by Sumner Willard and S.C.M. Southern. Amsterdam-New York, 1977. New edition, Woodbridge, 1997.

———. *De Krijgskunst in West-Europa in de Middeleeuwen, IXe tot begin XIVe eeuw.* Brussels, 1954.

———. *Het Leger en de Vloot van de Graven van Vlaanderen vanaf het Onstaat tot in 1305.* Brussels, 1960.

Waitz, Georg. *Deutsche Verfassungsgeschichte.* 4 vols. 1874–85. Reprint, Darmstadt, 1953–55.

———. *Jahrbücher des deutschen Reiches unter König Heinrich I.* 1885. Reprint, Darmstadt, 1963.

Walker, Gregg D., David A. Bella, Stephen J. Sprecher, eds. *The Military Industrial Complex: Eisenhower's Warning Three Decades Later.* New York, 1992.

Weinstein, Donald and Rudolph M. Bell. *Saints and Society.* Chicago, 1982.

Welsh, Douglas. *The History of the Vietnam War.* London, 1981.

Wiegand, Theodor, ed. *Baalbek Ergebnisse der Ausgrabungen und Untersuchungen in dem Jahren 1898–1905.* 3 vols. Berlin–Leipzig, 1921–25.

Wiet, Gaston, Jean Sauvaget, and Etienne Combe, eds. *Répertoire chronologique d'épigraphie arabe.* 17 vols. to date. Cairo, 1931– .

White, Lynn. *Medieval Technology and Social Change.* Oxford, 1962.

Wilson, Stephen. *Saints and their Cults.* Cambridge, 1983.

Winter, F.E. *Greek Fortifications.* Toronto, 1972.